BEGINNER'S CHINESE DICTIONARY

汉英入门词典

Hàn-Yīng Rùmén Cídiǎn

LI Dong

李 冬

TUTTLE PUBLISHING

Boston • Rutland, Vermont • Tokyo

Published by Tuttle Publishing,
an imprint of Periplus Editions (HK) Ltd.,
with editorial offices at 153 Milk Street, Boston, MA 02109 and
130 Joo Seng Road #06-01/03 Singapore 368357

Library of Congress Control Number: 2004103182
ISBN 0-8048-3551-9

First Edition 2004
Printed in Singapore

Distributed by:

North America, Latin America & Europe
Tuttle Publishing, 364 Innovation Drive,
North Clarendon, VT 05759-9436
Tel: (802) 773 8930 Fax: (802) 773 6993
Email: info@tuttlepublishing.com
www.tuttlepublishing.com

Japan
Tuttle Publishing, Yaekari Building, 3rd Floor
5-4-12 Osaki, Shinagawa-ku, Tokyo 141-0032
Tel: (03) 5437 0171 Fax: (03) 5437 0755
Email: tuttle-sales@gol.com

Asia Pacific
Berkeley Books Pte. Ltd.
130 Joo Seng Road #06-01/03, Singapore 368357
Tel: (65) 6280 1330 Fax: (65) 6280 6290
Email: inquiries@periplus.com.sg
www.periplus.com

08 07 06 05 04
6 5 4 3 2 1

Useful web sites for learners of Chinese
http://zhongwen.com/
http://www.ocrat.com/
http://www.csulb.edu/~txie/online.htm
http://www.webcom.com/~bamboo/chinese/chinese.html

Contents

A Guide for Beginning Students of Chinese

1 PRONUNCIATION

The pronunciation of Chinese words is transcribed in this dictionary using the *pinyin* transliteration scheme, the official, internationally recognized Chinese romanization scheme. Every Chinese character in this dictionary is accompanied by its *pinyin* spelling so users will know how it is pronounced.

Each Chinese syllable normally contains of three elements: vowels, consonants and tones. Modern standard Chinese, known as Putonghua, has in use about 400 syllables without tones and 1,382 syllables with tones.

1.1 Vowels

1.1.1 Single Vowels

There are seven basic single vowels:

a similar to *a* in *ah*
e similar to *a* in *ago*
ê similar to *e* in *ebb* (this sound never occurs alone and is transcribed **e**, as in **ei**, **ie**, **ue**)
i similar to *ee* in *cheese* (spelt **y**, when there is no consonant before it.)
o similar to *oe* in *toe*
u similar to *oo* in *boot* (spelt **w**, when there is no consonant before it.)
ü similar to German *ü* in *über* or French *u* in *tu*; you can also get *ü* by saying *i* and rounding your lips at the same time (spelt **u** after **j**, **q**, **x**; spelt **yu** when not preceded by a consonant).

1.1.2 Vowel Combinations (diphthongs)

These single vowels enter into combinations with each other or the consonants of *n* or *ng* to form what are technically known as *diphthongs*. These combinations are pronounced as a single sound, with a little more emphasis on the first part of the sound.

You can learn these combinations in four groups:

Group 1: diphthongs starting with a/e/ê

ai	similar to *y* in *my*
ao	similar to *ow* in *how*
an	
ang	
en	
eng	
ei	similar to *ay* in *may*

Group 2: diphthongs starting with i

ia	
ie	similar to *ye* in *yes*
iao	
iou	similar to *you* (spelt **iu** when preceded by a consonant)
ian	
ien	similar to *in* (spelt **in** when preceded by a consonant)
ieng	similar to *En* in *English* (spelt **ing** when preceded by a consonant)
iang	similar to *young*
iong	

Group 3: diphthongs starting with u/o

ua	
uo	
uai	similar to *why* in British English
uei	similar to *way* (spelt **ui** when preceded by a consonant)
uan	
uen	(spelt **un** when preceded by a consonant)
ueng	
uang	
ong	

Group 4: diphthongs starting with ü

üe	
üan	
üen	used only after **j**, **q**, **x**; spelt **un**

1.2 Consonants

Consonants may be grouped in the following ways.

Group 1: These consonants are almost the same in Chinese and English.

Chinese	English
m	*m*
n	*n*
f	*f*
l	*l*
s	*s*
r	*r*
b	pronounced as hard *p* (as in *speak*)
p	*p* (as in *peak*)
g	pronounced as hard *k* (as in *ski*)
k	*k* (as in *key)*
d	pronounced as hard *t* (as in *star*)
t	*t* (as in *tar*)

Group 2: Some modification is needed to get these Chinese sounds from English.

Chinese	English
j	as *j* in *jeep* (but unvoiced, not round-lipped)
q	as *ch* in *cheese* (but not round-lipped)
x	as *sh* in *sheep* (but not round-lipped)
c	as *ts* as in *cats* (make it long)
z	as *ds* as in *beds* (but unvoiced, and make it long)

Group 3: No English counterparts.
Chinese **zh**, **ch**, and **sh** have no English counterparts. It would be rather misleading to equate **zh** with *j* as in *jeep*, for example.

To make **sh**, curl the tip of the tongue up and back to the roof of yourmouth. With your tongue in that position, say *sh.* To make **zh,** curl the tip of the tongue up and back to the roof of your mouth, say *ch.* To make **zh,** curl the tip of the tongue up and back to the roof of your mouth and say *j*. For example, try saying something that sounds like **zhou**: curl the tip of the tongue up and back against the roof of your mouth, then, keeping your tongue in that position, say *joe*.

1.3 Tones

Chinese is a tonal language, i.e. a sound pronounced in different tones is understood as different words. So the tone is an indispensable component of the pronunciation of a word.

1.3.1 Basic Tones

There are four basic tones. The following five-level pitch graph shows the values of the four tones:

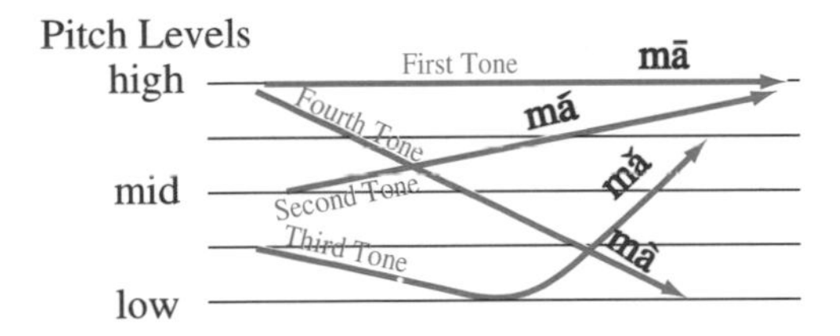

The **First Tone** is a high, level tone and is represented as ˉ, e.g. 妈 **mā** (meaning *mother*, *mom*).

The **Second Tone** is a high, rising tone and is represented by the tone mark ˊ, e.g. 麻 **má** (*hemp* or *sesame*).

The **Third Tone** is a falling and rising tone. As you can see from the pitch-graph it falls from below the middle of the voice range to nearly the bottom and then rises to a point near the top. It is represented by the tone mark ˇ, e.g. 马 **mǎ** (*horse*).

The **Fourth Tone** is a falling tone. It falls from high to low and is represented by the tone mark ˋ, e.g. 骂 **mà** (*curse*).

In Chinese speech, as in English speech, some sounds are unstressed, i.e. pronounced short and soft. They do not have any of the four tones. Such sounds are said to have **Neutral Tone**. Sounds with the neutral tone are not marked. For example in 爸爸 **bàba** (*daddy*) the first syllable is pronounced in the fourth tone and the second syllable in the neutral tone, that is, unstressed.

1.3.2 Tone Changes

Tones may undergo changes in actual speech ("tone sandhi"). The third tone, when followed by a first, second, fourth or neutral tone sound, loses its final rise and stops at the low pitch. Followed by another third tone sound, it becomes the second tone. This is a general rule and the notation of third tone sounds remains unchanged, even though the actualization is no longer that of a third-tone syllable.

For example, in 所以 **suǒyǐ** (*therefore*, *so*), the notation remains the third tone for both syllables, but the word is actually pronounced **suóyǐ**.

Two important words 不 **bù** (*no*) and 一 **yī** (*one*) also undergo tone changes. You will find the details of their tone changes under these entries.

2 WRITING CHINESE CHARACTERS

2.1 Strokes and Stroke Order

2.1.1 Strokes

Recognizing the strokes in a character is helpful for finding a character or radical in the Stroke Index, List of Radicals and Radical Index. Each of the following strokes is counted as one stroke.

Stroke	Writing the stroke	Examples
Héng	left to right 一	千 主 女
Shù	top to bottom 丨	千 山 北

Stroke	Writing the stroke	Examples
Piě	top (right) to bottom (left) 	千 人 么
Nā	top (left) to bottom (right) 	人 木 又
Diǎn	top to bottom	主 心 习
Tí	Bottom (left) to top (right)	习 打 北
Stroke with hook	left to right, top to bottom 	买 打 以 心
Stroke with turn(s)		山 马 女 么 又
Stroke with turn(s) and hook		北 习 认 马

2.1.2 Stroke Order

For the character to look correct, its strokes should be written in the correct order. Knowing the order will also help you remember characters. The general rules of stroke order are as follows, though there may be exceptions to the rules.

Rule	Example	Stroke order
Top before bottom	三	一 二 三
Left before right	什	丿 亻 仁 什
Horizontal before vertical/downward	天	一 二 于 天
"Enter the room, then close the door"	日	丨 冂 月 日
Vertical stroke before sides/bottom	小	亅 小 小

2.2 Composition of Chinese Characters

Most of Chinese characters are made up of two or more component parts. It is helpful to know something about those component parts rather than try to memorize each character as if it were a monolith.

Three kinds of components are recognized in contemporary scholarship:

- **Signific graphs** (shortened to "sign" in the dictionary listings) are meaningful components that suggest the meaning of the character. Of the three kinds of graphs the signific graph is the most important for learning characters. A list of common signific graphs used in this dictionary, with explanations and examples, is included on page 197. The first one, 冫, for example, suggests the meaning of "freezing, very cold." It pays to browse this list and memorize it.
- **Phonetic graphs** (shortened to "phon") are components that give some clue to the pronunciation of characters.

- **Symbols** (shortened to "symb") are components that are neither signific graphs nor phonetic graphs.

This dictionary shows the composition of each Chinese character in the headword when it is practical to do so. For example, the character 孩 (**hái**, meaning *child*) is composed of two parts: the left part 子 is a signific graph meaning "child" and the right part 亥 is a phonetic graph as 亥 **hài** is pronounced very similarly to 孩 **hái**. This is indicated thus:

hái 孩 (子 9) [子 sign + 亥 phon **hài**]

Here is another example. The character 海 (**hǎi**, meaning *sea*) is composed of 氵 and 每. While 氵 is a signific graph meaning *water*, 每 is just a symbol. So it is:

hǎi 海 (氵 10) [氵 sign + 每 symb]

In a few cases, the symbol or phonetic graph of a character is not shown. For example:

zǎo 澡 (氵 16) [氵 sign + phon]

xué 学 (子 8) [symb + 子 sign]

This means that the part less the signific graph is the phonetic graph or symbol.

2.3 How to Look Up a Word in a Chinese Dictionary

2.3.1 By *Pinyin* Romanization

To aid beginning learners of Chinese, this dictionary arranges headwords alphabetically according to *pinyin*. So if you know how a word is pronounced, you can find it easily, just the way you look up an English word in an English dictionary.

2.3.2 By Radical

Very often, however, you do not know the pronunciation of a word when you come across it in reading. In that case you can find it either by its radical or the number of its strokes. Radicals (部首 **bùshǒu** in Chinese) are certain component parts of characters that have been used in Chinese dictionary-making for nearly 2,000 years. Characters sharing a radical are grouped together under the heading of that radical. To find a character in a dictionary, just follow these steps:

(i) In the **List of Radicals**, look up the character's radical according to the number of strokes in the radical. This gives a Radical Index number.
(ii) Turn to the number in the **Radical Index** and locate the character according to the number of remaining strokes needed to write the character (i.e. number of: total strokes – radical strokes = remaining strokes). This gives the *pinyin* pronunciation.
(iii) Turn to the **Chinese-English Dictionary** section and find the character's meaning and usage in the relevant dictionary entry.

For example, to find 活:

(i) The radical group of 活 is 氵, which has three strokes. In the **List of Radicals**, look up 氵 in the section marked "3 strokes":

3 strokes
氵 31

(ii) Turn to number 31 in the **Radical Index**. There are nine strokes in 活. The radical has three strokes. Six strokes remain to complete the character 活 (9 – 3 = 6). Look in the section "6 strokes" and locate 活:

6 strokes
活 huó

(iii) Turn to **huó** in the dictionary:

huó 活 ...

2.3.3 By Number of Strokes

Unfortunately, looking for a character by its radical is not an entirely satisfactory method as learners may not always know which part of the character is the radical. Therefore, this dictionary includes a **Stroke Index** to aid the learner further. Simply look for the character according to the number of its strokes.

Entries indicate both the radical and the stroke number of each character to help the learner in consulting dictionaries at more advanced levels. For example, as 孩 **hái** belongs to the radical group of 子 and has nine strokes; this is shown as (子 9). Likewise after 海 you will find (氵 10), which means that 海 belongs to thc radical group of 氵 and has ten strokes. This information will also prove useful for your further studies.

2.3.4 By English Meaning

To find out the Chinese equivalent or near-equivalent of an English word, use the **English-Chinese Word Finder List**, which is practically a handy English-Chinese dictionary. Chinese equivalents or near-equivalents of over 1,500 English words are listed alphabetically in the Finder.

For example, to find out what *airport* is in Chinese, turn to "A" in the Finder and locate *airport* in the list of words beginning with "A":

airport **fēijīchǎng, jīchǎng** 飞机场, 机场 36, 56

The entry for 飞机场 **fēijīchǎng** is found on page 36 and the entry for 机场 **jīchǎng**, on page 56.

2.4 Simplified Characters

The Chinese government simplified hundreds of Chinese characters in mid-1950 by reducing the numbers of their strokes. Such simplified characters are called 简体字 **jiǎntǐzì**. This dictionary uses *jiantizi*, and the traditional or complicated version still used in Taiwan and Hong Kong is shown after "Trad" where applicable, e.g.:

xué 学 (子 8) [symb + 子 sign] Trad 學

3 VOCABULARY

This dictionary gives detailed description of the 1,033 words prescribed for Level A of the Hanyu Shuiping Kaoshi (汉语水平考试 **Hànyǔ Shuǐpíng Kǎoshì**). There are about fifty additional words, including:

- new words: 电脑 **diànnǎo**, 电子邮件 **diànzi yóujiàn**, 传真 **chuánzhēn**
- useful everyday words: 筷子 **kuàizi**, 功课 **gōngkè**, 丈夫 **zhàngfu**, 妻子 **qīzi**
- common Chinese family names: 李 **Lǐ**, 张 **Zhāng**, 王 **Wáng**, 陈 **Chén**
- names of countries and cities: 中国 **Zhōngguó**, 台湾 **Táiwān**, 新加坡 **Xīnjiāpō**, 北京 **Běijīng**, 上海 **Shànghǎi**, 香港 **Xiānggǎng**, 美国 **Měiguó**, 英国 **Yīngguó**.

3.1 Word-formation

Chinese words are very transparent, i.e. the way a word is formed reveals a lot about its meaning. Most Chinese words composed of two or more syllables belong to certain word-formation patterns. Knowledge of such patterns is useful because (1) it helps you understand the word, (2) it makes memorization easier, and (3) it reinforces your learning of individual characters.

This dictionary analyzes word-formation methods of headwords, whenever it is practical to do so. We recognize six methods of word-formation.

- Compounding (shortened to "compound"): the components of a word are complementary to each other in meaning and are of the same status. For example:

  yǎnjing 眼睛 [compound: 眼 *eye* + 睛 *eyeball*]

- Modification ("modif"): one component modifies the other. For example:

  wàiguó 外国 [modif: 外 *outside* + 国 *country*]

- Verb+object ("v+obj"): the word has a verb-and-object relationship. For example:

  fāshāo 发烧 [v+obj: 发 *develop* + 烧 *burning, fever*]

- Verb+complementation ("v+comp"): the word has a verb-and-complement relationship, that is, the first component is a verb and the second one modifies it. For example:

  tígāo 提高 [v+comp: 提 *raise* + 高 *high*]

- Suffixation ("suffix"): the word contains a suffix. For example:

  běnzi 本子 [suffix: 本 *a book* + 子 nominal suffix]

- Idioms ("idiom"): the word is an idiomatic expression. For example:

  mǎshàng 马上 [idiom]

3.2 Definitions

In most cases English equivalents or near-equivalents are given as definitions. For example:

> **cóngqián 从前** NOUN = past time, past, in the past

For grammatical words that have no English equivalents, concise explanations are given in brackets. For example:

> **de 的** (白 7) PARTICLE = (attached to a word, phrase or clause to indicate that it is an attribute; 的 **de** is normally followed by a noun)

After the definition of a noun, the specific measure word used with the noun is shown, if it is one of headwords in the dictionary. For example:

> **shū 书** (丨 4) Trad 書 NOUN = book (本 **běn**)

When the specific measure word is not within the scope of this dictionary and therefore is not shown, you can often use the default measure word 个 **gè**.

Antonyms are shown after the definition of most adjectives and some nouns, if they are headwords. For example:

> **duǎn 短** (矢 12) ADJECTIVE = (of length, time) short (antonym 长 **cháng**)

When a headword has more than one meaning, the different meanings are indicated by 1, 2, etc. For example:

> **yuè 月** (月 4) NOUN
> 1 = month
> ■ 我在那里住了八个月。**Wǒ zài nàlǐ zhùle bā ge yuè.** = *I stayed there for eight months.*
> 2 = the moon

3.3 Collocations

Certain words are habitually juxtaposed with each other. Such juxtapositions are called *collocations*. This dictionary shows approximately 2,000 common collocations, with clear definitions and necessary example sentences, if the components are headwords in this dictionary. For example:

> **bìng 病** (疒 10) [疒 sign + 丙 phon **bǐng**] ...
> shēng bìng 生病 = to fall ill
> bìng rén 病人 = sick person, patient
> bìngfáng 病房 = (hospital) ward

The result is that despite its modest title, this beginner's dictionary introduces you to many more words than the headwords, all learnt conveniently. In this way your word power will be significantly increased.

3.4 Words in Use: Sample Sentences

Words become really meaningful only when used in sentences. That is why this dictionary supplies a number of sample sentences for almost every headword. All the sentences are carefully constructed to be (1) idiomatic, (2) communicatively useful and (3) within the controlled vocabulary of this dictionary. Studying the sentences carefully will help you will learn how to use important Chinese words in everyday communication.

Care was taken to include sentences that are good examples of how words behave in communication. For example:

> **bàozhǐ 报纸** [modif: 报 *reporting* + 纸 *paper*] NOUN = newspaper (张 **zhāng**)
> ■ 今天报纸上有什么消息？ **Jīntiān bàozhǐ shang yǒu shénme xiāoxi?** = *What's the news in today's paper?*
> ■ 我很少看报纸。**Wǒ hěn shǎo kàn bàozhǐ.** = *I seldom read newspapers.*

Two sample sentences are given for the headword 报纸 **bàozhǐ**. In the first sentence, the headword 报纸 **bàozhǐ** is used in the subject position and is collocated with the preposition 上 **shàng**; in the second sentence, 报纸 **bàozhǐ** functions as an object after the common verb 看 **kàn**. Another example is the entry of 办法 **bànfǎ**. As many as five sample sentences are provided, encompassing almost all situations in everyday communication. If you understand and learn the sentences, you will be able to use 办法 **bànfǎ** with ease and confidence. All sample sentences in this dictionary are accompanied by its *pinyin* and English translation to aid learning. In some cases a second translation is provided in brackets to aid comprehension and idiomatic expression. → indicates a freer, more idiomatic translation and ←, a more literal translation. For example:

> **ràng 让** (讠 5) Trad 讓 VERB = let, allow
> ■ 你应该让那辆车先行。**Nǐ yīnggāi ràng nà liàng chē xiān xíng.** = *You should let that vehicle go first.* (→ *You should give way to that vehicle.*)

4 GRAMMAR

Grammar is simply a set of rules for the use of a language. To understand a language some knowledge of its grammar is helpful; this is particularly true if you are an adult learner of a foreign language such as Chinese. Chinese grammar and English grammar are of course different, but they share much common ground. Your knowledge of English grammar will be useful in understanding Chinese grammar (and vice versa).

Following are brief explanations of the basic terms in Chinese grammar used in this dictionary. (A word of warning: it is a rather complicated matter to define grammatical terms accurately. Here we will be content with some very general but useful ideas.)

4.1 Word Classes

ADJECTIVE	a describing word, a word that describes people, things or actions, typically used before a noun.
ADVERB	a word that modifies a verb, an adjective or another adverb.
CONJUNCTION	a word used to link two words, phrases or sentences, indicating certain relationships between them.
IDIOM	a set phrase, the meaning of which cannot be readily derived from its components.
INTERJECTION	a word that expresses strong emotions.
MEASURE WORD	a word that connects a numeral to a noun. Measure Words are a special feature of Chinese; a list of measure words is included on page 199.
MODAL VERB	a word used before a verb to indicate necessity, possibility, willingness, etc.
NOUN	a naming word, a word that names people, animals, plants, things, ideas, etc.
NUMERAL	a word that represents a number, typically used with a noun.
ONOMATOPOEIA	a word that imitates the sounds of a thing or an action.

PARTICLE	a word used with another word, phrase, or sentence to indicate certain grammatical meanings or to express strong emotions.
PREPOSITION	a word used before a noun or pronoun to indicate time, place, direction, manner, reason of an action, etc.
PRONOUN	a word that is used in the place of a noun, a verb, an adjective, etc.
VERB	an action word, a word that indicates what somebody does or feels.

4.2 Other Grammar Terms

ATTRIBUTE	the element that modifies the subject or object of a sentence; or, in word-formation analysis, a word that modifies a noun.
ADVERBIAL	the element that is used before the predicate of a sentence and modifies it; or, in word-formation analysis, a word that precedes a verb or adjective to modify it.
COMPLEMENT	the element that is used after the predicate of a sentence and modifies it; or, in word-formation analysis, a word that follows a verb or adjective to modify it.
IMPERATIVE SENTENCE	a command or a request.
OBJECT	the element that follows a predicative verb, typically to indicate the target of an action.
PREDICATE	the comment or information about the subject, typically a verb or adjective.
PREFIX	an additional element that immediately precedes the word it is attached to.
SUBJECT	the topic of a sentence, what the speaker wants to talk about, typically a noun or pronoun.
SUFFIX	an additional element that closely follows the word it is attached to.

5 CULTURAL AND USAGE NOTES

Essential information on cultural context, pronunciation, grammar and usage is given to help you use the language in a socially acceptable and idiomatic way. For example:

> **céng 层** (尸 7) Trad 層 MEASURE WORD
> = story (storey), floor
> ...
>
> NOTE: The Chinese way of numbering floors is the same as the American practice, e.g. 一层楼 **yī céng lóu** is "the first floor" in America, but "the ground floor" to the British.

A

ā 啊 (口 10) [口 sign + 阿 phon ā]
1 INTERJECTION = oh, ah (expressing strong emotions such as surprise, admiration, regret etc.)
■ 啊，这花儿真好看！ **Ā, zhè huār zhēn hǎokàn!** = *Oh, this flower is really beautiful!*
2 PARTICLE = (attached to a sentence to express strong emotion such as surprise, admiration, regret etc.)
■ 今天天气真好啊！ **Jīntiān tiānqì zhēn hǎo a!** = *What a fine day it is today!*
■ 北京的冬天真冷啊！ **Běijīng de dōngtiān zhēn lěng a!** = *How cold the winter in Beijing is!*

ǎi 矮 (矢 13) ADJECTIVE = of short stature (of a person or plant); short (antonym 高 gāo)
■ 你一点儿也不矮。**Nǐ yìdiǎnr yě bù ǎi.** = *You're not short at all.*
■ 他哥哥很高，他比哥哥矮多了。**Tā gēge hěn gāo. Tā bǐ gēge ǎi duō le.** = *His brother is tall. He's much shorter.*
ǎi gèzi 矮个子 = *a short person*
■ 那个矮个子是谁？ **Nà ge ǎi gèzi shì shéi?** = *Who's that short person?*

ài 爱 (爪 10) Trad 愛 VERB = love
■ 我爱你。**Wǒ ài nǐ.** = *I love you.*
■ 我爱我的国家。**Wǒ ài wǒ de guójiā.** = *I love my country.*
àiqíng 爱情 = romantic love
■ 她跟他结婚是为了爱情，不是为了钱。**Tā gēn tā jiéhūn shì wèile àiqíng, bú shì wèile qián.** = *She married him for love, not for money.*

àirén 爱人 [modif: 爱 *love* + 人 *person*] NOUN = husband or wife
■ 我和我爱人结婚十年了。**Wǒ hé wǒ àirén jiéhūn shí nián le.** = *My husband* (or *wife*) *and I have been married for ten years.*

NOTE: 爱人 **àirén** as *husband* or *wife* is only used in Mainland China as a colloquialism. On formal occasions 丈夫 **zhàngfu** and 妻子 **qīzi** are the words for *husband* and *wife*. Now there is a decreasing tendency to use 爱人 in China. In its place 先生 **xiānsheng** and 太太 **tàitai** are used to refer to husband and wife, a long established practice in Taiwan, Hong Kong and overseas Chinese communities. For example:
■ 你先生近来忙吗？ **Nǐ xiānsheng jìnlai máng ma?** = *Is your husband busy these days?*
■ 我太太要我买些菜回去。**Wǒ tàitai yào wǒ mǎi xiē cài huíqu.** = *My wife wants me to buy and bring home some vegetables.*

ān 安 (宀 6) [宀 sign + 女 sign]
ADJECTIVE = peaceful, safe

ānjìng 安静 [compound: 安 *peace* + 静 *quiet*] ADJECTIVE = quiet, peaceful, serene
■ 这儿很安静。**Zhèr hěn ānjìng.** = *It's very quiet here.*
■ 请大家安静！ **Qǐng dàjiā ānjìng!** = *Please be quiet, everyone!*

A

■ 我要一间安静的房间。**Wǒ yào yì jiān ānjìng de fángjiān.** = *I want a quiet room.*

NOTE: There are two important place names in 北京 **Běijīng**, the capital of China, which contain 安 **ān**: 天安门 **Tiān'ānmén** and 长安街 **Cháng'ān Jiē**, a boulevard that runs through the city from east to west. 安 **ān** is also found in the name of the ancient city of 西安 **Xī'ān**.

ānpái 安排 [compound: 安 *to settle, to arrange* + 排 *to arrange, to put in order*] VERB = arrange, make arrangement; plan

■ 下星期我们很忙，要安排好时间。**Xià xīngqī wǒmen hěn máng, yào ānpái hǎo shíjiān.** = *We'll be very busy next week and should plan our time well.*

■ 我想见周经理，请你安排一次会见。**Wǒ xiǎng jiàn Zhōu jīnglǐ, qǐng nǐ ānpái yí cì huìjiàn.** = *I want to see Mr Zhou, the manager. Would you please arrange an appointment for us?*

ào 澳 (氵 15) NOUN = deep waters

Àodàlìyà 澳大利亚 NOUN = Australia

B

bā 八 (八 2) NUMERAL = eight

■ 八八六十四 **Bā bā liùshísì.** = *Eight times eight is sixty-four.*

bǎ 把 (扌 7) [扌 sign + 巴 phon **bā**]

1 MEASURE WORD = (for objects with handles)

■ 一把刀 **yì bǎ dāo** = *a knife*

2 PREPOSITION = (used before a noun or pronoun to indicate it is the object of the sentence)

■ 他把菜都吃完了。**Tā bǎ cài dōu chīwán le.** = *He ate up the dishes.*

■ 我没有把这件事做好。**Wǒ méiyǒu bǎ zhè jiàn shì zuòhǎo.** = *I didn't do the job well.*

NOTE: Sentences with 把 **bǎ** are very common. In such sentences, emphasis is placed on the complement of the verb, e.g. 完了 **wǎn le** and 好 **hǎo** in the above examples.

bà 爸 (父 8) [父 sign + 巴 phon **bā**] NOUN = dad, papa

bàba 爸爸 NOUN = daddy, papa

■ 我爸爸是个工人。**Wǒ bàba shì ge gōngrén.** = *My daddy is a worker.*

■ 这件事别告诉我爸爸。**Zhè jiàn shì bié gàosu wǒ bàba.** = *Don't tell my father this.*

■ 爸爸，这个星期五晚上我想用一下你的车，行不行？ **Bāba, zhège Xīngqīwǔ wǎnshang wǒ xiǎng yòng yíxià nǐ de chē, xíng bu xíng?** = *Daddy, I'd like to use your car this Friday evening. Is it all right?*

ba 吧 (口 7) [口 sign + 巴 phon **bā**] PARTICLE = (expressing suggestion or supposition)

■ 时间不早了，我们走吧！ **Shíjiān bù zǎo le, wǒmen zǒu ba!** = *It's quite late. Let's go!*

■ 今天太冷了，别去游泳吧！ **Jīntiān tài lěng le, bié qù yóuyǒng ba!** = *It's too cold today. Don't go swimming, OK?*

■ 你是上海来的张先生吧？ **Nǐ shì Shànghǎi lái de Zhāng xiānsheng ba?** = *Aren't you Mr Zhang from Shanghai?*

■ 你学了一年多中文了吧？ **Nǐ xuéle yì nián duō Zhōngwén le ba?** = *You've been learning Chinese for over a year, haven't you?*

bái 白 (白 5) ADJECTIVE = white

■ 我家有一只白猫。**Wǒ jiā yǒu yì zhī bái māo.** = *I've got a white cat at home.*

■ 你穿白衣服真好看。**Nǐ chuān bái yīfu zhēn hǎokàn.** = *You really look good in white.*

báitiān 白天 = *daytime*

■ 这是我办公室的电话号码，你白天可以打这个电话。**Zhè shì wǒ bàngōngshì de diànhuà hàomǎ, nǐ báitiān kěyǐ dǎ zhège diànhuà.** = *This is my office telephone number. You can call this number in the daytime.*

bái kāishuǐ 白开水 = *plain boiled water*

■ 我不喝可乐，我喝白开水就行了。**Wǒ bù hē kělè, wǒ hē bái kāishuǐ jiù xíng le.** = *I don't drink Coke. Plain boiled water will do.*

NOTE: In Chinese tradition, white symbolizes death and is the color for funerals.

bǎi 百 (白 6) [一 symb + 白 phon **bái**] NUMERAL = hundred

■ 一年有三百六十五天。**Yì nián yǒu sānbǎi liùshíwǔ tiān.** = *A year has 365 days.*

NOTE: 百 **bǎi** may have the abstract sense of "a great deal," "a multitude of." This sense can be found in many expressions, e.g. 百闻不如一见 **Bǎi wén bùrú yí jiàn** which literally means *A hundred sounds are not as good as one sight,* and may be translated as *Seeing is believing.* Another example is 百忙 **bǎi máng**, meaning *very busy*:

■ 你百忙中还来看我，太好了。**Nǐ bǎi máng zhōng hái lái kàn wǒ, tài hǎo le.** = *It's very kind of you to come to see me when you're so busy.*

bǎi 摆 (扌 13) [扌 sign + 罢 phon **bà**] Trad 擺 VERB = put, place, arrange

■ 房间里摆着一些花。**Fángjiān li bǎizhe yìxiē huā.** = *Some flowers are arranged in the room.*

■ 吃饭了，你把碗筷摆好吧！ **Chīfàn le, nǐ bǎ wǎn kuài bǎihǎo ba!** = *It's mealtime, will you please set the table?*

bān 班 (王 10) NOUN = class (in school); shift (in a work place)

■ 我们班有十二个男生，十四个女生。**Wǒmen bān yǒu shí'èr ge nánshēng, shísì ge nǚshēng.** = *Our class has twelve male students and fourteen female students.*

■ 我父亲上个星期上白天班，这个星期上夜班。**Wǒ fùqin shàng ge xīngqī shàng báitiān bān, zhège xīngqī shàng yè bān.** = *My father was on day shift last week, and is on night shift this week.*

shàngbān 上班 = go to work

xiàbān 下班 = end/finish/leave work

B

B

■ 我妈妈每天九点上班，五点下班。**Wǒ māma měi tiān jiǔdiǎn shàngbān, wǔdiǎn xiàbān.** = *My mother goes to work at nine o'clock and ends work at five o'clock.*

bān 般 (舟 10) NOUN = kind, sort, class (See 一般 **yībān**.)

bān 搬 (扌 13) [扌 sign + 般 phon **bān**] VERB = move (heavy things)
■ 我们把这张桌子搬到房间外面去吧。**Wǒmen bǎ zhè zhāng zhuōzi bāndào fángjiān wàimian qù ba.** = *Let's move this table out of the room.*
bān de dòng 搬得动 = can move .../can be moved
bān bu dòng 搬不动 = cannot move .../ cannot be moved

bǎn 板 (木 8) [木 sign + 反 phon **fǎn**] NOUN = board (See 黑板 **hēibǎn**.)

bàn 办 (力 4) [力 sign + 八 symb] Trad 辦 VERB = handle, manage
■ 这件事不容易办。**Zhè jiàn shì bù róngyì bàn.** = *This matter is not easy to handle.*
■ 这件事我来办。**Zhè jiàn shì wǒ lái bàn.** = *Let me handle this matter.*

bànfǎ 办法 [modif: 办 *handle, manage* + 法 *method*] NOUN = way of doing things, method
■ 你的办法不行。**Nǐ de bànfǎ bù xíng.** = *Your method won't do.*
■ 你试试我的办法。**Nǐ shìshi wǒ de bànfǎ.** = *Will you try my method?*
xiǎng bànfǎ 想办法 = think up a plan/ find a way of doing things
■ 让我想想办法。**Ràng wǒ xiǎngxiang bànfǎ.** = *Let me try to find a way.*
yoǔ bànfǎ 有办法 = have a way with ..., resourceful
■ 他对小孩很有办法。**Tā duì xiǎohái hěn yoǔ bànfǎ.** = *He has a way with children.*
méiyǒu bànfǎ 没有办法 = there's nothing we can do
■ 飞机票全卖完了，我们明天不能走，没有办法。**Fēijī piào quán màiwán le, wǒmen míngtiān bù néng zǒu, méiyǒu bànfǎ.** = *All the air tickets are sold out. We won't be able to leave tomorrow. There's nothing we can do.*

bàngōngshì 办公室 [compound: 办 *handle* + 公 *public, public affairs* + 室 *room*] NOUN = office (间 **jiān**)
■ 老师的办公室在二楼。**Lǎoshī de bàngōngshì zài èrlóu.** = *Teachers' offices are on level two.*
■ 张先生不在办公室。**Zhāng xiānsheng bú zài bàngōngshì.** = *Mr Zhang is not in his office.*

bàn 半 (八 5) [八 sign + symb] NUMERAL = half
■ 我等她等了一个半小时。**Wǒ děng tā děngle yí ge bàn xiǎoshí.** = *I waited for her for one and a half hours.*

bàntiān 半天 [modif: 半 *half* + 天 *day*] NOUN = half a day; (a period of time felt to be very long) a very long time
■ 我等你等了半天了。**Wǒ děng nǐ děngle bàntiān le.** = *I've been waiting for you for a long time.*

■ 那本书我找了半天，还没找到。 **Nà běn shū wǒ zhǎole bàntiān, hái méi zhǎodào.** = *I've been looking for the book for a long time but I still haven't found it.*

bāng 帮 (巾 9) [邦 phon **bāng** + 巾 symb] VERB = help

bāngzhù 帮助 [compound: 帮 *help* + 助 *assist*] VERB = help, assist
■ 他常常帮助我。 **Tā chángcháng bāngzhù wǒ.** = *He often helps me.*
■ 李先生帮助我们解决了很多困难。 **Lǐ xiānsheng bāngzhù wǒmen jiějuéle hěn duō kùnnan.** = *Mr Li helped us overcome many difficulties.*

NOTE: In colloquial Chinese 帮 **bāng** is often used instead of 帮助 **bāng zhù**, for example:
■ 她常常帮妈妈做晚饭。 **Tā chángcháng bāng māma zuò wǎnfàn.** = *She often helps Mum prepare supper.*

bāo 包 (勹 5) NOUN = parcel (See 面包 **miànbāo**.)

bǎo 饱 (饣 8) [饣 sign + 包 phon **bāo**] Trad 飽 ADJECTIVE = having eaten one's fill, full (antonym 饿 **è**)
■ 谢谢，我饱了。 **Xièxie, wǒ bǎo le.** = *Thank you. I'm full.*
■ 您吃饱了吗？ **Nín chī bǎo le ma?** = *Have you had (← eaten) enough?*
chī de bǎo 吃得饱 = have enough to eat
chī bù bǎo 吃不饱 = not have enough to eat (→ not have enough food)

NOTE: It is customary for a Chinese host to ask a guest who seems to have finished the meal 您吃饱了吗？ **Nín chī bǎo le ma?** The guest is expected to reply, 吃饱了。多谢。您慢慢吃。 **Chī bǎo le. Duō xiè. Nín mànman chī.** = *Yes, I have. Thank you. Please take your time to eat.*

bào 抱 (扌 8) [扌 sign + 包 phon **bāo**] VERB = hold ... in arms, embrace, hug
■ 妈妈抱着孩子。 **Māma bàozhe háizi.** = *The mother is holding her baby in her arms.*
■ 让我抱抱你。 **Ràng wǒ bàobao nǐ.** = *Let me hug you.*

bào 报 (扌 7) Trad 報 VERB = report, announce

bàozhǐ 报纸 [modif: 报 *reporting* + 纸 *paper*] NOUN = newspaper (张 **zhāng**)
■ 今天报纸上有什么消息？ **Jīntiān bàozhǐ shang yǒu shénme xiāoxi?** = *What's the news in today's paper?*
■ 我很少看报纸。 **Wǒ hěn shǎo kàn bàozhǐ.** = *I seldom read newspapers.*

NOTE: Colloquially, 报 **bào** is often used instead of 报纸 **bàozhi**, e.g.
■ 你看得懂中文报吗？ **Nǐ kàn de dǒng Zhōngwén bào ma?** = *Do you understand Chinese newspapers?*

bēi 杯 (木 8) [木 sign + 不 phon **bù**] NOUN = cup, mug, glass (只 **zhī**)
bēizi 杯子 = cup, mug, glass
■ 这些杯子要洗一下。 **Zhèxiē bēizi yào xǐ yíxià.** = *These cups/mugs/ glasses need washing.*
chābēi 茶杯 = teacup
jiǔbēi 酒杯 = wine glass

B

yì bēi chá/jiǔ 一杯茶 / 酒 = a cup of tea/ a glass of wine

NOTE: (1) 杯 **bēi** may denote "cup," "mug" or "glass." (2) 杯 **bēi** is seldom used alone. It is usually suffixed with 子 **zi**: 杯子 **bēizi**, or combined with 茶 **chá** or 酒 **jiǔ**: 茶杯 **chābēi**, 酒杯 **jiǔbēi**.

běi 北 (匕 5) NOUN = north, northern
■ 在北半球，刮北风，天就冷。**Zài běibànqiú, guā běifēng, tiān jiù lěng.** = *In the north hemisphere, the weather becomes cold when a north wind blows.*
běijí 北极 = the North Pole (← the north extreme)
běijí xīng 北极星 = the North Star, Polaris

běibiān 北边 [modif: 北 *north* + 边 *side*] NOUN = north side, to the north, in the north
■ 山的北边是一个农场。**Shān de běibiān shì yí ge nóngchǎng.** = *North of the hill is a big farm.*
■ 加拿大在美国的北边。**Jiānádà zài Měiguó de běibiān.** = *Canada is to the north of America.*

Běijīng 北京 NOUN = Beijing (Peking) (the capital of the People's Republic of China)

bèi 备 (夂 8) Trad 備 VERB = prepare (See 准备 **zhǔnbèi**.)

bèi 被 (衤 10) PREPOSITION = by (introducing the doer of an action)
■ 花瓶被小明打破了。**Huāpíng bèi Xiǎo Míng dǎ pòle.** = *The vase was broken by Xiao Ming.*
■ 他被老师批评了。**Tā bèi lǎoshī pīpíng le.** = *He was criticized by the teacher.*

bèi 倍 (亻 10) MEASURE WORD = fold, time
yí bèi 一倍 = twice as ... as
■ 这个农场比那个农场大一倍。**Zhège nóngchǎng bǐ nàge nóngchǎng dà yí bèi.** = *This farm is twice as big as that one.*
■ 他爸爸的年龄是他的两倍。**Tā bāba de niánling shì tāde liǎng beì.** = *His daddy's age is twice as much as his.* (→ *His daddy is twice as old as he is.*)

NOTE: The concept "A is twice as big as B" can be expressed in two ways: A 比 B 大一倍 **A bǐ B dà yí bèi** or A 是 B 的两倍 **A shì B de liǎng bèi**.

běn 本 (木 5) MEASURE WORD = (for books, etc.)
■ 一本书 **yì běn shū** = *a book*

běnzi 本子 [suffix: 本 *a book* + 子 nominal suffix] NOUN = notebook (本 **běn**)
■ 这本本子记了很多重要的事情。**Zhè běn běnzi jìle hěn duō zhòngyào de shìqing.** = *Many important things are recorded in this notebook.*
■ 他丢了一个很重要的本子。**Tā diūle yí ge hěn zhòngyào de běnzi.** = *He's lost an important notebook.*

bǐ 比 (比 4)

1 VERB = compete, compare, contrast
■ 你们两个谁个子高？比一比！**Nǐmen liǎng ge shéi gèzi gāo? Bǐ yì bǐ!** = *Of you two, who is taller? Let's see!*

2 PREPOSITION = than (introducing the object that is compared with the subject of a sentence)
■ 你比他高。**Nǐ bǐ tā gāo.** = *You're taller than he is.*
■ 今天比昨天冷一点儿。**Jīntiān bǐ zuótiān lěng yìdiǎnr.** = *Today is a bit colder than yesterday.*
■ 我跑得比你快。**Wǒ pǎo de bǐ nǐ kuài.** = *I run faster than you.*
■ 你说中文说得比我好。**Nǐ shuō Zhōngwén shuō de bǐ wǒ hǎo.** = *You speak Chinese better than I do.*

bǐsài 比赛 [compound: 比 *compare* + 赛 *compete*]

1 VERB = compete, have a match
■ 我们比赛一下，看谁跑得快！**Wǒmen bǐsài yíxià, kàn shéi pǎo de kuài!** = *Let's have a race to see who runs fastest.*

hé/gēn ... bǐsài 和 / 跟...比赛 = have a match/race with
■ 今天晚上我们和他们比赛篮球。**Jīntiān wǎnshang wǒmen hé tāmen bǐsài lánqiú.** = *This evening we'll have a basketball match with them.*

2 NOUN = match, contest (场 **chǎng**)
■ 昨天晚上的篮球比赛精彩极了！**Zuótiān wǎngshang de lánqiú bǐsài jīngcǎi jíle!** = *The basketball match yesterday evening was wonderful!*
■ 他喜欢看足球比赛。**Tā xǐhuan kàn zúqiú bǐsài.** = *He likes to watch football matches.*

kàn bǐsài 看比赛 = watch a game/competition
cānjiā bǐsài 参加比赛 = participate in a game/competition

bǐ 笔 (竹 10) [竹 sign + 毛 sign]
Trad 筆

1 NOUN = writing instrument, pen, pencil (支 **zhī**)
■ 这支笔很好写。**Zhè zhī bǐ hěn hǎoxiě.** = *This pen writes well.*
■ 我可以借用你的笔吗？ **Wǒ kěyǐ jièyòng nǐ de bǐ ma?** = *May I borrow your pen?*

máobǐ 毛笔 = Chinese writing brush
huàbǐ 画笔 = paintbrush (for art)

2 MEASURE WORD = (for a sum of money)
yì bǐ qián 一笔钱 = a sum of money
yí dà bǐ qián 一大笔钱 = a big sum of money

bì 必 (心 5) ADVERB = must

bìxū 必须 [compound: 必 *must* + 须 *need, have to*] MODAL VERB = must
■ 你明天必须早一点儿来。**Nǐ míngtiān bìxū zǎo yìdiǎnr lái.** = *You must come a bit earlier tomorrow.*

biān 边 (辶 5) [辶 sign + 力 symb]
Trad 邊 NOUN = side, border
■ 山的这一边有很多树，那一边没有树。**Shān de zhè yì biān yǒu hěn duō shù, nà yì biān méiyǒu shù.** = *On this side of the hill there are lots of trees, and there are no trees on the other side.*

NOTE: The most frequent use of 边 **biān** is to form "compound location nouns" with words like 东 **dōng**,

B

B

南 **nán**, 西 **xī**, 北 **běi**, 里 **lǐ**, 外 **wài** etc., e.g. 东边 **dōngbiān** = east side, 南边 **nánbiān** = south side, 西边 **xībiān** = west side, 北边 **bēibiān** = north side, 里边 **lǐbiān** = inside, 外边 **wàibiān** = outside. 边 **biān** is often pronounced in the neutral tone.

biàn 变 (亦 8) Trad 變 VERB = transform, change
■ 这些年这个地方变了不少。**Zhèxiē nián zhège dìfang biànle bùshǎo.** = *This place has changed a lot over the years.*

biànchéng 变成 [v+comp: 变 *change* + 成 *into*] VERB = change into
■ 几年不见，小女孩变成了一个大姑娘。**Jǐnián bújiàn, xiǎo nǚhái biànchéngle yí ge dà gūniang.** = *After several years' absence, the little girl had changed into a young lady.*

biànhuà 变化 [compound: 变 *change* + 化 *transform*]
1 VERB = transform, change
■ 这些年这个地方变化不少。**Zhèxiē nián zhè ge dìfang biànhuà bù shǎo.** = *This place has changed a lot over the years.*

NOTE: As a verb, 变化 **biànhuà** is interchangeable with 变 **biàn**, 变化 **biànhuà** being a little more formal than 变 **biàn**.

2 NOUN = transformation, change
■ 这里的变化真大呀！ **Zhèlǐ de biànhuà zhēn dà ya!** = *How great the changes here are!*
■ 这些年来这个城市没有多大变化。**Zhèxiē nián lai zhè ge chéngshì méiyǒu duō dà biànhuà.** = *This city has not had much change over these years.*

biàn 便 (亻 9) See 方便 **fāngbiàn**.

biàn 遍 (辶 12) [辶 sign + 扁 phon **biǎn**] MEASURE WORD = time(s) (indicating the frequency of an action done in its complete duration from the beginning to the end)
■ 这本书我看了三遍了。**Zhè běn shū wǒ kànle sān biàn le.** = *I've read this book three times.*

biǎo 表 (衣 8) NOUN = watch (块 **kuài**/只 **zhī**)
■ 我的表丢了！ **Wǒ de biǎo diū le!** = *I've lost my watch!*
■ 我的表停了，你的表几点？ **Wǒ de biǎo tíng le, nǐ de biǎo jǐ diǎn?** = *My watch has stopped. What time is it by your watch?*
■ 去年生日爸爸送给我一块表。**Qùnián shēngrì bàba sòng gěi wǒ yí kuài biǎo.** = *Daddy gave me a watch on my last birthday.*
dài biǎo 戴表 = wear a watch
■ 他戴了一块新表。**Tā dàile yí kuài xīn biǎo.** = *He wears a new watch.*
nán biǎo 男表 = men's watch
nǚ biǎo 女表 = ladies' watch

biǎoshì 表示 [compound: 表 *show, express* + 示 *show, indicate*] VERB = express, show, indicate
■ 她点点头，表示同意。**Tā diǎndiǎn tóu, biǎoshì tóngyì.** = *She nodded, indicating agreement.*

biǎoxiàn 表现 [compound: 表 *show, express* + 现 *display*] VERB = display, show
■ 他表现得很热情。**Tā biǎoxiàn de hěn rèqíng.** = *He appeared to be enthusiastic.*

biǎoyǎn 表演 [compound: 表 *show* + 演 *act*]
1 VERB = put on (a show), perform, demonstrate
■ 他们星期六在这里表演。**Tāmen Xīngqīliù zài zhèli biǎoyǎn.** = *They perform here on Saturday.*
2 NOUN = (theatrical) performance
■ 他们的表演很精彩。**Tāmen de biǎoyǎn hěn jīngcǎi.** = *Their performance was wonderful.*
kàn biǎoyǎn 看表演 = watch a performance/demonstration
■ 今天晚上你去看表演吗？**Jīntiān wǎnshang nǐ qù kàn biǎoyǎn ma?** = *Are you going to see the performance tonight?*
cānjiā biǎoyǎn 参加表演 = participate in a performance/demonstration

biǎoyáng 表扬 [compound: 表 *display* + 扬 *raise, make known*] VERB = praise, commend (antonym 批评 **pīpíng**)
■ 你做了一件好事，应该表扬。**nǐ zuòle yí jiàn hǎo shì, yīnggāi biǎoyáng.** = *You've done a good deed and should be praised.*
biǎoyáng hǎo rén hǎo shì 表扬好人好事 = praise good people and commend good deeds

bié 别 (刂 7) ADVERB = don't
■ 别说话了，电影开始了！**Bié shuōhuà le, diànyǐng kāishǐ le!** = *Don't talk. (→ Stop talking.) The movie has started.*
■ 你不愿意去，就别去了。**Nǐ bú yuànyì qù, jiù bié qù le.** = *If you don't want to go, then don't go.*

NOTE: 别 **bié** is a contraction of 不要 **bú yaò** in an imperative sentence, e.g. ■ 请别在这里抽烟。**Qǐng bié zài zhèli chōuyān.** = *Don't smoke here.* It is used colloquially only.

biéde 别的 PRONOUN = *other*
■ 我们这里这本书卖完了，您去别的书店看看。**Wǒmen zhèli zhè běn shū màiwán le, nín qù biéde shūdiàn kànkan.** = *We've sold out the book here. You could go to other bookshops to have a look.*

biérén 别人 [modif: 别 *other* + 人 *person, people*] PRONOUN = other people, others
■ 你不能只想自己，不想别人。**Nǐ bù néng zhǐ xiǎng zìjǐ, bù xiǎng biérén.** = *You shouldn't think of yourself only, and not of others.*
■ 别人都说这部电影好看，只有你说不好看。**Biérén dōu shuō zhè bù diànyǐng hǎokàn, zhǐyǒu nǐ shuō bù hǎokàn.** = *All the other people say this film is good, only you say it's not.*

bìng 病 (疒 10) [疒 sign + 丙 phon **bǐng**]
1 VERB = fall ill, be ill

■ 我爸爸病了，在家休息。**Wǒ bàba bìng le, zài jiā xiūxi.** = *My father's ill and is resting at home.*

2 NOUN = illness, disease

■ 你的病很重，要住医院。**Nǐ de bìng hěn zhòng, yào zhù yīyuàn.** = *You're seriously ill and need to be hospitalized.*

■ 这一点儿小病，没关系。**Zhè yìdiǎnr xiǎo bìng, méiguānxi.** = *This is a mild case (of illness); it doesn't matter.*

■ 张先生什么病？ **Zhāng xiānsheng shénme bìng?** = *What is Mr Zhang ill with?* (→ *What's wrong with Mr Zhang?*)

shēng bìng 生病 = to fall ill
bìng rén 病人 = sick person, patient
bìngfáng 病房 = (hospital) ward

B

bō 播

(扌 15) [扌 sign + 番 symb] VERB = sow (See 广播 **guǎngbō**.)

búcuò 不错

ADJECTIVE = not wrong, quite right; not bad, quite good

■ 这个电影不错。**Zhè ge diànyǐng búcuò.** = *This movie is not bad.*

■ 你说得不错。**Nǐ shuō de búcuò.** = *You've spoken correctly.* (→ *You're right.*)

■ 这孩子画得真不错。**Zhè háizi huà de zhēn búcuò.** = *This child really doesn't draw badly.* (→ *This child draws quite well.*)

■ 你这个字写得不错。**Nǐ zhè ge zì xiě de búcuò.** = (This sentence is ambiguous. It may mean either *You wrote this character correctly.* or *You wrote this character quite well.*)

búdàn 不但

CONJUNCTION = not only ... (but also)

búdàn ... érqie 不但… 而且… = not only... but also

■ 我不但会说一点儿汉语，而且会写一些汉字。**Wǒ búdàn huì shūo yìdiǎnr Hànyǔ, érqiě huì xiě yìxiē hànzì.** = *I can not only speak a little Chinese but also write a few Chinese characters.*

■ 这间房间不但整齐，而且很舒服。**Zhè jiān fāngjiān búdàn zhěngqí, érqiě hěn shūfu.** = *This room is not only tidy but also very comfortable.*

búyào 不要

ADVERB = do not (used in an imperative sentence or as advice)

■ 请您不要在这里抽烟。**Qǐng nín búyào zài zhèli chōuyān.** = *Please don't smoke here.*

■ 你不要着急，你孩子的病很快会好的。**Nǐ búyào zháojí, nǐ háizi de bìng hěn kuài huì hǎo de.** = *Don't be worried; your child will recover soon.*

NOTE: 不要 **búyào** has the same meaning and syntactic function as 别 **bié**, but 别 **bié** is only used colloquially. See note under 别 **bié**.

búyòng 不用

ADVERB = no need, there's no need, don't have to

■ 如果明天下雨，你就不用来了。**Rúguǒ míngtiān xià yǔ, nǐ jiù búyòng lái le.** = *If it rains tomorrow, you don't have to come.*

■ 不用麻烦了，我们一会儿就走。**Búyòng máfan le, wǒmen yīhuìr jiù zǒu.** = *Don't bother. We're leaving soon.*

bù 不 (一 4) ADVERB = no, not
■ 今天不热。**Jīntiān bú rè.** = *Today is not hot.*
■ 我不同意你的话。**Wǒ bù tóngyì nǐ de huà.** = *I don't agree with what you said.*
■ "你是澳大利亚人吗?" "不是，我是新西兰人。" **"Nǐ shì Àodàlìyà rén ma?" "Bú shì, wǒ shì Xīnxīlán rén."** = *Are you an Australian?" "No, I'm a New Zealander."*

NOTE: When followed by a syllable in the fourth (falling) tone, 不 **bù** undergoes tone change—from the normal fourth tone to the second (rising) tone, e.g. 不热 **bú rè,** 不是 **bú shì**.

bùjiǔ 不久 NOUN = not long, near future, soon
■ 我们不久就要毕业了。**Wǒmen bùjiǔ jiùyào bìyè le.** = *We will soon graduate.*

bùrú 不如 VERB = be not as good as, not as ... as
■ 走路不如骑车快。**Zǒulù bùrú qíchē kuài.** = *Walking is not as fast as riding a bicycle.*

bùtóng 不同 ADJECTIVE = not the same, different
■ 我们来自不同的国家，但都在学习中文。**Wǒmen láizì bùtóng de guójiā, dàn dōu zài xuéxí Zhōngwén.** = *We came from different countries, but we're all studying Chinese.*
...hé/gēn ... bùtóng ...和 / 跟... 不同 = ... *is/are different from ...*
■ 人和人不同，不能比较。**Rén hé rén bùtóng, bù néng bǐjiào.** = *People are different and cannot be compared.*

bù 布 (巾 5) NOUN = cotton or linen cloth (块 **kuài**)
■ 这块布很好看，做一条裙子正合适。**Zhè kuài bù hěn hǎokàn, zuò yì tiáo qúnzi zhèng héshì.** = *This piece of cotton cloth looks good, just right for a skirt.*

bù 步 (止 7) See 跑步 **pǎobù**, 散步 **sànbù**.

bù 部 (阝 10) NOUN = part

bùfen 部分 [compound: 部 *part* + 分 *division*] NOUN = portion, part
■ 这本语法书有五个部分，每个部分讲一个问题。**Zhè běn yǔfǎ shū yǒu wǔ ge bùfen, měi ge bùfen jiǎng yí ge wèntí.** = *This grammar book has five parts, each dealing with a grammatical topic.*

C

cā 擦 (扌 17) [扌 sign + 察 phon **chá**] VERB = clean or erase by wiping or rubbing
■ 在中国的学校里，学生擦黑板，在这个学校，谁擦黑板? **Zài Zhōngguó de xuéxiào li, xuésheng cā hēibǎn, zài zhège xuéxiào, shuí cā hēibǎn?** = *In Chinese schools, students clean the blackboard. In this school, who cleans the blackboard?*
cā gānjìng 擦干净 = wipe ... clean

C

■ 我的自行车太脏了，我要把它擦干净。**Wǒ de zìxíngchē tài zāng le, wǒ yào bǎ tā cā gānjing.** = *My bike is dirty. I'll wipe it clean.*

cái 才 (一 3) ADVERB
1 = (before a verb) a short time ago, just
■ 我才来，不知道这件事。**Wǒ cái lái, bù zhīdào zhè jiàn shì.** = *I've just arrived; I don't know about this matter.*
■ 他才起床，还没有吃早饭。**Tā cái qǐchuáng, hái méiyǒu chī zǎofàn.** = *He's just gotten up and hasn't eaten breakfast yet.*
2 = (before a word of time or quantity, indicating that the speaker feels the time is too early, too short or the quantity is too little) only, as early as, as few/little as
■ 我中文学了才一年，讲得不好。**Wǒ Zhōngwén xuéle cái yì nián, jiǎng de bù hǎo.** = *I've learned Chinese for only a year, and can't speak it very well.*
■ 这本书才十块钱，太便宜了。**Zhè běn shū cái shí kuài qián, tài piányì le.** = *This book is only ten dollars; it's really cheap.*
3 = (after a word of time) indicating that the speaker feels the time is too late or there is too much delay; as late as
■ 他每天晚上十二点才睡觉。**Tā měi tiān wǎnshang shí'èr diǎn cái shuìjiào.** = *Every night he goes to bed as late as twelve o'clock.*
■ 这个小孩三岁才会走。**Zhège xiǎohái sān suì cái huì zǒu.** = *This child learned to walk as late as three years old.*

cǎi 彩 (彡 11) [采 phon **cǎi** + 彡 symb]
See 精彩 **jīngcǎi**.

cài 菜 (艹 11) [艹 sign + 采 phon **cǎi**]
NOUN
1 = vegetable
■ 我喜欢吃菜，不喜欢吃肉。**Wǒ xǐhuan chī cài, bù xǐhuan chī ròu.** = *I like eating vegetables, not meat.*
zhòng cài 种菜 = grow vegetables
■ 我们在花园里种了不少菜。**Wǒmen zài huāyuán li zhòngle bùshǎo cài.** = *We grow quite a lot of vegetables in our garden.*
2 = any non-staple food such as vegetables, meat, fish, eggs, etc.
■ 妈妈每个星期五都要买很多菜，有鱼、有肉、还有鸡。**Māma měi ge Xīngqīwǔ dōu yào mǎi hěn duō cài, yǒu yú, yǒu ròu, háiyǒu jī.** = *Every Friday Mum buys lots of food: fish, meat and chicken.*
mǎi cài 买菜 = buy non-staple food, do grocery shopping
■ 我每个星期买两次菜。**Wǒ měi ge xīngqī mǎi liǎng cì cài.** = *I do grocery shopping twice a week.*
3 = (cooked) dish
■ 请别客气，多吃点菜！ **Qǐng bié kèqi duō chī diǎnr cài!** = *Please don't be so polite, eat more food!*
■ 这个菜又好看又好吃，是谁做的？ **Zhège cài yòu hǎokàn yòu hǎochī, shì shuí zuò de?** = *This dish looks inviting and tastes delicious. Who cooked it?*
Zhōngguó cài 中国菜 = Chinese dishes, Chinese food
■ 你会做中国菜吗？ **Nǐ huì zuò Zhōngguó cài ma?** = *Can you cook Chinese dishes?*

cān 参 (厶 8) Trad 參 VERB = call on

cānguān 参观 [compound: 参 *call on* + 观 *watch, see*] VERB = visit (a place, not a person)
■ 我在中国的时候，参观了很多学校。**Wǒ zài Zhōngguó de shíhou, cānguānle hěn duō xuéxiào.** = *I visited many schools when I was in China.*
■ 明天有几位中国朋友要来参观我们的农场。**Míngtiān yǒu jǐ wèi Zhōngguó péngyou yào lái cānguān wǒmen de nóngchǎng.** = *A group of Chinese friends will visit our farm tomorrow.*

cānjiā 参加 [v+comp: 参 *enter* + 加 *add*] VERB = join, participate, attend
■ 我可以参加中文班吗？ **Wǒ kěyǐ cānjiā Zhōngwén bān ma?** = *May I join the Chinese class?*
■ 欢迎您参加我们的晚会。**Huānyíng nín cānjiā wǒmen de wǎnhuì!** = *You're welcome to our evening party!*

cāo 操 (扌 16) [扌 sign + phon] NOUN = drill, exercise

cāochǎng 操场 [modif: 操 *drill, exercise* + 场 *ground*] NOUN = sports ground, playground
■ 我们学校的操场很大。**Wǒmen xuéxiào de cāochǎng hěn dà.** = *Our school's sports ground is very big.*
(zài) cāochǎng shang (在) 操场上 = on the sports ground
■ 很多学生在操场上玩。**Hěn duō xuésheng zài cāochǎng shang wán.** = *Many students are playing on the sports ground.*

cǎo 草 (艹 9) [艹 sign + 早 phon **zǎo**] NOUN = grass, weed (棵 **kē**)
■ 几只羊在吃草。**Jǐ zhī yáng zài chī cǎo.** = *Several sheep are grazing.*
cǎodì 草地 = lawn, grassland, pasture
■ 我家房前有一大片草地。**Wǒ jiā fáng qián yǒu yí dà piàn cǎodì.** = *There is a big lawn in front of my house.*

céng 层 (尸 7) Trad 層 MEASURE WORD = story (storey), floor
■ 那个大楼有八层，我住在第三层。**Nàge dà lóu yǒu bā céng, wǒ zhù zài dì-sān céng.** = *That building has eight floors. I live on the third floor.*

NOTE: The Chinese way of numbering floors is the same as the American practice, e.g. 一层楼 **yī céng lóu** is "the first floor" in America, but "the ground floor" to the British.

chá 茶 (艹 9) [艹 sign + symb] Trad 茶 NOUN = tea
■ 这杯茶是你的。**Zhè bēi chá shì nǐ de.** = *This cup of tea is yours.*
■ 茶凉了，快喝吧。**Chá liáng le, kuài hē ba.** = *The tea is no longer hot. Please drink it.*
■ 您喝红茶还是绿茶？ **Nín hē hóngchá háishì lǜchá?** = *Do you drink black tea or green tea?*
hóngchá 红茶 = black tea
lǜchá 绿茶 = green tea
nǎi chá 奶茶 = tea with milk
chá bēi 茶杯 = tea cup
hē chá 喝茶 = drink tea

C

chá 查 (木 9) VERB = check, look up
■ 我可以用一下你的词典吗？我想查一个字。 **Wǒ kěyǐ yòng yíxià nǐ de cídiǎn ma? Wǒ xiǎng chá yí ge zì.** = *May I use your dictionary? I want to look up a word.*
chá cídiǎn 查词典 = look up words in a dictionary
■ 你会查中文词典吗？ **Nǐ huì chá Zhōngwén cídiǎn ma?** = *Do you know how to look up words in a Chinese dictionary?*

C

chà 差 (羊 10) VERB = be short of, lack
■ 我还差二十块钱，你可以借给我吗？ **Wǒ hái chà èrshí kuài qián, nǐ kěyǐ jiè gei wǒ ma?** = *I'm still short of twenty dollars. Can you give me a loan?*
■ 现在是十一点差五分。**Xiànzài shì shíyī diǎn chà wǔ fēn.** = *It's five to eleven now.*

chǎn 产 (立 6) Trad **產** VERB = produce (See 生产 **shēngchǎn**.)

cháng 长 (丿 4) Trad **長** ADJECTIVE = long (antonym 短 **duǎn**)
■ 中国的历史很长。**Zhōngguó de lìshǐ hěn cháng.** = *China has a long history.*
chángpǎo 长跑 = long distance running
■ 他是一名长跑运动员。**Tā shì yì míng chángpǎo yùndòngyuán.** = *He is a long-distance athlete.*

NOTE: 长 **cháng** occurs in two Chinese icons: 长城 **chángchéng** (← *the long wall*) = *the Great Wall*, arguably the most famous place of historical interest in China and 长江 **chángjiāng** (← *the long river*) = *the Yangtze River*, her longest river.

cháng 常 (巾 11) ADVERB = often
■ 我常给他打电话。**Wǒ cháng gěi tā dǎ diànhuà.** = *I often ring him.*
chángcháng 常常 = often
■ 我们常常到他家去玩。**Wǒmen chángcháng dào tā jiā qù wán.** = *We often go to his home to have a good time.*
bùcháng 不常 = not often, seldom
■ 他不常看电影。**Tā bùcháng kàn diànyǐng.** = *He seldom goes to the movies.*

NOTE: Colloquially, 常常 **chángcháng** is often used instead of 常 **cháng**.

chǎng 厂 (厂 2) Trad **廠** NOUN = factory (See 工厂 **gōngchǎng**.)

chǎng 场 (土 6) [土 sign + symb] Trad **場**
1 MEASURE WORD = (for movies, sport events, etc.)
yì chǎng diànyǐng 一场电影 = a film show
■ 这个电影院一天放六场电影。**Zhè ge diànyǐngyuàn yìtiān fàng liù chǎng diànyǐng.** = *This cinema has six film shows a day.*
yì chǎng qiúsài 一场球赛 = a ball game
■ 昨天我看了一场精彩的球赛。**Zuótiān wǒ kànle yì chǎng jīngcǎi de qiúsài.** = *I watched a wonderful ball game yesterday.*
2 NOUN = ground, field
tǐyù chǎng 体育场 = sports ground, stadium
fēijī chǎng 飞机场 = airport

chàng 唱 (口 11) [口 sign + 昌 phon **chāng**] VERB = sing
■ 你会唱中文歌吗？ **Nǐ huì chàng Zhōngwén gē ma?** = *Can you sing Chinese songs?*
chànggē 唱歌 = sing songs, sing
■ 你唱歌唱得真好听！ **Nǐ chànggē chàng de zhēn hǎotīng!** = *You really sing well!*

cháo 朝 (月 12)
1 VERB = face
■ 中国人的房子大都朝南。**Zhōngguórén de fángzi dàdōu cháo nán.** = *Chinese people's houses usually face south.*
2 PREPOSITION = towards, to
■ 你一直朝前走十分钟左右，就到公园了。**Nǐ yìzhí cháo qián zǒu shí fēnzhōng zuǒyòu, jiù dào gōngyuán le.** = *Walk straight ahead for about ten minutes and you'll reach the park.*

chē 车 (车 4) Trad 車 NOUN = vehicle, traffic (辆 **liàng**)
■ 我的车坏了。**Wǒ de chē huài le.** = *My car* (or *bicycle*) *has broken down.*
■ 路上车很多。**Lùshang chē hěn duō.** = *There is lots of traffic on the road.*
■ 我可以借用你的车吗？ **Wǒ kěyǐ jièyòng nǐ de chē ma?** = *May I borrow your car* (or *bicycle*)*?*
kāi chē 开车 = drive an automobile
qí chē 骑车 = ride a bicycle
xué chē 学车 = learn to drive (or to ride a bicycle)

chēzhàn 车站 [modif: 车 *vehicle* + 站 *station*] NOUN = (bus) stop, (railway or coach) station (座 **zuò**, 个 **gè**)
■ "车站离这里远不远？" "不远，开车去只要十分钟。" **"Chēzhàn lí zhèli yuǎn bu yuǎn?" "Bù yuǎn, kāichē qù zhǐyào shí fēnzhōng."** = *"Is the railway* (or *bus*) *station far from here?" "No, it's only ten minutes' drive."*
■ 王先生去车站接朋友了。**Wáng xiānsheng qù chēzhàn jiē péngyou le.** – *Mr Wang has gone to the railway* (or *coach*) *station to meet a friend.*

Chén 陈 (阝 7) Trad 陳 NOUN = a common family name

chén 晨 (日 11) [日 sign + 辰 phon **chén**] NOUN = early morning (See 早晨 **zǎochén**.)

chéng 成 (戈 6) VERB = become, turn into
■ 几年没见，她成了一个漂亮的大姑娘了。**Jǐnián méi jiàn, tā chénle yí ge piàoliang de dàgūniang le.** = *After several years' absence, she had become a pretty young lady.*

chéngjì 成绩 [compound: 成 *accomplish* + 绩 *result*] NOUN = achievement, examination result
■ 他去年的考试成绩不太好。**Tā qùnián de kǎoshì chéngjì bú tài hǎo.** = *His examination results last year were not very good.*
■ 我们取得了很大成绩。**Wǒmen qǔdé le hěn dà chéngjì.** = *We've made great achievements.*
kǎoshì chéngjì 考试成绩 = examination result
qǔdé chéngjì 取得成绩 = make achievement, get (positive, good) results

C

C

chéng 城 (土 9) [土 sign + 成 phon **chéng**] NOUN = city, town (**座 zuò**)
jìn chéng 进城 = go to town, go to the city center
■ 我今天下午进城，有什么事要我办吗？ **Wǒ jīntiān xiàwǔ jìn chéng, yǒu shénme shì yào wǒ bàn ma?** = *I'm going to town this afternoon. Is there anything you want me to do for you?*
chéngli 城里 = in town, downtown
chéngwài 城外 = out of town, suburban area

chéngshì 城市 [compound: 城 *city wall, city* + 市 *market*] NOUN = city, urban area (as opposed to rural area) (座 **zuò**)
■ 这座城市不大，但是很漂亮。 **Zhè zuo chéngshì bú dà, dànshì hěn piàoliang.** = *This city is not big, but it's quite beautiful.*
■ 我喜欢住在大城市里。 **Wǒ xǐhuan zhù zài dà chéngshì li.** = *I like to live in big cities.*
chéngshì shēnghuó 城市生活 = city life

chī 吃 (口 6) [口 sign + 乞 phon **qǐ**] VERB = eat
■ "你吃过早饭没有？" "吃过了。" **"Nǐ chīguo zǎofàn méiyoǔ?" "Chīguo le."** = *"Have you had breakfast?" "Yes, I have."*

chí 迟 (辶 7) Trad 遲 ADJECTIVE = late

chídào 迟到 [modif: 迟 *late* + 到 *arrive*] VERB = come late, be late (for work, school, etc.)
■ 对不起，我迟到了。 **Duìbuqǐ, wǒ chídào le.** = *I'm sorry I'm late.*
■ "你今天迟到了二十分钟，明天不要再迟到了。" "请您原谅。我明天一定不迟到。" **"Nǐ jīntiān chídàole èrshí fēnzhōng, míngtiān búyào zài chídào le." "Qǐng nín yuánliàng. Wǒ míngtiān yídìng bù chídào."** = *"You were late twenty minutes today. Don't be late tomorrow." "My apologies. I'll definitely not be late tomorrow."*

chí 持 (扌 9) [扌 sign + 寺 phon **shì**] VERB = persevere (See 坚持 **jiānchí**.)

chū 出 (凵 5) VERB = emerge from, get out of
chūlái 出来 = come out
■ 请你出来一下。 **Qǐng nǐ chūlái yíxià.** = *Would you please step out for a while.*
chūqù 出去 = go out
■ 请你出去一下。 **Qǐng nǐ chūqù yíxià.** = *Please go out for a while (→Please leave us for a while.)*
chūguó 出国 = go abroad, go overseas
■ 我爸爸每年都要出国开会。 **Wǒ bàba měi nián dōu yào chūguó kāihuì.** = *My father goes overseas for conferences every year.*

chūfā 出发 [compound: 出 *depart* + 发 *discharge*] VERB = set off, start (a journey)
■ "我们明天什么时候出发？" "早上八点。" **"Wǒmen míngtiān shénme shíhou chūfā?" "Zǎoshang bā diǎn."** = *"When do we set off tomorrow?" "Eight o'clock in the morning."*

chūxiàn 出现 [compound: 出 *emerge* + 现 *appear*] VERB = come into view, appear, emerge
■ 开车两小时，一座漂亮的小山城出现在我们面前。**Kāichē liǎng xiǎoshí, yí zuò piàoliang de xiǎo shānchéng chūxiàn zài wǒmen miànqián.** = *After two hours' drive, a beautiful small mountain town came into our view.*

chūzū 出租 [compound: 出 *out* + 租 *rent*] VERB = let, rent, hire
■ 这家商店出租电视机。**Zhè jiā shāngdiàn chūzū diànshìjī.** = *This store has TV sets for hire.*
chūzū qìchē 出租汽车 = taxi
■ 我要一辆出租汽车去飞机场。**Wǒ yào yí liàng chūzū qìchē qù fēijīchǎng.** = *I want a taxi to go to the airport.*

NOTE: The slang expression 打的 **dǎdī**, which means "to call a taxi" or "to travel by taxi," is very popular in everyday Chinese.

chū 初 (衤 7) See 最初 **zuìchū**.

chú 除 (阝 9) VERB = remove, eliminate

chúle...(yǐwài) 除了…(以外) PREPOSITION = except, besides
■ 我们除了星期六和星期天每天都上学。**Wǒmen chúle Xīngqīliù hé Xīngqītiān měi tiān dōu shàngxué.** = *We go to school every day except Saturday and Sunday.*
■ 我除了英文以外，还会说一点儿中文。**Wǒ chúle Yīngwén yǐwài, háihuì shuō yìdiǎnr Zhōngwén.** = *Besides English I speak a little Chinese.*

NOTE: While "except" and "besides" are two distinct words in English, 除了…(以外) **chúle...(yǐwài)** is the equivalent of both words, as the examples show. 以外 **yǐwài** may be omitted, i.e. 除了…以外 **chúle... yǐwài** and 除了… **chúle...** have the same meaning.

chǔ 础 (石 10) [石 sign + 出 phon **chū**] Trad 礎 NOUN = plinth (See 基础 **jīchǔ**.)

chǔ 楚 (疋 13) ADJECTIVE = clear, neat (See 清楚 **qīngchu**.)

chù 处 (夂 5) Trad 處 NOUN = place, spot (See 好处 **hǎochu**.)

chuān 穿 (穴 9) VERB = put on (clothes or shoes), wear (clothes or shoes)
■ 这个小孩会穿衣服了，可是还不会穿鞋子。**Zhège xiǎohái huì chuān yīfu le, kěshì hái bú huì chuān xiézi.** = *This child can put on clothes, but still can't put on shoes.*
chuānzhe 穿着 = be dressed in
■ 那个穿着红衣服的女孩子是我哥哥的女朋友。**Nàge chuānzhe hóng yīfu de nǚháizi shì wǒ gēge de nǚ péngyou.** = *The girl in red is my elder brother's girlfriend.*

chuán 传 (亻 5) Trad 傳 VERB = transmit, pass on

chuánzhēn 传真 [v+obj: 传 *transmit* + 真 *true*] NOUN = fax (份 **fèn**)
■ 这份传真是给你的。**Zhè fèn**

chuánzhēn shì gěi nǐ de. = *This fax is for you.*
■ 我发了一份传真给他。**Wǒ fāle yí fèn chuánzhēn gěi tā.** = *I sent him a fax.*

C

chuán 船 (舟 11) [舟 sign + symb]
NOUN = boat, ship
zuòchuán 坐船 = travel by boat (ship)
■ 从香港坐船到上海去，只要两天。**Cóng Xiānggǎng zuòchuán dào Shànghǎi qu, zhǐ yào liǎng tiān.** = *It takes only two days to travel from Hong Kong to Shanghai by sea.*

chuāng 窗 (穴 12) [穴 sign + symb]
NOUN = window

chuānghu 窗户 [compound: 窗 *window* + 户 *door*] NOUN = window
■ 我房间的窗户朝东。**Wǒ fángjiān de chuānghu cháo dōng.** = *The window in my room faces east.*
■ 马上要下雨了，把窗户关上吧。**Mǎshàng yào xià yǔ le, bǎ chuānghu guānshang ba.** = *It's going to rain. Let's close the window.*
dǎkāi/guānshang chuānghu 打开 / 关上 窗户 = open/close a window

chuáng 床 (广 7) [广 sign + 木 sign]
Trad 床 NOUN = bed (张 **zhāng**)
■ 这张床很舒服。**Zhè zhāng chuáng hěn shūfu.** = *This bed is very comfortable.*
■ 你的衣服在床上。**Nǐ de yīfu zài chuáng shang.** = *Your clothes are on the bed.*

chuī 吹 (口 7) [口 sign + 欠 symb]
VERB = blow, puff
■ 风吹草动 **Fēng chuī cǎo dòng** = *Winds blow and the grass stirs.* (→ *There are faint signs of trouble.*)
chuīniú 吹牛 = brag, boast
■ 你别相信他，他在吹牛。**Nǐ bié xiāngxìn tā, tā zài chuīniú.** = *Don't believe him. He's bragging.*

chūn 春 (日 9) [日 sign + symb]
NOUN = spring

chūnjié 春节 [modif: 春 *spring* + 节 *festival*] NOUN = Spring Festival (the Chinese New Year)
■ 小明的哥哥、姐姐都要回家过春节。**Xiǎomíng de gēge, jiějie dōu yào huí jiā guò chūnjié.** = *Xiao Ming's elder brothers and sisters will come home for the Spring Festival.*

chūntiān 春天 [modif: 春 *spring* + 天 *days*] NOUN = spring
■ 春天来了，花园里的花都开了。**Chūntiān lái le, huāyuán li de huā dōu kāi le.** = *Spring has come. The flowers in the garden are in full bloom.*
■ 我最喜欢春天，不太冷，也不太热。**Wǒ zuì xǐhuan chūntiān, bú tài lěng, yě bú tài rè.** = *I like spring best; it's neither too hot nor too cold.*
■ 他们去年春天结婚的。**Tāmen qùnián chūntiān jiéhūn de.** = *They were married in spring last year.*

cí 词 (讠 7) [讠 sign + 司 phon **sī**]
Trad 詞 NOUN = word
■ 中文里有的词是两个字，所以字不一定是词。**Zhōngwén li yǒude cí shì liǎng ge zì, suǒyǐ zì bù yídìng shì cí.** = *In Chinese some words have two*

characters, so a character is not necessarily a word.
■ 我没有听说过这个词。**Wǒ méiyǒu tīngshuōguo zhège cí.** = *I haven't heard of this word.*

cídiǎn 词典 NOUN = dictionary (本 **běn**)
■ 这本词典对我们很有帮助。**Zhè běn cídiǎn duì wǒmen hěn yǒubāngzhù.** = *This dictionary is very helpful to us.*
■ 你看，我买了一本新词典。**Nǐ kàn, wǒ mǎile yì běn xīn cídiǎn.** = *Look, I've bought a new dictionary.*
chá cídiǎn 查词典 = look up a word in a dictionary
■ 你会查中文词典吗？ **Nǐ huì chá Zhōngwén cídiǎn ma?** = *Can you look up a word in a Chinese dictionary?*

cí 磁 (石 14) [石 sign + 兹 phon **zī**] NOUN = magnetism

cídài 磁带 [modif: 磁 *magnetic* + 带 *tape*] NOUN = magnetic tape, audio tape
■ 你要的磁带，我借给一个朋友了。**Nǐ yào de cídài, wǒ jiè gei yí ge péngyou le.** = *I've lent the tape you want to a friend.*
■ 她一边听磁带，一边看报纸。**Tā yìbiān tīng cídài, yìbiān kàn bàozhǐ.** = *She listened to a tape while reading the newspaper.*

cì 次 (冫 6) MEASURE WORD = time (expressing frequency of an act)
■ 我去过他家两次。**Wǒ qùguo tā jiā liǎngcì.** = *I've been to his home twice.*

cóng 从 (人 4) [人 sign + 人 sign] Trad **從** PREPOSITION = following, from
■ "你从哪里来？" "我从城里来。" **"Nǐ cóng nǎlǐ lái?" "Wǒ cóng chéngli lái."** = *"Where did you come from?" "I came from the town."*

cóng ... dào ... 从…到… PREPOSITION = from ... to ... , from ... till ...
■ 我从上午九点到下午三点都要上课。**Wǒ cóng shàngwǔ jiǔ diǎn dào xiàwǔ sān diǎn dōu yào shàngkè.** = *I have classes from nine o'clock in the morning till three o'clock in the afternoon.*
■ 从中国到英国要经过许多国家。**Cóng Zhōngguó dào Yīngguó yào jīngguò xǔduō guójiā.** = *Travelling from China to England, one has to pass through many countries.*
cóng-zǎo-dào-wǎn 从早到晚 = from morning till night, long hours each day
■ 夏天他从早到晚都在农场工作。**Xiàtiān tā cóng-zǎo-dào-wǎn dōu zài nóngchǎng gōngzuò.** = *In summer he works on the farm from dawn to dusk.*

cóng ... qǐ 从…起 PREPOSITION = starting from ...
■ 我决定从明年一月一日起每天早上跑步。**Wǒ juédìng cóng míngnián Yīyuè yīrì qǐ měi tiān zǎoshang pǎobù.** = *I resolve to jog every morning starting from January 1 next year.*

cóngqián 从前 NOUN = past time, past, in the past
■ 这里从前是个大农场。**Zhèli**

C

cóngqián shì ge dà nóngchǎng. = *In the past there was a big farm here.*
■ 我从前不知道学中文多么有意思。**Wǒ cóngqián bù zhīdào xué Zhōngwén duōme yǒuyìsi.** = *I did not know before how interesting it is to learn Chinese.*

C

cūn 村 (木 7) [木 sign + 寸 phon **cùn**] NOUN = village (See 农村 **nóngcūn.**)

cuò 错 (钅 13) Trad **錯** ADJECTIVE = wrong (antonym 对 **duì**)
■ 你错了。**Nǐ cuò le.** = *You're wrong.*
■ 你这个字写错了。**Nǐ zhè ge zì xiě cuò le.** = *You've written this character wrong.*
■ 他说错了。**Tā shuō cuò le.** = *He's said the wrong thing.* (→ *He's wrong.*)

NOTE: It is very common to use 错 **cuò** after a verb. Here are more examples:
■ 他做错了。**Tā zuò cuò le.** = *He did something wrong.*
■ 他想错了。**Tā xiǎng cuò le.** = *He thought wrongly.* (→ *He was mistaken.*)

cuòwù 错误 [compound: 错 *wrong* + 误 *miss*]
1 NOUN = mistake, error
■ 这个错误很大。**Zhège cuòwù hěn dà.** = *This is a serious mistake.*
■ 你这次作业有很多错误。**Nǐ zhè cì zuòyè yǒu hěn duō cuòwù.** = *You've made many mistakes in this assignment.*
2 ADJECTIVE = wrong, mistaken
■ 这是一个错误的决定。**Zhè shì yí ge cuòwù de juédìng.** = *This is a wrong decision.*

D

dǎ 打 (扌 6) [扌 sign + 丁 symb] VERB = strike, hit; play (certain games)
■ 不能打人！ **Bù néng dǎ rén.** = *You can't hit people.*
dǎ qiú 打球 = play basketball/volleyball/netball
■ 小王正在打球。**Xiǎo Wáng zhèngzài dǎ qiú.** = *Xiao Wang is playing a ball game.*

dǎsuàn 打算 [compound: 打 *act* + 算 *calculate*] VERB = plan, contemplate
■ 你打算明年做什么？ **Nǐ dǎsuàn míngnián zuò shénme?** = *What do you plan to do next year?*
■ 我不打算买什么。= **Wǒ bù dǎsuàn mǎi shénme.** = *I don't intend to buy anything.*

dà 大 (大 3) ADJECTIVE = big (antonym 小 **xiǎo**)
■ 他们家的农场很大。**Tāmen jiā de nóngchǎng hěn dà.** = *Their family farm is very big.*
■ 这双鞋太大了，请给我小一号的。**Zhè shuāng xié tài dà le, qǐng gěi wǒ xiǎo yí hào de.** = *This pair of shoes is too big. Please give me a smaller size.*
■ 我夏天常常在那棵大树下睡一会儿。**Wǒ xiàtiān chángcháng zài nà kē dà shù xià shuì yíhuìr.** = *In summer I often have a nap under that big tree.*
dàren 大人 = adult (antonym 小孩儿 **xiǎoháir**)
■ 小孩儿都希望很快变成大人。**Xiǎoháir dōu xīwàng hěn kuài biànchéng dàren.** = *All children hope to grow up quickly.*

dàgài 大概

1 ADJECTIVE = general, more or less

■ 他的话我没听清楚，但是大概的意思还是懂的。**Tā de huà wǒ méi tīng qīngchu, dànshì dàgài de yìsi háishì dǒng de.** = *I did not catch his words clearly, but I understood the general idea.*

2 ADVERB = probably

■ 下这么大的雨，他大概不会来了。**Xià zhème dà de yǔ, tā dàgài bú huì lái le.** = *It's raining so hard. He probably won't come.*

dàjiā 大家 PRONOUN = all, everybody

■ 大家都说好，只有他说不好。**Dàjiā dōu shuō hǎo, zhǐyǒu tā shuō bù hǎo.** = *Everybody says it's good, only he says it's not good.*

■ 请大家安静，我有一件重要的事对大家说。**Qǐng dàjiā ānjìng, wǒ yǒu yí jiàn zhòngyào de shì duì dàjiā shuō.** = *Please be quiet, everybody. I've something important to say to you all.*

wǒmen dàjiā 我们大家 = all of us

nǐmen dàjiā 你们大家 = all of you

tāmen dàjiā 他们大家 = all of them

■ 我们大家明天都去动物园，你去吗？ **Wǒmen dàjiā míngtiān dōu qù dòngwùyuán, nǐ qù ma?** = *We're all going to the zoo tomorrow. Will you join us?*

dàxué 大学 [modif: 大 *big* + 学 *school*] NOUN = university (座 **zuò**)

■ 这座大学很有名。**Zhè zuò dàxué hěn yǒumíng.** = *This university is well known.*

■ 我爸爸没有上过大学。**Wǒ bàba méiyǒu shàngguo dàxué.** = *My father has never studied in a university.*

shàng dàxué 上大学 = go to university, study in a university

kǎo dàxué 考大学 = sit for university entrance examination

■ 他在准备考大学。**Tā zài zhǔnbèi kǎo dàxué.** = *He's preparing for the university entrance examination.*

kǎoshàng dàxué 考上大学 = pass university entrance examination

■ 我今年一定要考上大学。**Wǒ jīnnián yídìng yào kǎoshàng dàxué.** *I'm determined to pass the university entrance examination this year.*

dàifu 大夫 NOUN = (medical) doctor (位 **wèi**)

> NOTE: Same as 医生 **yīshēng**.

dài 代 (亻 5) VERB = substitute, take the place of

dàibiǎo 代表 [compound: 代 *substitute* + 表 *manifest*]

1 NOUN = representative, delegate (位 **wèi**)

■ 代表们从各地来北京参加一个重要的会议。**Dàibiǎomen cóng gèdì lái Běijīng cānjiā yí ge zhòngyào de huìyì.** = *Delegates from all over the country came to Beijing to attend an important conference.*

■ 谁是你们的代表？ **Shéi shì nǐmen de dàibiǎo?** = *Who is your representative?*

2 VERB = represent, indicate

■ 他说的话代表了我们大家的意见。**Tā shuō de huà dàibiǎole wǒmen dàjiā de yìjiàn.** = *What he said represented the opinion of us all.*

D

dài 带 (巾 9) [symb + 巾 sign]
Trad **帶** VERB = bring, take
■ 明天来上课的时候，请把词典带来。**Míngtiān lái shàngkè de shíhou, qǐng bǎ cídiǎn dàilai.** = *Please bring your dictionary when you come to class tomorrow.*
dàilai/dài ...lái 带来 / 带…来 = bring
■ 带你妹妹来参加星期五的晚会。**Dài nǐ mèimei lái cānjiā Xīngqīwǔ de wǎnhuì.** = *Bring your sister to our party on Friday evening!*
dàiqu/dài ... qù 带去 / 带…去 = take
■ 你不知道图书馆在哪里？我带你去！ **Nǐ bù zhīdào túshūguǎn zài nǎlǐ? Wǒ dài nǐ qù!** = *You don't know where the library is? I'll take you there.*

dài 戴 (戈 17) VERB = put on/wear (hat, gloves, spectacles)
■ 外面很冷，戴上帽子吧！
Wàimian hěn lěng, dàishang màozi ba! = *It's cold outside. Do put on your cap.*

dān 单 (八 8) Trad **單** ADJECTIVE = single (See 简单 **jiǎndān.**)

dàn 但 (亻 7) CONJUNCTION = but

dànshì 但是 CONJUNCTION = but, yet
■ 这个房间很大，但是不舒服。
Zhège fángjiān hěn dà, dànshì bù shūfu. = *This room is big, but not comfortable.*
■ 他星期天不工作，但是好象比哪一天都忙。**Tā Xīngqītiān bù gōngzuò, dànshì hǎoxiàng bǐ nǎ yì tiān dōu máng.** = *He does not work on Sundays, but seems to be busier than on any other day.*
■ 这个女孩子长得很漂亮，但是大家都不喜欢她。**Zhège nǚ háizi zhǎng de hěn piàoliang, dànshì dàjiā dōu bù xǐhuan tā.** = *This girl is very pretty, but nobody likes her.*

NOTE: In written Chinese 但是 **dànshì** can be shortened to 但 **dàn.**

dàn 蛋 (虫 11) NOUN = egg (See 鸡蛋 **jīdàn.**)

dāng 当 (小 6) Trad **當**
1 PREPOSITION = at the time of, when ...
■ 当我回到家的时候，天已经黑了。
Dāng wǒ huídào jiā de shíhou, tiān yǐjīng hēi le. = *When I got back home, it was already dark.*
dāng ... de shíhou 当…的时候 = when ...
2 VERB = work as, serve as
■ "你长大了想当什么？" "我想当医生。" **"Nǐ zhǎngdàle xiǎng dāng shénme?" "Wǒ xiǎng dāng yīshēng."** = *"What do you want to be when you grow up?" "A doctor."*

dāngrán 当然 ADVERB = of course
■ "到了上海你一定要给我写信啊！" "当然。" **"Dàole Shànghǎi nǐ yídìng yào gěi wǒ xiě xìn a!" "Dāngrán."** = *"You must write to me when you're in Shanghai." "Of course."*

dāo 刀 (刀 2) NOUN = knife (把 **bǎ**)
■ "我可以借用一下你的刀吗？" "可以。" **"Wǒ kěyǐ jièyòng yíxià nǐ de dāo ma?" "Kěyǐ."** = *"May I use your knife?" "Yes."*
qiānbǐ dāo 铅笔刀 = pencil sharpener
shuǐguǒ dāo 水果刀 = penknife

dǎo 倒 (亻 10) [亻 sign + 到 phon **dào**] VERB = fall, topple
■ 风大极了，把树刮倒了。**Fēng dà jíle, bǎ shù guā dǎo le.** = *The winds were so strong that they blew the tree over.*

dǎo 导 (巳 6) Trad **導** VERB = lead, guide (See 辅导 **fǔdǎo**, 领导 **lǐngdǎo**.)

dào 到 (刂 8) [至 sign + 刂 phon **dāo**] VERB = arrive, come to; up to
■ 北京来的飞机什么时候到？ **Běijīng lái de fēijī shénme shíhou dào?** = *When will the flight from Beijing arrive?*
■ 我们已经学到第十八课了。 **Wǒmen yǐjīng xuédào dì-shíbā kè le.** = *We've studied up to Lesson 18.*

dào 道 (辶 12) [辶 sign + 首 symb] NOUN = way, path

dàolǐ 道理 [compound: 道 *way, principle* + 理 *pattern, reason*] NOUN = principle, reason, hows and whys
■ 这个道理人人都懂。**Zhège dàolǐ rénren dōu dǒng.** = *Everybody understands this principle.* (→ *Everybody understands why this is true/correct.*)

yǒu dàolǐ 有道理 = truthful, reasonable
■ 你说的话很有道理。**Nǐ shuō de huà hěn yǒu dàolǐ.** = *What you said is reasonable/true.*

jiǎng dàolǐ 讲道理 = (of a person) reasonable
■ 他这个人很不讲道理。**Tā zhège rén hěn bù jiǎng dàolǐ.** = *This man is very unreasonable.*

NOTE: 道 **dào** and 理 **lǐ** are two important concepts in Chinese thought. The original meaning of 道 **dào** is "path, way." By extension it denotes "the fundamental principle of the universe." 理 **lǐ** originally meant "the grain of a piece of jade" and came to mean "the underlying logic of things."

dé 得 (彳 11) VERB = get, obtain
■ 她去年英文考试得了A。**Tā qùnián Yīngwén kǎoshì déle A.** = *She got an A for the English examination last year.*

dédào 得到 = succeed in getting/ obtaining
■ 他得到一个去中国学汉语的机会。**Tā dédào yí ge qù Zhōngguó xué Hànyǔ de jīhuì.** = *He got a chance to go to China to study Chinese.*

NOTE: The verb 得 **dé** is seldom used alone. It is often followed by 到 **dào**, grammatically a complement: 得到 **dédào** = get/obtain.

dé 德 (彳 15) Trad **悳** NOUN = virtue

Déguó 德国 NOUN = Germany

de 的 (白 7) PARTICLE = (attached to a word, phrase or clause to indicate that it is an attribute; 的 **de** is normally followed by a noun)
■ 我的书 **wǒ de shū** = *my book(s)*
■ 张先生的书 **Zhāng xiānsheng de shū** = *Mr Zhang's book(s)*
■ 桌子上的书 **zhuōzi shang de shū** = *the book(s) on the desk*

■ 你要借的书 **nǐ yào jiè de shū** = *the book(s) you want to borrow*

de 地 (土 6) [土 sign + 也 symb] PARTICLE = (attached to a word or phrase to indicate that it is an adverbial; 地 is normally followed by a verb or adjective)

■ 慢慢地走 **mànman de zǒu** = *walk slowly*

■ 努力地学习 **nǔlì de xuéxí** = *study hard*

■ 非常高兴地知道 **fēicháng gāoxìng de zhīdào** = *learn (of something) happily*

NOTE: 地 is pronounced **dì** for emphasis.

de 得 (彳 11) PARTICLE = (introducing a word, phrase or clause to indicate that it is a complement; 得 **de** follows a verb or adjective)

■ 玩得非常高兴 **wán de fēicháng gāoxìng** = *play happily*

■ 说得大家笑了起来 **shuō de dàjiā xiàole qǐlai** = *speak in such a way that everybody starts laughing*

■ 冷得很 **lěng de hěn** = *very cold*

NOTE: 的, 地, and 得 play different syntactic functions and are three distinct words. However, as they are pronounced the same (**de**) in everyday speech, many Chinese speakers do not distinguish them.

děi 得 (彳 11) MODAL VERB = have to, has to

■ 时间不早了，我们得走了。**Shíjiān bù zǎi le, wǒmen děi zǒu le.** = *It's quite late. We've got to go.*

■ 这件事怎么办，我得想一想。**Zhè jiàn shì zěnme bàn, wǒ děi xiǎng yi xiǎng.** = *I'll have to think over how to deal with this matter.*

NOTE: 得 **děi** is a common colloquial word. It is used together with a verb, and is equivalent to "have to…" or "has to...".

dēng 灯 (火 6) [火 sign + 丁 phon **dīng**] Trad 燈 NOUN = lamp, lighting

■ 这个房间的灯坏了。**Zhège fángjiān de dēng huài le.** = *The light in this room is out of order.*

■ 最后一个离开办公室的人，别忘了关灯。**Zuìhòu yí ge líkāi bàngōngshì de rén, bié wàngle guān dēng.** = *The last one to leave the office, please turn off the light.*

kāi dēng 开灯 = turn on the light

guān dēng 关灯 = turn off the light

děng 等 (竹 12)

1 VERB = wait for

■ 晚上八点钟我在电影院门口等你。**Wǎnshang bā diǎnzhōng wǒ zài diànyǐngyuàn ménkǒu děng nǐ.** = *I'll be waiting for you at eight o'clock this evening by the gate of the cinema.*

děng yíxià 等一下 = wait a minute

■ 等一下，我马上就来。**Děng yíxia, wǒ mǎshàng jiù lái.** = *Wait a minute, I'll come soon.*

2 PARTICLE = and so on, etc.

■ 我们在中国参观了北京、上海、西安等地。**Wǒmen zài Zhōngguó cānguānle Běijīng, Shànghǎi, Xī'ān děng dì.** = *While in China we visited Beijing, Shanghai, Xi'an and other places.*

dī 低 (亻 7)

1 ADJECTIVE = low (antonym 高 **gāo**)
■ 这把椅子太低了，坐着不舒服。**Zhè bǎ yǐzi tài dī le, zuòzhe bù shūfu.** = *This chair is too low, it's uncomfortable to sit on.*

2 VERB = lower
■ 她低着头，一句话也不说。**Tā dīzhe tóu, yí jù huà yě bù shuō.** = *She hung her head, not saying a word.*

dì 第 (竹 11) PREFIX = (used before a number to form an ordinal numeral)

dì-yī 第一 = the first
■ 第一天 **dì-yī tiān** = *the first day*

dì-èr 第二 = the second
■ 第二个房间 **dì-èr ge fángjiān** = *the second room*

dì-shí 第十 = the tenth
■ 第十课 **dì-shí kè** = *Lesson Ten*

dì 弟 (八 7)

dìdi 弟弟 (八 7) NOUN = younger brother
■ 我弟弟比我小两岁。**Wǒ dìdi bǐ wǒ xiǎo liǎng suì.** = *My younger brother is two years younger than I am.*
■ "你有没有弟弟?" "没有，我只有一个哥哥。" **"Nǐ yǒu méiyǒu dìdi?" "Méiyǒu, wǒ zhǐyǒu yí ge gēge."** = *"Do you have a younger brother?" "No, I only have an elder brother."*

dì 地 (土 6) [土 sign + 也 symb] NOUN = earth, ground

dìfang 地方 [compound: 地 *earth* + 方 *place*] NOUN = place, location, space (个 **ge**)
■ 这个地方很安静，我们就在这里坐一会儿吧。**Zhège dìfang hěn ānjìng, wǒmen jiù zài zhèlǐ zuò yìhuìr ba.** = *This place is quiet. Let's sit here for a while.*
■ 我这里没有地方放这些书。**Wǒ zhèlǐ méiyǒu dìfang fàng zhèxiē shū.** = *There is no room here for these books.*
■ 他们正在找开会的地方。**Tāmen zhèngzài zhǎo kāihuì de dìfang.** = *They're looking for a place for their conference.*

NOTE: 地方 **dìfang** is a word of wide application. It can denote any "place, location, space" either in a concrete or abstract sense. As such, it is a very common word. More examples:
■ 医生：你什么地方不舒服？**Yīshēng: Nǐ shénme dìfang bù shūfu?** = *Doctor: What spot ails you?* (-> *What's wrong with you?*)
■ 这本书我有些地方不大明白。**Zhè běn shū wǒ yǒuxiē dìfang búdà míngbai.** = *I'm not quite clear about parts of the book.*
■ 照顾不到的地方，请多多原谅。**Zhàogù búdào de dìfang, qǐng duōduo yuánliàng.** = *If there's anything not well attended to, please accept my sincere apology.*

diǎn 点 (灬 9) Trad 點

1 NOUN = drop, point, dot, o'clock
■ 雨点打在窗户上。**Yǔdiǎn dǎ zài chuānghu shang.** = *Raindrops beat on the window pane.*
■ "点"字下面有四点。**"Diǎn" zì xiàmian yǒu sì diǎn.** = *There're four dots at the bottom of the character* 点.

D

■ "现在几点？" "三点正。" **"Xiànzài jǐ diǎn?" "Sān diǎn zhěng."** = *"What time is it?" "Three o'clock sharp."*

2 VERB = drip, put a dot, touch

■ 你给我点眼药水，行吗？ **Nǐ gěi wǒ diǎn yǎnyàoshuǐ, xíng ma?** = *Could you please put my eye drops in for me?*

3 MEASURE WORD = a little, a bit

yǒu (yī) diǎnr 有（一）点儿… = (used before noun and adjective) a bit, a little

■ 我有一点儿累，想休息一会儿。 **Wǒ yǒu yìdiǎnr lèi, xiǎng xiūxi yíhuìr.** = *I'm a bit tired. I want to have a short break.*

■ 他喜欢在睡觉前喝一点儿酒。 **Tā xǐhuan zài shuìjiào qián hē yìdiǎnr jiǔ.** = *He is fond of drinking a little wine before going to bed.*

■ 我去商店买一点儿东西，很快就回来。 **Wǒ qù shāngdiàn mǎi yìdiǎnr dōngxi, hěn kuài jiù huílai.** = *I'm going to the store to do a little shopping and will be back soon.*

D

diǎnxīn 点心 [v+obj: 点 *touch* + 心 *the heart*] NOUN = snack, light refreshments

■ 有点儿饿了吧？ 吃点儿点心吧！ **Yǒudiǎnr èle ba? Chī diǎnr diǎnxīn ba!** = *Aren't you a bit hungry? Have a snack!*

■ 这些点心都很好吃。 **Zhèxiē diǎnxīn dōu hěn hǎochī.** = *All these refreshments are delicious.*

NOTE: The Cantonese pronunciation of 点心 **diǎnxīn** is "dim sum." Many Chinese restaurants outside China sell Cantonese-style refreshments known as "dim sum." To have such a meal is "yum cha," the Cantonese pronunciation of 饮茶 **yǐnchá**, which literally means "drink tea."

diǎnzhōng 点钟 NOUN = o'clock

■ "现在几点钟？" "三点钟。" **"Xiànzài jǐ diǎnzhōng?" "Sān diǎnzhōng."** = *"What time is it?" "Three o'clock."*

■ 我每天十点钟睡觉，七点钟起床。 **Wǒ měitiān shí diǎnzhōng shuìjiào, qī diǎnzhōng qǐchuáng.** = *Every day I go to bed at ten o'clock and get up at seven o'clock.*

NOTE: In colloquial Chinese, …点钟 ... **diǎnzhōng** can be shortened to …点 ... **diǎn**, e.g. "现在几点？" "三点。" **"Xiànzài jǐ diǎn?" "Sān diǎn."**

diǎn 典 (八 8) NOUN = standard work (See 词典 **cídiǎn**.)

diàn 电 (田 5) Trad 電 NOUN = electricity, power; electronics

■ 我们这里电比较便宜。 **Wǒmen zhèli diàn bǐjiào piányi.** = *Power is rather cheap here.*

■ 今天停电。 **Jīntiān tíng diàn.** = *No power today.* (*→There's a blackout/ power failure today.*)

diànchē 电车 [modif: 电 *electricity* + 车 *vehicle*] NOUN = trolley bus, streetcar (辆 **liàng**)

■ 这辆电车去哪儿？ **Zhè liàng diànchē qù nǎr?** = *Where does this trolley bus go?*

■ 他每天坐电车上班。**Tā měitiān zuò diànchē shàngbān.** = *He goes to work by trolley bus every day.*

diàndēng 电灯 [modif: 电 *electricity* + 灯 *lamp*] NOUN = electric light (个 **ge**)

■ 这个房间的电灯坏了。**Zhège fángjiān de diàndēng huài le.** = *The lights in this room are out of order.*

■ 你会装电灯吗? **Nǐ huì zhuāng diàndēng ma?** = *Do you know how to install an electric light?*

kāi diàndēng 开电灯 = turn on the light

guān diàndēng 关电灯 = turn off the light

diànhuà 电话 [modif: 电 *electricity* + 话 *speech*] NOUN = telephone, telephone call (个 **ge**)

■ "电话在哪里?" "在桌子上。" **"Diànhuà zài nǎlǐ?" "Zài zhuōzi shang."** = *"Where's the telephone?" "It's on the table."*

■ "我可以用一下你的电话吗?" "当然可以。" **"Wǒ kěyǐ yòng yíxià nǐ de diànhuà ma?" "Dāngrán kěyǐ."** = *"May I use your telephone?" "Sure."*

dǎ diànhuà 打电话 = make a telephone call

■ 王先生在打电话。**Wáng xiānsheng zài dǎ diànhuà.** = *Mr Wang is on the phone.*

gěi ... dǎ diànhuà 给…打电话 = call ... on the telephone, ring ...

■ "你常常给你妈妈打电话吗?" "常常打。" **"Nǐ chángcháng gěi nǐ māma dǎ diànhuà ma?" "Chángcháng dǎ."** = *"Do you often ring your mother?" "Yes."*

tīng diànhuà 听电话 = answer a telephone call

■ 李小姐，请你听电话。**Lǐ xiǎojiě, qǐng nǐ tīng diànhuà.** = *Miss Li, you're wanted on the phone.*

diànnǎo 电脑 [modif: 电 *electronics* + 脑 *brain*] NOUN = computer (个 **ge**)

■ 电脑很有用。**Diànnǎo hěn yǒuyòng.** = *Computers are very useful.*

■ 我会用电脑写汉字。**Wǒ huì yòng diànnǎo xiě hànzì.** = *I can write Chinese characters on a computer.*

diànshì 电视 [modif: 电 *electricity* + 视 *view*] NOUN = television

■ "今天晚上的电视有没有好节目?" "没有。" **"Jīntiān wǎnshang de diànshì yǒu méiyǒu hǎo jiémù?" "Méiyǒu."** = *"Are there any good programs on TV tonight?" "No."*

■ 我很少看电视。**Wǒ hěn shǎo kàn diànshì.** = *I seldom watch TV.*

kàn diànshì 看电视 = watch TV

diànshì jī 电视机 = TV set

diànyǐng 电影 [modif: 电 *electricity* + 影 *shadow*] NOUN = film, movie (场 **cháng**, 个 **ge**)

■ 我昨天看的电影很有意思。**Wǒ zuótiān kàn de diànyǐng hěn yǒu yìsi.** = *The film I saw yesterday was very interesting.*

kàn diànyǐng 看电影 = see a film, go to the movies

■ 他常常和女朋友一起看电影。**Tā chángcháng hé nǚpéngyou yìqǐ kàn diànyǐng.** = *He often goes to the movies with his girlfriend.*

diànyǐng piào 电影票 = film ticket

D

diànzǐ 电子 [suffix: 电 *electricity, electron* + 子 nominal suffix] NOUN = electron
diànzǐ yóuxì 电子游戏 = electronic game
diànzǐ gōngyè 电子工业 = electronic industry

diànzǐ yóujiàn 电子邮件 [modif: 电子 *electronic* + 邮件 *mail*] NOUN = e-mail (个 **ge**)
■ 我今天收到两个电子邮件。**Wǒ jīntiān shōudào liǎng ge diànzǐ yóujiàn.** = *I received two e-mail messages today.*

diàn 店 (广 8) [广 sign + 占 symb] NOUN = shop, store (家 **jiā**)
■ 这家店是卖书的。**Zhè jiā diàn shì mài shū de.** = *This store sells books.*

diào 调 (讠 10) Trad **調** NOUN = tune (See 声调 **shēngdiào**.)

diào 掉 (扌 11) [扌 sign + 卓 symb] VERB = fall, drop
■ 杯子从桌子上掉到地上。**Bēizi cóng zhuōzi shang diào dào dì shang.** = *The cup fell from the table to the floor.*
chīdiào 吃掉 = eat up
■ 水果都吃掉了。**Shuǐguǒ dōu chīdiào le.** = *The fruit is all eaten up.*
yòngdiào 用掉 = use up
■ 我上个月用掉了一千块钱。**Wǒ shàng ge yuè yòngdiàole yìqiān kuài qián.** = *I used up one thousand dollars last month.* (→*I spent a thousand dollars last month.*)
màidiào 卖掉 = sell out
■ 那些书还没有卖掉。**Nàxiē shū hái méiyǒu màidiào.** = *Those books have not been sold out.*
wàngdiào 忘掉 = forget
■ 这件事我怎么也忘不掉。**Zhè jiàn shì wǒ zěnme yě wàng bú diào.** = *I can't forget this incident, no matter how hard I try.*
diūdiào 丢掉 = throw away, discard
■ 这件衣服太小了，不能穿了，你丢掉吧！ **Zhè jiàn yīfu tài xiǎo le, bù néng chuān le, nǐ diūdiào ba!** = *This dress is too small for you. You should throw it away.*

dìng 定 (宀 8) VERB = fix, set (See 决定 **juédìng**, 一定 **yídìng**.)

diū 丢 (去 6) VERB = lose, throw away
■ 我的手表丢了！ **Wǒ de shǒubiǎo diū le!** = *I've lost my watch!*

dōng 东 (一 5) Trad **東** NOUN = east
■ 我在体育馆东门等你。**Wǒ zài tǐyùguǎn dōng mén děng nǐ.** = *I'll be waiting for you at the east gate of the gymnasium.*
■ 一直往东走，就 是我们的学校。**Yìzhí wàng dōng zǒu, jiùshì wǒmen de xuéxiào.** = *Walk straight towards the east and you'll come to our school.*
dōngběi 东北 = the Northeast (the northeastern part of China, which used to be known in the West as Manchuria)

dōngbian 东边 NOUN = east side, east
■ 我们学校的东边是一个公园。**Wǒmen xuéxiào de dōngbian shì yí ge gōngyuán.** = *To the east of our school is a park.*

■ 日本在中国的东边。**Rìběn zài Zhōngguō de dōngbian.** = *Japan lies to the east of China.*

dōngxi 东西 NOUN = thing, things (个 **ge,** 件 **jiān,** 种 **zhǒng**)

■ 这些东西都是小明的。**Zhèxie dōngxi dōu shì Xiǎo Míng de.** = *All these things are Xiao Ming's.*

■ 我没有看到过这种东西。**Wǒ méiyǒu kàndàoguo zhè zhǒng dōngxi.** = *I've never seen such things.*

NOTE: 东西 **dōngxi**, which literally means "east and west," is an extremely common "all-purpose" noun that can denote any object or objects in Chinese. More everyday examples:

■ 图书馆里不能吃东西。**Túshūguǎn li bù néng chī dōngxi.** = *No food in the library.*

■ 我想喝点儿东西。**Wǒ xiǎng hē diǎnr dōngxi.** = *I want to have a drink.*

■ 妈妈出去买东西了。**Māma chūqu mǎi dōngxi le.** = *Mother's gone shopping.*

dōng 冬 (夂 5) [冫 sign + 夂 symb] NOUN = winter

dōngtiān 冬天 NOUN = winter

■ 今年的冬天比去年冷。**Jīnnián de dōngtiān bǐ qùnián lěng.** = *Winter this year is colder than last year.*

■ 这一对老人喜欢在暖和的地方过冬天。**Zhè yí duì lǎorén xǐhuan zài nuǎnhuo de dìfang guò dōngtiān.** = *This old couple likes to spend winter in a mild place.*

■ 我妈妈冬天常常生病。**Wǒ māma dōngtiān chángcháng shēngbìng.** = *My mother is often sick in winter.*

dǒng 懂 (忄 15) [忄 sign + 董 phon **dǒng**] VERB = comprehend, understand

■ 我不懂你的意思。**Wǒ bù dǒng nǐ de yìsi.** = *I don't understand what you mean.*

■ 我听得懂一些简单的中文。**Wǒ tīng de dǒng yīxiē jiǎndān de Zhōngwén.** = *I can understand some simple spoken Chinese.*

tīngdǒng 听懂 = listen and understand

kàndǒng 看懂 = see (or read) and understand

■ 这个电影我没有看懂。**Zhège diànyǐng wǒ méiyǒu kàndǒng.** = *I didn't understand the movie.*

dúdǒng 读懂 = read and understand

■ 这本书我读了两遍才读懂。**Zhè běn shū wǒ dúle liǎng biàn cái dúdǒng.** = *I understood this book only after reading it twice.*

dòng 动 (力 6) [云 symb + 力 sign] Trad 動 VERB = move

■ 别动，我给你照张相。**Bié dòng, wǒ gěi nǐ zhào zhāng xiàng.** = *Stay put. I'll take your picture.*

dòngwù 动物 [modif: 动 *moving* + 物 *object*] NOUN = animal (只 **zhī**)

■ 这些小动物真可爱！ **Zhèxiē xiǎo dòngwù zhēn kě'ài!** = *These little animals are really lovable!*

■ 小孩子特别喜欢动物。**Xiǎo háizi tèbié xǐhuan dòngwù.** = *Children are particularly fond of animals.*

dòngwùyuán 动物园 = zoo

■ 下星期五我们班参观动物园。**Xià Xīngqīwǔ wǒmen bān cānguān dòngwùyuán.** = *Our class will visit the zoo next Friday.*

dōu 都 (阝 10) ADVERB = all, both, without exception

■ 学生们都喜欢上中文课。**Xuéshengmen dōu xǐhuan shàng Zhōngwén kè.** = *All the students like having Chinese classes.*

■ 我每天都跑步。**Wǒ měi tiān dōu pǎobù.** = *I jog every day.*

NOTE: When words like 每天 **měi tiān**, 每个 **měi ge**, 大家 **dàjiā** or 所有的 **suǒyǒu de** are used, we usually use the adverb 都 **dōu** to form the common collocations 每…都 **měi ... dōu**, 大家…都 **dàjiā ... dōu**, 所有的…都 **suǒyǒu de ... dōu**, e.g.:
■ 大家都说这个主意好。**Dàjiā dōu shuō zhè ge zhǔyi hǎo.** *Everybody said it's a good idea.*
■ 我所有的朋友都来了。**Wǒ suǒyǒu de péngyou dōu lái le.** = *All my friends have come.*

D

dú 读 (讠 10) [讠 sign + 卖 symb] Trad 讀 VERB = read, read aloud; attend (a school)

■ 他们在图书馆读书。**Tāmen zài túshūguǎn dúshū.** = *They're reading in the library.*

dú xiǎoxuē 读小学 = attend primary school

dú zhōngxuē 读中学 = attend high school

dú dàxuē 读大学 = attend university

■ 他们的大儿子在读中学，小女儿在读小学。**Tāmen de dà érzi zài dú zhōngxúe, xiǎo nǚ'er zài dú xiǎoxuē.** = *Their elder son is studying in a high school and their young daughter is studying in a primary school.*

NOTE: In colloquial Chinese, 读 **dú** may be replaced by 看 **kàn** when used in the sense of "read," e.g.看书 **kàn shū** = read books, 看报 **kàn bào** = read the newspaper. In 读小学 / 中学 / 大学 **dú xiǎoxuē/zhōngxúe/dàxuē**, 读 may be replaced by 念 **niàn**: 念小学 / 中学 / 大学 **niàn xiǎoxuē/zhōngxúe/dàxue** in colloquial Chinese.

dù 度 (广 9) NOUN = limit, extent (See 态度 **tàidu**.)

duǎn 短 (矢 12) ADJECTIVE = (of length, time) short (antonym 长 **cháng**)

■ 这条街很短，只有十几座房子。**Zhè tiáo jiē hěn duǎn, zhǐyǒu shí jǐ zuò fángzi.** = *This is a short street, with only a dozen houses.*

■ 我在上海的时间很短，没有好好玩。**Wǒ zài Shànghǎi de shíjiān hěn duǎn, méiyǒu hǎohǎo wán.** = *I stayed in Shanghai for only a short time and did not have much time for fun* [e.g. sightseeing, window-shopping, dining out].

duàn 锻 (钅 14) [钅 sign + 段 phon **duàn**] Trad 鍛 VERB = forge, shape metal

duànliàn 锻炼 [compound: 锻 *shape metal* + 炼 *smelt*] VERB = have physical training, do physical exercise

■ 你要成为一个好运动员，就得天天锻炼。**Nǐ yào chéngwéi yí ge hǎo yùndòngyuán, jiùděi tiāntiān duànliàn.** = *If you want to become a good athlete, you have to train every day.*

duàn 段 (殳 9) MEASURE WORD = section (of something long)
yí duàn lù 一段路 = *a section of a road (street), part of a journey*
■ 这段路不平，开车要特别小心。**Zhè duàn lù bù píng, kāi chē yào tèbié xiǎoxīn.** = *This section of the road is quite rough. One should be particularly careful when driving.*
yí duàn shíjiān 一段时间 = a period of time

duì 对 (又 5) Trad **對**
1 VERB = treat, deal with
■ 她对我很好。**Tā duì wǒ hěn hǎo.** = *She treats me well. (→She is nice to me.)*
2 PREPOSITION = to, towards
■ 他对我说："请进来。" **Tā duì wǒ shuō: "Qǐng jìnlai."** = *He said to me, "Please come in."*
■ 你对他的批评很有道理。**Nǐ duì tā de pīpíng hěn yoǔ dàolǐ.** = *Your criticism of him is reasonable.*
3 ADJECTIVE = correct, true (antonym 错 **cuò**)
■ 你的话很对。**Nǐ de huà hěn duì.** = *Your words are correct. (→You're right.)*
■ 你说得很对。**Nǐ shuō de hěn duì.** = *You spoke correctly. (→You're right.)*
■ 他回答得不对。**Tā huídāo de bú duì.** = *He answered wrongly. (→ He gave a wrong answer.)*

duìbuqǐ 对不起 IDIOM = I'm sorry. I beg your pardon

NOTE: 对不起 **duìbuqǐ** is a very useful idiomatic expression in colloquial Chinese. It is used when you've done something wrong or caused some inconvenience to others, e.g.:
■ 对不起，打错电话了。**Duìbuqǐ, dǎ cuò diànhuà le.** = *Sorry, I've dialed a wrong number.*
■ 对不起，我迟到了。**Duìbuqǐ, wǒ chídào le.** = *Sorry, I'm late.*

dùn 顿 (页 10) Trad **頓** MEASURE WORD = (for meals)
■ 我们一天吃三顿饭：早饭、午饭、晚饭。**Wǒmen yì tiān chī sān dùn fàn: zǎofàn, wǔfàn,wǎnfàn.** = *We have three meals a day: breakfast, lunch and supper.*
■ 他好好地吃了一顿晚饭。**Tā hǎohǎo de chīle yí dùn wǎnfàn.** = *He has a nice meal for supper.*

duō 多 (夕 6)
1 ADJECTIVE = many, much (antonym 少 **shǎo**)
■ 今天的作业不多。**Jīntiān de zuòyè bù duō.** = *There isn't much homework today.*
■ 他有很多中国朋友。**Tā yǒu hěn duō Zhōngguó péngyou.** = *He has many Chinese friends.*
■ 他昨天酒喝得太多，今天头疼。**Tā zuótiān jiǔ hē de tài duō, jīntiān tóu tēng.** = *He drank too much last night. Today he has a headache.*
bǐ ... de duō 比…得多 = much more ... than

D

■ 今天比昨天热得多。**Jīntiān bǐ zuótiān rè de duō.** = *Today's much hotter than yesterday.*

2 ADVERB = how ...! how ...?

■ 要是我能去北京学中文，多好啊！ **Yàoshì wǒ néng qù Běijīng xué Zhōngwén, duō hǎo a!** = *How nice it would be if I could go to Beijing to study Chinese!*

■ 老先生，您多大了？ **Lǎo xiānsheng, nín duō dà le?** = *How old are you, sir?* (to an elderly man)

3 NUMERAL = more, over

■ 我们学了五百多个汉字。**Wǒmen xuéle wǔbǎi duō ge hànzì.** = *We've learned more than five hundred Chinese characters.*

■ 他在台湾住了八个多月。**Tā zài Táiwān zhùle bā ge duō yuè.** = *He lived in Taiwan for over eight months.*

duōme 多么 ADVERB = How ...!

■ 要是我能去北京学中文，多么好啊！ **Yàoshì wǒ néng qù Běijīng xué Zhōngwén, duōme hǎo a!** = *How nice it would be if I could go to Beijing to study Chinese!*

NOTE: 多么…! **duōme...!** and 多…! **duō...!** are interchangeable when meaning "How ...!". 多…! **duō...!** is more colloquial.

duōshǎo 多少 [compound: 多 *many, much* + 少 *few, little*] PRONOUN = how many, how much

■ 你们班多少人学中文？ **Nǐmen bān duōshǎo rén xué Zhōngwén?** = *How many in your class are studying Chinese?*

...**duōshǎo qián? ... 多少钱?** = How much is ...?

■ 这本书多少钱？ **Zhè běn shū duōshǎo qián?** = *How much is this book?*

E

è 饿 (饣 10) [饣 sign + 我 phon **wǒ**] Trad 餓 ADJECTIVE = hungry (antonym 饱 **bǎo**)

■ 我饿了，我们去吃饭吧！ **Wǒ è le, wǒmen qù chī fàn ba!** = *I'm hungry. Let's go and eat.*

ér 而 (一 6) CONJUNCTION = yet, on the other hand

érqie 而且 CONJUNCTION = moreover, what's more

■ 这件衣服大了一点儿，而且比较贵，所以还是不买吧。**Zhè jiàn yīfu dàle yìdiǎnr, érqiě bǐjiào guì, suóyǐ háishì bù mǎi ba.** = *This dress is a bit too big and also expensive, so it's better not to buy it.*

búdàn ..., érqiě .. 不但 …，而且 … = not only..., but also…

■ 我爸爸不但会开车，而且会修车。**Wǒ bàba búdàn huì kāi chē, érqǐe huì xiū chē.** = *My daddy can not only drive but also fix cars.*

■ 这个电子游戏不但小孩爱玩，而且大人也爱玩。**Zhège diànzǐ yóuxì búdàn xiǎohái ài wán, érqiě dàren yě ài wán.** = *Not only children but also grown-ups like to play this electronic game.*

ér 儿 (丿 2) Trad 兒 NOUN = child, son (个 gè)

érzi 儿子 [suffix: 儿 *son* + 子 *nominal suffix*] NOUN = son (个 ge)
■ 儿子长大了，有时候会不听父母的话。**Érzi zhǎng dà le, yoǔ shíhou huì bù tīng fùmǔ de huà.** = *When a son grows up, he will not listen to his parents sometimes.*
■ 他希望妻子生一个儿子。**Tā xīwàng qīzǐ shēng yí ge érzi.** = *He hopes that his wife will give birth to a son.*

èr 二 (二 2) NUMERAL = second, two
■ 一千二百二十二 **yìqiān èrbǎi èrshí èr** = *one thousand, two hundred and twenty-two*
■ 我二哥去年结婚了。**Wǒ èrgē qùnián jiéhūn le.** = *My second elder brother got married last year.*

NOTE: See note on 两 **liǎng**.

F

fā 发 (又 5) Trad 發 VERB = send out
■ 我上个星期给他发了一封信，今天上午又发了一个传真。**Wǒ shàng ge xīngqī gěi tā fāle yì fēng xìn, jīntiān shàngwǔ yòu fāle yí ge chuángzhēn.** = *I sent him a letter last week and sent him a fax this morning.*

fāshāo 发烧 [v+obj: 发 *develop* + 烧 *burning, fever*] VERB = run a fever
■ 她昨天着凉了，夜里就发烧了。**Tā zuótiān zhāoliáng le, yèli jiù fāshāo le.** = *She got a cold yesterday and began to run a fever at night.*

fāshēng 发生 [compound: 发 *develop* + 生 *grow*] VERB = take place, happen
■ 这里发生了什么事？ **Zhèlǐ fāshēngle shénme shì?** = *What happened here?*

fāxiàn 发现 [compound: 发 *develop* + 现 *show*] VERB = discover, find out
■ 谁先发现新西兰的？ **Shuí xiān fāxiàn Xīnxīlán de?** = *Who first discovered New Zealand?*

fāzhǎn 发展 [compound: 发 *develop* + 展 *unfold*] VERB = develop (economy)
■ 经济要发展，政治要民主。**Jīngjì yào fāzhǎn, zhēngzhì yào mínzhǔ.** = *Economy should be developed, and politics should be democratized.*

fāzhǎnzhōng guójia 发展中国家 = developing country
■ 中国是世界上最大的发展中国家。**Zhōngguó shì shìjiè shang zuì dà de fāzhǎnzhōng guójiā.** = *China is the largest developing country in the world.*

fǎ 法 (氵 8) NOUN = method, law

Fǎguó 法国 [modif: 法 *France* + 国 *state, country*] NOUN = France
■ 法国是一个重要的国家。**Fǎguó shì yí ge zhòngyào de guójiā.** = *France is an important country.*

Fǎyǔ 法语 [compound: 法 *France* + 语 *speech*] NOUN = the French language

F

■ 法语难学吗? **Fǎyǔ nán xué ma?** = *Is French difficult to learn?*
■ 她法语说得很漂亮。**Tā Fǎyǔ shuō de hěn piàoliang.** = *She speaks French beautifully.*

Fǎwén 法文 [compound: 法 *France* + 文 *writing*] NOUN = the French language (especially the writing)

fān 翻 (羽 18) VERB = turn, turn over
■ 请把书翻到二十页。**Qǐng bǎ shū fāndào èrshí yè.** = *Please turn your books to page twenty.*

fānyì 翻译
1 VERB = translate, interpret
■ 你能不能把这封信翻译成中文? **Nǐ néng bù néng bǎ zhè fēng xìn fānyì chéng Zhōngwén?** = *Can you translate this letter into Chinese?*
2 NOUN = translator, interpreter
■ 这位翻译中文英文都好极了。**Zhè wèi fānyì Zhōngwén Yīngwén dōu hǎo jíle.** = *This translator* (or *interpreter) has very good command of both Chinese and English.*
dāng fāngyi 当翻译 = to work as a translator (or interpreter)
■ 明天有中国朋友来参观我们工厂，请你当翻译。**Míngtiān yǒu Zhōngguó péngyou lái cānguān wǒmen gōngchǎng, qǐng nǐ dāng fāngyì.** = *Tomorrow some Chinese friends will come to visit our factory. I'll ask you to act as interpreter.*

fán 烦 (火 10) [火 sign + 页 symb] Trad 煩 ADJECTIVE = vexing (See 麻烦 **máfan.**)

fǎn 反 (又 4) VERB = oppose

fǎnduì 反对 [modif: 反 *opposing* + 对 *deal with*] VERB = oppose, object (antonym 同意 **tóngyì**)
■ 我不反对你的计划，但是我觉得很难做到。**Wǒ bù fǎnduì nǐ de jìhuà, dànshì wǒ juéde hěn nán zuòdào.** = *I don't object to your plan, but I think it'll be difficult to implement.*

fàn 饭 (饣 7) [饣 sign + 反 phon **fǎn**] Trad 飯 NOUN = cooked rice; meal (顿 **dùn**)
■ 小王每顿吃两碗饭。**Xiǎo Wáng měi dùn chī liǎng wǎn fàn.** *Xiao Wang eats two bowls of rice for each meal.*
■ 他们常常在外面吃饭。**Tāmen chángcháng zài wàimian chīfàn.** = *They often dine out.*
■ 我请你吃饭。**Wǒ qǐng nǐ chīfàn.** = *I'll treat you to a meal.*

fàndiàn 饭店 [modif: 饭 *meal* + 店 *shop, store*] NOUN = restaurant; hotel (家 **jiā**)
■ 这家饭店饭菜好吃，价钱便宜。**Zhè jiā fàndiàn fàncài hǎochī, jiàqián piányì.** = *The dishes in the restaurant are delicious and affordable.*
■ 他住在一家大饭店里。**Tā zhù zài yì jiā dà fàndiàn lǐ.** = *He stays in a big hotel.*

NOTE: The original meaning of 饭店 **fàndiàn** is "restaurant," but it is also used to denote a hotel. For example, 北京饭店 **Běijīng Fàndiàn** may mean "Beijing Restaurant" or "Beijing Hotel."

F

fāng 方 (方 4) ADJECTIVE = square

fāngbiàn 方便 ADJECTIVE = convenient, handy (antonym 麻烦 **máfan**)
■ 住在城里买东西很方便。**Zhù zài chéngli mǎi dōngxi hěn fāngbiàn.** = *Shopping is convenient in town.*

NOTE: A euphemism for "going to the toilet" is 方便一下 **fāngbiàn yíxià** for example:
■ 我要方便一下. **Wǒ yào fāngbiàn yíxià.** = *I'm going to the toilet.*

fāngfǎ 方法 [compound: 方 *method, way of doing things* + 法 *method*] NOUN = method
■ 这个方法不行。**Zhège fāngfǎ bù xíng.** = *This method won't do.*
■ 学中文有没有什么好方法? **Xué Zhōngwén yǒu méiyǒu shénme hǎo fāngfǎ?** = *Are there any good ways of learning Chinese?*

fāngmiàn 方面 [compound: 方 *side* + 面 *face, surface*] NOUN = side, aspect
■ 这方面他很有经验。**Zhè fāngmiàn tā hěn yǒu jīngyàn.** = *He's got lots of experience in this respect.*

fāngxiàng 方向 NOUN = direction, orientation
■ 你的方向错了。**Nǐ de fāngxiàng cuò le.** = *You're in the wrong direction.*

fáng 房 (户 8) [户 sign + 方 phon **fāng**] NOUN = room, house

fángjiān 房间 [compound: 房 *room, house* + 间 *space*] NOUN = room (间 **jiān**)
■ 这间房间不大，但是挺舒服。**Zhè jiān fángjiān bú dà, dànshì tǐng shūfu.** = *This room is not big, but it's very comfortable.*
■ 楼上有几个房间? **Lóu shang yǒu jǐ ge fángjiān?** = *How many rooms are there upstairs?*

fángzi 房子 [suffix: 房 *house* + 子 nominal suffix] NOUN = house, building (座 **zuò**)
■ 这座房子有多少年了? **Zhè zuò fángzi yǒu duōshǎo nián le?** = *How old is this house?*
■ 山上有很多漂亮的房子。**Shān shang yǒu hěn duō piàoliang de fángzi.** = *There're many beautiful houses on top of the hill.*

fǎng 访 (讠 6) [讠 sign + 方 phon **fāng**] Trad 訪 VERB = visit

fǎngwèn 访问 [compound: 访 *visit* + 问 *ask, ask after*] VERB = visit, interview
■ 这位老人很有名，经常有人来访问他。**Zhè wèi lǎorén hěn yǒumíng, jīngcháng yǒu rén lái fǎngwèn tā.** = *This old man is famous. People often come to visit him.*

fàng 放 (方 8) [方 phon **fāng** + 攵 sign] VERB = put, put in
■ 请你不要把你的书放在我的桌子上。**Qǐng nǐ bú yào bǎ nǐ de shū fàng zài wǒ de zhuōzi shang.** = *Please don't put your books on my desk.*

F

■ 你的咖啡里要不要放糖？ **Nǐ de kāfēi li yào bu yào fàng táng?** = *Shall I put sugar in your coffee?*

fàngjià 放假 [v+obj: 放 *release* + 假 *holiday*] VERB = be on holiday, have a day off
■ 我们学校从十二月十五日到一月二十日放假。**Wǒmen xuéxiào cóng Shí'èryuè shíwǔ rì dào Yīyuè èrshí rì fàngjià.** = *We have school holidays from December 15 to January 20.*
■ 爸爸明天放假，他要带孩子去动物园。**Bàba míngtiān fàngjià, tā yào dài háizi qù dòngwùyuán.** = *Father will be having a day off tomorrow. He'll take the children to the zoo.*

F

fēi 非 (非 8) ADJECTIVE = not, non-, un- (See 非常 **fēicháng**.)

fēicháng 非常 [modif: 非 *not* + 常 *usual*] ADVERB = unusually, very
■ 中国非常大。**Zhōngguó fēicháng dà.** = *China is very big.*
■ 我非常想去新加坡旅行。**Wǒ fēicháng xiǎng qù Xīnjiāpō lǚxíng.** = *I very much want to take a trip to Singapore.*

fēi 飞 (乙 3) Trad **飛** VERB = fly
■ 小鸟飞走了。**Xiǎo niǎo fēi zuǒ le.** = *The little bird flew away.*

fēijī 飞机 [modif: 飞 *flying* + 机 *machine*] NOUN = airplane
■ 从北京来的飞机什么时候到？**Cóng Běijīng lái de fēijī shénme shíhou dào?** = *When does the plane from Beijing arrive?*
■ 我们全家明天坐飞机去上海。**Wǒmen quánjiā míngtiān zuò fēijī qù Shànghǎi.** = *My family will go to Shanghai tomorrow by air.*
fēijī jiào 飞机票 = air ticket
fēijī chǎng 飞机场 = airport

fēn 分 (八 4) [八 sign + 刀 sign]
1 VERB = divide
■ 今天是你的生日，你来分生日蛋糕。**Jīntiān shì nǐ de shēngrì, nǐ lái fēn shēngrì dàogāo.** = *Today's your birthday, come and cut your birthday cake.*
2 NOUN = point; minute
■ 你去年中文考试得了多少分？ **Nǐ qùnián Zhōngwén kǎoshì déle duōshǎo fēn?** = *What marks did you get for the Chinese examination last year?*
■ 现在是十点二十分。**Xiànzài shì shí diǎn èrshí fēn.** = *It's ten twenty now.*
...fēnzhī... **···分之···** = (way of indicating fraction)
■ 三分之二 **sān fēnzhī èr** = *two thirds*
■ 八分之一 **bā fēnzhī yī** = *one eighth*
...bǎi fēnzhī... **···百分之···** = ...percent
■ 百分之七十 **bǎi fēnzhī qīshí** = *seventy percent*
■ 百分之四十五 **bǎi fēnzhī sìshíwǔ** = *forty-five percent*
3 MEASURE WORD = (Chinese currency) 0.01 yuan or 0.1 jiao (mao), cent
■ 五分钱 **wǔ fēn qián** = *five cents*

fēnzhōng 分钟 NOUN = minute (of an hour)
■ 五分钟不是一段很长的时间。**Wǔ fēnzhōng bú shì yí duàn hěn cháng de shíjiān.** = *Five minutes is not a long time.*

■ 我等你等了四十多分钟。**Wǒ děng nǐ děngle sìshí duō fēnzhōng.** = *I waited for you for over forty minutes.*

fēng 丰 (一 4) Trad 豐 ADJECTIVE = abundant

fēngfù 丰富 [compound: 丰 *abundance* + 富 *wealth*] ADJECTIVE = abundant, rich
■ 我们的生活很丰富。**Wǒmen de shēnghuó hěn fēngfù.** = *Our life is very rich.* (→ *We live a full life.*)
■ 这位老师有丰富的经验。**Zhè wèi lǎoshī yǒu fēngfù de jīngyàn.** = *This teacher has rich experience.*

fēng 封 (寸 9) MEASURE WORD = (for letters)
■ 一封信 **yì fēng xìn** = *a letter*
■ 王先生，有你一封信。**Wáng xiānsheng, yǒu nǐ yì fēng xìng.** = *Mr Wang, here's a letter for you.*

fēng 风 (风 4) Trad 風 NOUN = wind
■ 今天风很大。**Jīntiān fēng hěn dà.** = *It's very windy today.*
■ 冬天中国常常刮西北风。**Dōngtiān Zhōngguó chángcháng guā xīběi fēng.** = *In winter a northwestern wind prevails in China.*

fū 夫 (大 4) [symbol + 大 sign] NOUN = husband

fūrén 夫人 NOUN = (formal term for another person's) wife

fú 服 (月 8) VERB = obey

fúwù 服务 [compound: 服 *obey* + 务 *work*] VERB = serve, work for
■ 我能为大家服务，感到很高兴。**Wǒ néng wèi dàjiā fúwù, gǎn dào hěn gāoxìng.** = *I'm happy to be able to serve you all.*
wèi ... fúwu 为…服务 = serve, work for

fúwùyuán 服务员 [suffix: 服务 *serve* + 员 *person*] NOUN = attendant, waiter/waitress (个 **ge**, 位 **wèi**)
■ 这位服务员态度不大好。**Zhè wèi fúwùyuán tàidù bú dà hǎo.** = *This attendant's work attitude is not very good.*
■ 请你叫一下服务员。**Qǐng nǐ jiào yíxià fúwùyuán.** = *Please call the attendant.*

NOTE: 服务员 **fúwùyuán** is the word to refer to or address an attendant, a waiter or waitress. However, if the attendant is a woman, 小姐 **xiǎojiě** is more common in everyday usage.

fǔ 辅 (车 11) Trad 輔 VERB = assist

fǔdǎo 辅导
1 VERB = coach, tutor
■ 王小姐辅导我们学中文。**Wáng xiǎojiě fǔdǎo wǒmen xuě Zhōngwěn.** = *Miss Wang tutors us in Chinese.*
2 NOUN = coaching, tutorial
■ 王老师，您的辅导对我们很有帮助。**Wáng lǎoshī, nín de fǔdǎo duì wǒmen hěn yǒu bāngzhù.** = *Teacher Wang, your tutorial is helpful to us.*
■ 谢谢您的辅导。**Xièxie nín de fǔdǎo.** = *Thank you for your tutorial.*
fǔdǎo ke 辅导课 = tutorial class, tutorial
■ 我们一星期上两次辅导课。

F

Wǒmen yì xīngqī shàng liǎng cì fǔdǎo kè. = *We have two tutorials every week.*

fǔdǎo lǎoshī 辅导老师 = tutor, teaching assistant

■ 王小姐是我们的辅导老师。**Wáng xiǎojiě shì wǒmen de fǔdǎo lǎoshī.** *Miss Wang is our tutor.*

fú 福 (礻 13) NOUN = blessing (See 幸福 **xìngfú**.)

fǔ 府 (广 8) [广 sign + 付 phon **fù**] NOUN = prefecture (See 政府 **zhèngfǔ**.)

fù 复 (丿 9) VERB = repeat, compound

fùxí 复习 [modif: 复 *repeat* + 习 *study*] VERB = review (one's lesson)

■ 下星期要考试，这几天我在复习。**Xià xīngqī yào kǎoshì, zhè jǐ tiān wǒ zài fùxí.** = *I'll be having an examination next week. I'm reviewing my lessons these days.*

fùzá 复杂 [compound: 复 *multiple* + 杂 *miscellaneous*] ADJECTIVE = complicated, complex (antonym 简单 **jiǎndān**)

■ 这件事很复杂，我说不清楚。**Zhè jiàn shì hěn fùzá, wǒ shuō bu qīngchu.** = *This is a complicated matter. I can't explain it clearly.*

■ 这样复杂的中文句子，我不会说。**Zhèyàng fùzá de Zhōngwén jùzi, wǒ bú huì shuō.** = *I can't say such a complicated sentence in Chinese.*

fù 富 (宀 12) ADJECTIVE = wealthy (See 丰富 **fēngfù**.)

fù 父 (父 4) NOUN = father

fùqin 父亲 [modif: 父 *father* + 亲 *parent*] NOUN = father

■ 您父亲做什么工作？ **Nín fùqin zuò shénme gōngzuò?** = *What does your father do?*

■ 我爱我父亲。**Wǒ ài wǒ fùqin.** = *I love my father.*

■ 父亲的话，有的有道理，有的没有什么道理。**Fùqin de huà, yǒude yǒudàolǐ, yǒude méiyǒu shénme dàolǐ.** = *Some of my father's words are reasonable, others are not so reasonable.*

NOTE: 爸爸 **bàba** and 父亲 **fùqin** denote the same person. While 爸爸 **bàba** is colloquial, like "daddy," 父亲 **fùqin** is formal, equivalent to "father." When referring to another person's father, 父亲 **fùqin** is preferred. As a form of address to your own father, only 爸爸 **bàba** is normally used.

fù 负 (刀 6) Trad 負 VERB = carry on the back

fùzé 负责 VERB = be responsible, be in charge

■ 这件事我负责。**Zhè jiàn shì wǒ fùzé.** = *I'm responsible for this matter.* (or *I'm in charge of this matter.*)

■ 他做事非常负责。**Tā zuò shì fēicháng fùzé.** = *He has a strong sense of responsibility.*

fùzérén 负责人 = the person in charge

■ 我很不满意，我要见你们的负责人。**Wǒ hěn bù mǎnyì, wǒ yào jiàn nǐmen de fùzérén.** = *I'm very dissatis-*

F

fied (or *disappointed*). *I want to see the person in charge here.*

fū 附 (阝 7) [阝 sign + 付 phon **fù**] VERB = be close to

fùjìn 附近 [compound: 附 *close to* + 近 *close by*] NOUN = the area nearby
■ 附近有没有邮局? **Fùjìn yǒu méiyǒu yóujú?** = *Is there a post office nearby?*
■ 李先生就住在这里附近。**Lǐ xiānsheng jiù zhù zài zhèli fùjìn.** = *Mr Li lives near here.*
■ 附近的学校都很好。**Fùjìn de xuéxiào dōu hěn hǎo.** = *The schools nearby* (or *in this area*) *are all very good.*

fù 傅 (亻 12) NOUN = teacher, advisor (See 师傅 **shīfu**.)

G

gāi 该 (讠 8) Trad **該**
1 MODAL VERB = should, ought to
■ 你不该常常迟到。**Nǐ bù gāi chángcháng chídào.** = *You shouldn't be late so often.*
2 VERB = be somebody's turn to do something
■ 今天该你洗碗。**Jīntiān gāi nǐ xǐ wǎn.** = *It's your turn to wash the dishes today.*

gǎi 改 (攵 7) [己 symb + 攵 sign] VERB = alter, change, correct
■ 你这个字写错了，要改一下。**Nǐ zhège zì xiě cuò le, yào gǎi yíxià.** = *You've written a wrong character. You should correct it.*

gǎibiàn 改变 [compound: 改 *alter* + 变 *change*]
1 VERB = transform, change
■ 青年人要改变世界，老年人知道得改变自己。**Qīngnián rén yào gǎibiàn shìjiè, lǎonián rén zhīdào děi gǎibiàn zìjǐ.** = *Young people want to change the world, and old people know they have to change themselves.*
2 NOUN = change, transformation
■ 你明年的计划有没有什么改变? **Nǐ míngnián de jìhuà yǒu méiyǒu shénme gǎibiàn?** = *Is there any change in your plans for next year?*

gài 概 (木 12) ADJECTIVE = probable (See 大概 **dàgài**.)

gān 干 (干 3) Trad **乾** ADJECTIVE = dry

gānjìng 干净 [compound: 干 *dry* + 净 *clean*] ADJECTIVE = clean (antonym 脏 **zāng**)
■ 这些衣服很干净，不用洗。**Zhèxiē yīfu hěn gānjing, búyòng xǐ.** = *These clothes are clean. They don't need washing.*
■ 这些是干净的衣服。**Zhèxiē shì gānjing de yīfu.** = *These are clean clothes.*
■ 这件衣服洗不干净了。**Zhè jiàn yīfu xǐ bù gānjing le.** = *This dress cannot be washed clean.*

G

gǎn 感 (心 13) [咸 symb + 心 sign] VERB = feel

gǎndào 感到 [v+comp: 感 *feel* + 到 *arrive* (as a complement)] VERB = feel
■ 我有机会访问你们的国家，感到很高兴。**Wǒ yǒu jīhuì fǎngwèn nǐmen de guójiā, gǎndào hěn gāoxìng.** = *I feel very happy to have the opportunity to visit your country.*

gǎnmào 感冒 VERB = catch a cold
■ 突然变冷，很多人感冒了。**Tūrán biàn lěng, hěn duō rén gǎnmào le.** = *It suddenly became cold, so quite a few people caught colds.*

gǎnxiè 感谢 [v+obj: 感 *feel* + 谢 *gratitude*] VERB = be grateful, appreciate
■ 我感谢你对我的帮助。**Wǒ gǎnxiè nǐ duì wǒ de bāngzhù.** = *I'm grateful for your help.*

gǎn 敢 (攵 11) MODAL VERB = dare
■ 这么多人，我不敢讲话。**Zhème duō rén, wǒ bù gǎn jiǎnghuà.** = *There're so many people here, I don't dare to speak.*

gàn 干 (干 3) Trad 幹 VERB = do, work
■ 你干了一下午了，该休息休息了。**Nǐ gànle yí xiàwǔ le, gāi xiūxi xiūxi le.** = *You've been working for the entire afternoon. You should take a break.*

gànbù 干部 NOUN = cadre, official (位 **wèi**)

NOTE: 干部 **gànbù** is a communist party term, denoting party (or government) officials. It is not commonly used today.

gāng 刚 (刂 6) Trad 剛 ADVERB = just, only a short while ago
■ 我刚借来这本书，还没开始看呢。**Wǒ gāng jièlai zhè běn shū, hái méi kāishǐ kàn ne.** = *I've just borrowed this book. I haven't begun reading it.*

gāngcái 刚才 [compound: 刚 *just* + 才 *only*] NOUN = a short time ago, just now
■ 我刚才看见小明到图书馆去，你去那儿一定能找到他。**Wǒ gāngcái kànjiàn Xiǎo Míng dào túshūguǎn qu, nǐ qù nàr yídìng néng zhǎodào tā.** = *I saw Xiao Ming going to the library just now. You're sure to find him there.*

gāng 钢 (钅 9) [钅 sign + 冈 phon **gāng**] Trad 鋼 NOUN = steel

gāngbǐ 钢笔 [modif: 钢 *steel* + 笔 *pen*] NOUN = fountain pen (支 **zhī**)
■ 你的钢笔我用一下，行吗？**Nǐ de gāngbǐ wǒ yòng yíxià, xíng ma?** = *I'll use your fountain pen for a while, is that OK?* (→ *May I use your fountain pen for a while?*)
■ 我上中学的时候，爸爸送给我一支钢笔。**Wǒ shàng zhōngxué de shíhou, bàba sòng gei wǒ yì zhī gāngbǐ.** = *When I entered high school, daddy gave me a fountain pen.*

gǎng 港 (氵 11) [氵 sign + 巷 phon **xiàng**] NOUN = harbor (See 香港 **Xiānggǎng**.)

gāo 高 (亠 10) ADJECTIVE = tall, high (antonym 矮 **ǎi**, 低 **dī**)
■ 我哥哥比我高得多。**Wǒ gēge bǐ wǒ gāo de duō.** = *My elder brother is much taller than I am.*
■ 那座高高的楼房是一座新医院。**Nà zuò gāogāo de lóufáng shì yí zuò xīn yīyuàn.** = *That tall building is a new hospital.*
■ 一年不见，那孩子长高了不少。**Yì nián bú jiàn, nà háizi zhǎng gāole bùshǎo.** = *I haven't seen the child for a year. He's grown much taller.*

gāoxìng 高兴 [compound: 高 *high* + 兴 *excited*] ADJECTIVE = happy, delighted
■ 见到你，我很高兴。**Jiàndào nǐ, wǒ hěn gāoxìng.** = *I'm delighted to see you.*
■ 这个学校一定很好，你看，孩子们每天都高高兴兴地到学校来。**Zhège xuéxiào yídìng hěn hǎo, nǐ kàn, háizimen měi tiān dōu gāo-gāo-xìng-xìng de dào xuéxiào lái.** = *This school must be good. Look, the children come to school happily every day.*

gǎo 搞 (扌 13) [扌 sign + 高 phon **gāo**] VERB = do, be engaged in (a trade, profession, etc.)
■ "你父亲搞什么工作?" "他搞农业。" **"Nǐ fùqin gǎo shénme gōngzuò?" "Tā gǎo nóngyè."** = *"What does your father do?" "He's engaged in farming."*

NOTE: 搞 **gǎo** is only used in very colloquial, informal style.

gào 告 (口 7) [symb + 口 sign] VERB = tell

gàosu 告诉 [compound: 告 *tell* + 诉 *inform*] VERB = tell, inform
■ 他告诉我一个很重要的消息。**Tā gàosu wǒ yí ge hěn zhòngyào de xiāoxi.** = *He told me a very important piece of news.*

gē 哥 (一 10) NOUN = elder brother

gēge 哥哥 NOUN = elder brother
■ 我哥哥踢足球踢得很好。**Wǒ gēge tī zúqiú tī de hěn hǎo.** = *My elder brother plays soccer very well.*
■ 她把哥哥介绍给自己最好的朋友。**Tā bǎ gēge jièshào gěi zìjǐ zuì hǎo de péngyou.** = *She introduced her elder brother to her best friend.*

gē 歌 (欠 14) [哥 phon **gē** + 欠 symb] NOUN = song
■ 这个歌很好听，我想再听一遍。**Zhège gē hěo hǎotīng, wǒ xiǎng zài tīng yí biàn.** = *This song is beautiful. I want to hear it once more.*
■ 你会唱中文歌吗? **Nǐ huì chàng Zhōngwén gē ma?** = *Can you sing Chinese songs?*
chàng gē 唱歌 = sing a song
gēshǒu 歌手 = professional singer

gè 个 (个 3) Trad **個** MEASURE WORD = (the most commonly used measure word for nouns that do not take

G

special measure words, or in default of any other measure word)
■ 一个人 **yí ge rén** = *a person*
■ 两个苹果 **liǎng ge píngguǒ** = *two apples*
■ 三个工厂 **sān ge gōngchǎng** = *three factories*

gè 各 (夂 6) PRONOUN = each, every
■ 各人的事，各人自己负责。**Gè rén de shì, gè rén zìjǐ fùzé.** = *Everyone should be responsible for his own affairs.*
gè zhǒng 各种 = all kinds of
■ 我各种水果都喜欢吃。**Wǒ gè zhǒng shuǐguǒ dōu xǐhuan chī.** = *I like to eat all kinds of fruit.*

gěi 给 (纟 9) Trad 給
1 VERB = give, give as a gift
■ 妈妈每两个星期给小明五十块钱。**Māma měi liǎng ge xīngqī gěi Xiǎo Míng wǔshí kuài qián.** = *Mum gives Xiao Ming fifty dollars every fortnight.*
2 PREPOSITION = for, to
■ 她给我们做了一顿很好吃的中国饭。**Tā gěi wǒmen zuòle yí dùn hěn hǎochī de Zhōngguó fàn.** = *She cooked us a delicious Chinese meal.*

gēn 根 (木 10) [木 sign + 艮 phon **gēn**]
1 NOUN = root
■ 这棵树非常大，根一定很深。**Zhè kē shù fēicháng dà, gēn yídìng hěn shēn.** = *This tree is very big; its roots must be deep.*
2 MEASURE WORD = (for long, thin things)
■ 一根筷子 **yì gēn kuàizi** = *a chopstick*

gēn 跟 (足 13) [足 sign + 艮 phon **gēn**]
1 VERB = follow
■ 我在前面走，我的小狗在后面跟。**Wǒ zài qiánmiàn zǒu, wǒ de xiǎo gǒu zài hòumiàn gēn.** = *I walked in front and my puppy followed behind.*
2 PREPOSITION = with
■ 我常常跟爸爸一起去看足球赛。**Wǒ chángcháng gēn bàba yìqǐ qù kàn zúqiú sài.** = *I often go to watch soccer games with my father.*
gēn ... yìqǐ 跟…一起 = together with ...
3 CONJUNCTION = and
■ 我跟我的男朋友都在学中文。**Wǒ gēn wǒ de nán péngyou dōu zài xué Zhōngwén.** = *My boyfriend and I are both learning Chinese.*

gèng 更 (一 7) ADVERB = more, even more
■ 美国很大，加拿大更大。**Měiguó hěn dà, Jiānádà gèng dà.** = *America is big and Canada is even bigger.*

gōng 功 (工 5) [工 phon **gōng** + 力 sign] NOUN = skill

gōngkè 功课 [compound: 功 *skill* + 课 *lesson*] NOUN = school work, homework
■ 他功课不错。**Tā gōngkè búcuò.** = *His schoolwork is quite good.*

gōng 工 (工 3) NOUN = work

gōngrén 工人 [modif: 工 *work* + 人 *person*] NOUN = workman, worker (个 **ge**, 位 **wèi**)

G

■ 工人在建一座新学校。**Gōngrén zài jiàn yí zuò xīn xuéxiào.** = *Workers are building a new school.*

■ 他十九岁就当工人了。**Tā shíjiǔ suì jiù dāng gōngrén le.** = *He began working as a worker when he was nineteen years old.*

gōngchǎng 工厂 [modif: 工 *work* + 厂 *factory*] NOUN = factory, works (座 **zuò**, 家 **jiā**)

■ 这座工厂生产什么? **Zhè zuò gōngchǎng shēngchǎn shénme?** = *What does this factory make?*

■ 他在中国参观了三家工厂。**Tā zài Zhōngguó cānguānle sān jiā gōngchǎng.** = *He visited three factories in China.*

gōngyè 工业 [modif: 工 *work* + 业 *industry*] NOUN = (manufacturing) industry

■ 工业发展了，国家才能富。**Gōngyè fāzhǎn le, guójiā cái néng fù.** = *Only when industry is developed, can a country be rich.*

■ 这个国家没有汽车工业。**Zhège guójiā méiyǒu qìchē gōngyè.** = *This country does not have automobile industry.*

gōngzuò 工作 [compound: 工 *work* + 作 *do*]

1 VERB = work

■ 我们一星期工作五天。**Wǒmen yì xīngqī gōngzuò wǔ tiān.** = *We work five days a week.*

2 NOUN = work, job (件 **jiàn**, 个 **ge**)

■ 这件工作不太难。**Zhè jiàn gōngzuò bú tài nán.** = *This job is not too difficult.*

■ 他找工作找了两个月了。**Tā zhǎo gōngzuò zhǎole liǎng ge yuè le.** = *He's been looking for a job for two months.*

gōng 公 (八 4) ADJECTIVE = public

gōnggòng 公共 [compound: 公 *public* + 共 *shared*] ADJECTIVE = public

■ 这是一座公共图书馆，任何人都可以进去看书。**Zhè shì yí zuò gōnggòng túshūguǎn, rènhé rén dōu kěyǐ jìnqù kàn shū.** = *This is a public library. Anybody can go in and read.*

gōnggòng qìchē 公共汽车 = bus

■ 我的车卖了，我现在坐公共汽车上班。**Wǒ de chē mài le, wǒ xiànzài zuò gōnggòng qìchē shàngbān.** = *I've sold my car. Now I go to work by bus.*

gōngjīn 公斤 [modif: 公 *metric* + 斤 a traditional Chinese measurement of weight] MEASURE WORD = kilogram

■ 这里有五公斤苹果，我送给你。**Zhèli yǒu wǔ gōngjīn píngguǒ, wǒ sòng gei nǐ.** = *Here're five kilograms of apples, my gift to you.*

gōnglǐ 公里 [modif: 公 *metric* + 里 a traditional Chinese measurement of distance] MEASURE WORD = kilometer

■ 从城里到飞机场大概有十公里。**Cóng chéngli dào fēijīchǎng dàgài yǒu shí gōngli.** = *It's about ten kilometers from town to the airport.*

gōngyuán 公园 [modf: 公 *public* + 园 *garden*] NOUN = public garden, park (座 **zuò**)

■ 这个公园春天特别美。**Zhège gōngyuán chūntiān tèbié měi.** = *This park is especially beautiful in spring.*

■ 早上很多人在公园里跑步。 **Zǎoshang hěn dōu rén zài gōngyuáng lǐ pǎobù.** = *Many people jog in the park early in the morning.*

gòng 共 (八 6) ADVERB = together, jointly (See 公共 **gōnggòng**, 一共 **yígòng**.)

goǔ 狗 (犭 8) NOUN = dog (只 **zhī**)
■ 弟弟的小狗是他最好的朋友。**Dìdi de xiǎogoǔ shì tā zuìhǎo de péngyou.** = *My younger brother's little dog is his best friend.*

gòu 够 (丿 11) ADJECTIVE = enough, sufficient
■ 够了，够了，谢谢你! **Gòu le, gòu le, xièxie nǐ!** = *That's enough. Thank you!*

G

gū 姑 (女 8) [女 sign + 古 phon **gǔ**) NOUN = woman

gūniang 姑娘 [compound: 姑 *woman* + 娘 *girl*] NOUN = unmarried young woman, girl
■ 那个姑娘是谁家的孩子? **Nàge gūniang shì shuí jiā de háizi?** = *Whose child is that girl?*
■ 我不认识那个姑娘。**Wǒ bú rènshi nàge gūniang.** = *I don't know that girl.*
xiǎo gūniang 小姑娘 = little girl
■ 小姑娘一般比小男孩懂事。**Xiǎo gūniang yìbān bǐ xiǎo nánhái dǒng shì.** = *Little girls are generally more sensible than little boys.*
dà gūniang 大姑娘 = young woman (usually unmarried)

gù 故 (攵 9) [古 phon **gǔ** + 攵 symb] ADJECTIVE = old, former

gùshi 故事 [modif: 故 *old, past* + 事 *happening, event*] NOUN = story, tale
■ 这个故事是真的吗? **Zhège gùshi shì zhēn de ma?** = *Is this story true?*
■ 他每天晚上都给孩子讲一个故事。**Tā měi tiān wǎnshang dōu gěi háizi jiǎng yí ge gùshi.** = *He tells his child* (or *children*) *a story every evening.*
jiǎng gùshi 讲故事 = tell a story
tīng gùshi 听故事 = listen to a story

gù 顾 (页 10) Trad 顧 VERB = attend to (See 照顾 **zhàogù**.)

guā 刮 (刂 8) VERB = (of wind) blow
■ 这儿冬天常常刮西北风。**Zhèr dōngtiān chángcháng guā xīběi fēng.** = *A northwestern wind often blows here in winter.*

guà 挂 (扌 9) [扌 sign + 圭 symb] VERB = hang up
■ 墙上挂着一张画。**Qiáng shang guàzhe yì zhāng huà.** = *A picture was hanging on the wall.*

guān 官 (宀 8) NOUN = government official

guānyuán 官员 [suffix: 官 *official* + 员 nominal suffix] NOUN = official (位 **wèi**)
■ 这位官员很负责任。**Zhè wèi guānyuán hěn fù zérèn.** = *This official has a strong sense of responsibility.*

■ 我想见一下这里的负责官员。**Wǒ xiǎng jiàn yíxià zhèli de fùzé guānyuán.** = *I'd like to see the official in charge here.*

guān 关 (八 6) Trad 關 VERB = close; turn off

■ 你离开的时候，请把灯关掉，把门关上。**Nǐ líkāi de shíhou, qǐng bǎ dēng guāndiao, bǎ mén guānshang.** = *When you leave, please turn off the light and close the door.*

bǎ diàndēng guāndiao 把电灯关掉 = turn off the light

bǎ lùyīngjī guāndiao 把录音机关掉 = turn off the recorder

bǎ diànshìjī guāndiao 把电视机关掉 = turn off the TV

bǎ jīqì guāndiao 把机器关掉 = turn off the machine

bǎ mén guānshang 把门关上 = close the door

bǎ chuāng guānshang 把窗关上 = close the window

guānxì 关系 [compound: 关 *related* + 系 *connected*]

1 NOUN = connection, relation

■ 这两件事有没有关系？**Zhè liǎng jiàn shì yǒu méiyǒu guānxì?** = *Is there any connection between these two matters?* (→ *Are these two matters related?*)

hé ... yǒu guānxi 和…有关系 = have something to do with

■ 这件事和大家都有关系。**Zhè jiàn shì hé dàjiā dōu yǒu guānxì.** = *This matter concerns everybody.*

méi(yǒu)guānxi 没(有)关系 = *It doesn't matter. It's OK.*

■ "对不起。" "没关系。" **"Duìbuqǐ." "Méiguānxì"** = *"I'm sorry* [for an unintentional, minor offence]*." "It's OK."*

> NOTE: Right connections are believed to be very important in business and social dealings in Chinese culture. Sometimes the Pinyin form of the word (*guanxi*) appears in English texts.

2 VERB = affect, have bearing on

■ 睡得好不好，关系到你的健康。**Shuì de hǎo bu hǎo, guānxì dào nǐ de jiànkāng.** = *Whether you sleep well or not affects your health.*

guānxīn 关心 [v+obj: 关 *connected* + 心 *the heart*] VERB = be concerned about, care for

■ 妈妈总是关心孩子的健康。**Māma zǒngshì guānxīn háizi de jiànkāng.** = *Mothers are always concerned about their children's health.*

guān 观 (见 6) [又 symb + 见 sign] Trad 觀 VERB = watch, observe (See 参观 **cānguān**.)

guǎn 馆 (饣 11) [饣 sign + 官 phon **guān**) Trad 館 NOUN = building (for a specific purpose)

fànguǎn 饭馆 = restaurant

guǎnzi 馆子 = restaurant

túshūguǎn 图书馆 = library

tǐyùguǎn 体育馆 = gymnasium

guàn 惯 (忄 11) Trad 慣 ADJECTIVE = accustomed to (See 习惯 **xíguàn**.)

G

guǎng 广 (广 3) Trad 廣 ADJECTIVE = extensive, wide

guǎngbō 广播 [modif: 广 *extensively, wide* + 播 *sow, spread*]
1 VERB = broadcast
■ 今天早上广播了一条重要新闻。**Jīntiān zǎoshang guǎngbōle yì tiáo zhòngyào xīnwén.** = *A piece of important news was broadcast early this morning.*
2 NOUN = broadcasting
■ 这位老人每天都听新闻广播。**Zhè wèi lǎorén měi tiān duō tīng xīnwén guǎngbō.** = *This old man listens to the news broadcast every morning.*

guì 贵 (贝 9) [symb + 贝 sign] Trad 貴 ADJECTIVE = expensive, of great value (antonym 便宜 **piányi**)
■ 这家商店的东西都很贵。**Zhè jiā shāngdiàn de dōngxi dōu hěn guì.** = *The goods in this shop are all very expensive.*
■ 什么？要一千块？太贵了！**Shénme? Yào yìqiān kuài? Tài guì le.** = *What? One thousand dollars? Too expensive.*

guìxìng 贵姓 [modif: 贵 *valuable* + 姓 *family name*] IDIOM = your family name
■ "请问，您贵姓？" "我姓王。" **"Qǐngwèn, nín guìxìng?" "Wǒ xìng Wáng."** = *"What's your family name, please?" "Wang."*

NOTE: (1) The word 贵 **guì** in the sense of "valuable" is added to certain nouns to mean "your ...," e.g. 贵姓 **guìxìng** = *your family name*, 贵国 **guìguó** = *your country*, 贵校 **guìxiào** = *your school*. They are only used in formal and polite contexts.

(2) While 贵姓 **guìxìng** is the polite form in asking somebody's family name, the polite way to ask for somebody's given name is "请问，您大名是…？" **"Qǐngwèn, nín dàmíng shì...?"** 大名 **dàmíng** literally means "big name." The answer to this question is "我叫 XX," e.g.:
■ "请问，您贵姓？" "我姓王。" **"Qǐngwèn, nín guìxìng?" "Wǒ xìng Wáng."** = *"May I ask what your family name is?" "Wang."*
■ "您大名是…？" "我叫小明。" **"Nín dàmíng shì ...?" "Wǒ jiào Xiǎomíng."** = *"And your given name is...?" "It's Xiao Ming."*
■ "您是王小明先生？" "是，是。" **"Nín shì Wáng Xiǎomíng xiānsheng?" "Shì, shì."** = *"Oh, you're Mr Wang Xiaoming?" "That's right."*

guó 国 (口 8) [口 sign + 玉 sign] Trad 國 NOUN = country
Zhōngguó 中国 = China
Yīngguó 英国 = England, the United Kingdom
Fǎguó 法国 = France
Déguó 德国 = Germany
Měiguó 美国 = the United States of America

guójiā 国家 [compound: 国 *country* + 家 *family*] NOUN = country, state
■ 这个国家历史很长。**Zhège guójiā lìshǐ hěn cháng.** = *This country has a long history.*

G

■ 他代表国家参加运动会。**Tā dàibiǎo guójiā cānjiā yùndònghuì.** = *He represented his country in the sports meet.*

NOTE: It is significant that the Chinese word meaning "country"—国家 **guójia**—is composed of the word 国 **guó** = *country* and the word 家 **jiā** = *family*. In traditional Chinese thought, China was one big family and the country was ruled as such, with the emperor acting as patriarch.

guǒ 果 (木 8) [木 sign + 田 sign] NOUN = fruit (See 结果 **jiéguǒ**, 苹果 **píngguǒ**, 如果 **rúguǒ**, 水果 **shuǐguǒ**.)

guò 过 (辶 6) [辶 sign + 寸 symb] Trad 過

1 VERB = pass, cross

■ 过马路，一定要小心。**Guò mǎlù, yídìng yào xiǎoxīn.** = *You must be very careful when crossing the street.*

guòlai 过来 = come over, come across (towards the speaker)

■ 他正从马路那边过来。**Tā zhèng cóng mǎlù nà biān guòlai.** = *He's coming over from the other side of the street.*

■ 公共汽车开过来了。**Gōnggòng qìchē kāi guòlai le.** = *A bus is coming over.*

guòqu 过去 = go over, go across (away from the speaker)

■ 街上车太多，很难过去。**Jiē shang chē tài duō, hěn nán guòqu.** = *Traffic's too heavy in the street. It's very difficult to go across.*

■ 河水很急，我游不过去。**Hě shuǐ hěn jí, wǒ yóu bu guòqu.** = *The river runs swiftly. I can't swim across it.*

2 PARTICLE = (used after a verb or adjective to emphasize a past experience)

■ "你去过中国没有?" "去过，我去过中国很多地方。" **"Nǐ qùguo Zhōnguó méiyǒu?" "Qùguo, wǒ qùguo Zhōngguó hěn duō dìfang."** = *"Have you been to China?" "Yes, I've been to many places in China."*

guòqù 过去 [compound: 过 *pass* + 去 *gone*] NOUN = (sometime) in the past

■ 过去的事，不要多想了。**Guòqù de shì, bú yào duō xiǎng le.** = *Don't keep thinking about what's past.* (→ *Let bygones be bygones.*)

■ 他过去常常生病，现在身体好多了。**Tā guòqù chángcháng shēng bìng, xiànzài shēntǐ hǎo duō le.** = *He was often sick in the past. Now he's much healthier.*

H

hā 哈 (口 9) [口 sign + 合 phon **hé**] ONOMATOPOEIA = sound of loud laughter

hāhā 哈哈 ONOMATOPOEIA = representing loud laughter

■ 他听了我的笑话，哈哈大笑起来。**Tā tīngle wǒ de xiàohua, hāhā dà xiào qǐlai.** = *Hearing my joke, he burst into laughter.*

hái 还 (辶 7) Trad **還** ADVERB = as before, still
■ 已经九点钟了，爸爸还没有回来。 **Yǐjīng jiǔ diǎnzhōng le, bāba hái méiyǒu huílai.** = *It's already nine o'clock. Daddy still hasn't come back.*

háishì 还是
1 ADVERB = (same as 还 **hái**)
2 CONJUNCTION = or (only used in a question of alternatives)
■ 你要喝茶，还是喝咖啡？ **Nǐ yào hē chá, háishì hē kāfēi?** = *Do you want to drink tea or coffee?*

hái 孩 (子 9) [子 sign + 亥 phon **hài**] NOUN = child

háizi 孩子 [suffix: 孩 *child* + 子 nominal suffix] NOUN = child; son or daughter
■ 这个孩子真聪明！ **Zhège háizi zhēn cōngmíng!** = *This child is really smart!* (-> *What a bright child!*)
■ 他们有一个男孩子，两个女孩子。 **Tāmen yǒu yí ge nán háizi, liǎng ge nǚ háizi.** = *They've got a son and two daughters.*

hǎi 海 (氵 10) [氵 sign + 每 symb] NOUN = sea
■ 没有风，海很平静。 **Méiyǒu fēng, hǎi hěn píngjìng.** = *There's no wind. The sea is calm.*
■ 我爱大海。 **Wǒ aì dà hǎi.** = *I love the sea.*
■ 海水冷吗？可以游泳吗？ **Hǎishuǐ lěng ma? Kěyǐ yóuyǒng ma?** = *Is the seawater cold? May I swim?*
dà hǎi 大海 = vast sea, sea
hǎi fēng 海风 = sea breeze, winds from the sea
hǎi biān 海边 = seaside
Dōng Hǎi 东海 = the East China Sea
Nán Hǎi 南海 = the South China Sea
Huáng Hǎi 黄海 = the Yellow Sea

NOTE: The word 海 **hǎi** is seldom used alone. It is often used together with 洋 **yáng** = *ocean* to form the noun 海洋 **hǎiyáng** = *ocean*. It is also often modified by 大 **dà**: 大海 **dà hǎi**, which means *sea* with poetic connotations.

hán 寒 (宀 12) [symb + 冫 sign] ADJECTIVE = cold

hánjià 寒假 [modif: 寒 *cold* + 假 *holiday, vacation*] NOUN = winter vacation
■ 寒假快到了！ **Hánjià kuài dàole!** = *The winter vacation is coming soon.*
■ 你们学校什么时候放寒假？ **Nǐmen xuéxiào shénme shíhou fàng hánjià?** = *When will your school have its winter vacation?*
■ 我们寒假要去南方旅行。 **Wǒmen hánjià yào qù nánfāng lǚxíng.** = *For winter vacation we're going to make a trip to the south.*

hǎn 喊 (口 12) [口 sign + 咸 symb] VERB = shout, call out
■ 有人在窗外喊你。 **Yǒu rén zài chuāng wài hǎn nǐ.** = *There's someone outside calling for you.*

hàn 汉 (氵 5) Trad **漢** NOUN = the Han people

H

Hānyǔ 汉语 [modif: 汉 *the Han people* + 语 *language*] NOUN = Chinese, the language of the Han Chinese
■ 汉语不难学。**Hānyǔ bù nán xué.** = *Chinese is not difficult to learn.*
■ 我会说一点儿汉语。= **Wǒ huì shuō yìdiǎnr Hānyǔ.** = *I can speak a little Chinese.*

NOTE: In Chinese there are a number of words denoting "the Chinese language." 汉语 **Hānyǔ** literally means *the language of the Han Chinese people*, in contrast with the many other languages of the non-Han ethnic peoples in China. 汉语 **Hānyǔ** is therefore the accurate, scientific term for the language this dictionary describes. However, the most popular term for "Chinese" is 中文 **Zhōngwén**. In Singapore and other Southeast Asian countries, the Chinese language is often referred to as 华语 **Huáyǔ.**

hànzì 汉字 [modif: 汉 *the Han people* + 字 *word, character*] NOUN = Chinese character
■ 这个汉字我不认识。**Zhège hànzì wǒ bú rènshi.** = *I don't know this Chinese character.*
■ 你会写多少汉字？ **Nǐ huì xiě duōshǎo hànzì?** = *How many Chinese characters can you write?*

hǎo 好 (女 6) [女 sign + 子 sign]
1 ADJECTIVE = good, all right (antonym 坏 **huài**)
■ 我身体非常好。**Wǒ shēntǐ fēicháng hǎo.** = *I'm in very good health.*
■ 他是个好学生。**Tā shì ge hǎo xuésheng.** = *He's a good student.*
■ 你中文说得很好。**Nǐ Zhōngwén shuō de hěn hǎo.** = *You speak Chinese very well.*
2 ADVERB = very much, very; how...!
■ 今天好冷。**Jīntiān hǎo lěng!** = *How cold it is today!*
hǎoduo 好多 = a good many, many
■ 他有好多中国朋友。**Tā yǒu hǎoduō Zhōngguó péngyou.** = *He has many Chinese friends.*
hǎoxīn 好心 = kindhearted, with good intentions
■ 她是个好心人。**Tā shì ge hǎoxīn rén.** = *She is a kindhearted person.*

hǎochī 好吃 ADJECTIVE = delicious
■ 那家饭店的菜不好吃。= **Nà jiā fàndiàn de cài bù hǎochī.** *The food in that restaurant is not tasty.*
■ 妈妈买了很多好吃的东西。 **Māma mǎile hěn duō hǎochī de dōngxi.** = *Mum's bought lots of yummy food.*

hǎochu 好处 NOUN = benefit, being beneficial
■ 经常锻炼身体的好处，大家都知道。**Jīngcháng duànliàn shēntǐ de hǎochu, dàjiā dōu zhīdào.** = *We all know the benefits of regular physical exercise.*
duì ... yǒu hǎochu 对…有好处 = be beneficial to ...
■ 经常锻炼对身体有好处。 **Jīngcháng duànliàn duì shēntǐ yǒu hǎochu.** = *Regular exercise is beneficial to your health.*

hǎokàn 好看 NOUN
1 = good-looking, pretty, beautiful
■ 你穿这件衣服不好看。**Nǐ chuān zhè jiàn yīfu bù hǎokàn.** = *You don't look good in this dress.*
■ 她看到好看的衣服就想买。**Tā kàndao hǎokàn de yīfu jiù xiǎng mǎi.** = *Whenever she sees beautiful clothes, she wants to buy them.*
2 = interesting to read (to watch)
■ 我借给你一本好看的书。**Wǒ jiè gei nǐ yì běn hǎokàn de shū.** = *I'll lend you an interesting book.*
■ 你昨天看的电影好看吗？ **Nǐ zuótiān kàn de diànyǐng hǎokàn ma?** = *Was the film you saw yesterday interesting?*

hǎoxiàng 好像 VERB = be like, similar to
■ 她今天好像不高兴。你知道为什么吗？ **Tā jīntiān hǎoxiàng bù gāoxìng. Nǐ zhīdào wèi shénme ma?** = *She looks unhappy today. Do you know why?*
hǎoxiàng shì 好像是 = seem to be
■ 听他说话，他好像是美国人。**Tīng tā shuōhuà, tā hǎoxiàng shì Měiguórén.** *Judging from his accent, he seems to be an American.*

hào 号 (口 5) Trad **號** NOUN
1 = order of sequence;
■ 张先生住在三号房间。**Zhāng xiānsheng zhù zài sān hào fángjiān.** = *Mr Zhang lives in Room No. 3.*
2 = date of the month
■ 今天是五月十八号。**Jīntiān shì Wǔ yuè shíbā hào.** = *It's the eighteenth of May today.*

NOTE: The other word for "a date of the month" is 日 **rì**, e.g. 五月十八日 **Wǔ yuè shí bā rì**. While 号 **hào** is normally used in speech, 日 **rì** is more common in writing. So for May 18, for example, we usually say 五月十八号 **Wǔyuè shíbā hào**, but write 五月十八日 **Wǔyuè shíbā rì**.

hē 喝 (口 12) [口 sign + 曷 symb] VERB = drink
■ 我不喝酒，就喝水吧。 **Wǒ bù hē jiǔ, jiù hē shuǐ ba.** = *I don't drink wine. Just some water, please.*

hé 合 (人 6) VERB = suit, be in harmony with

héshì 合适 [compound: 合 *harmony* + 适 *fit*] ADJECTIVE = suitable, appropriate, just right
■ 这件衣服你穿正合适。**Zhè jiàn yīfu nǐ chuān zhèng héshì.** = *This dress suits you well.*
■ 合适的工作不容易找到。**Héshì de gōngzuò bù róngyì zhǎodào.** = *It's not easy to find a suitable job.*
duì ... héshì 对…合适 = suitable (appropriate) to...
■ 这种运动对老年人不合适。**Zhè zhǒng yùndòng duì lǎoniánrén bù héshì.** = *This sport is not suitable for old people.*

hé 何 (亻 7) PRONOUN = which, what (See 任何 **rènhé**.)

hé 和 (禾 8)
1 PREPOSITION = with

■ 我想和你谈谈。**Wǒ xiǎng hé nǐ tántan.** = *I'd like to have a word with you.*

hé ... yìqǐ 和…一起 = together with

■ 他星期日有时候和朋友一起看球赛。**Tā Xīngqīrì yǒushíhou hé péngyou yìqǐ kàn qiú sài.** = *He sometimes watches ball games together with his friends on Sunday.*

2 CONJUNCTION = and

■ 他到过北京、上海和香港。**Tā dàoguo Běijīng, Shànghǎi hé Xiānggǎng.** = *He's been to Beijing, Shanghai and Hong Kong.*

hé 河 (氵 8) [氵 sign + 可 phon **kě**] NOUN = river (条 **tiáo**)

■ 这条河水太急，不能游泳。**Zhè tiáo hé shuǐ tài jí, bù néng yóuyǒng.** = *The current of this river is too swift. You cannot swim in it.*

NOTE: The most famous 河 **hé** in China is 黄河 **Huánghé** = *the Yellow River*, which is the second longest river in China.

hēi 黑 (黑 12) ADJECTIVE = black, dark

■ 天黑了，我们回家吧！**Tiān hēi le, wǒmen huí jiā ba!** = *It's getting dark. Let's go home.*

■ 那辆黑汽车是谁的？**Nà liàng hēi qìchē shì shuíde?** = *Whose is that black car?*

Hēirén 黑人 = Black people, a Black person

hēibǎn 黑板 [modif: 黑 *black* + 板 *board*] NOUN = blackboard (块 **kuài**)

■ 这块黑板太小了，有没有大一点儿的？**Zhè kuài hēibǎn tài xiǎo le, yǒu méiyǒu dà yìdiǎnr de?** = *This blackboard is too small. Do you have a bigger one?*

■ 请到黑板这里来！**Qǐng dào hēibǎn zhèli lái!** = *Come to the blackboard, please!*

hēibǎn shang 黑板上 = on the blackboard

■ 黑板上的字你看得清吗？**Hēibǎn shang de zì nǐ kàn de qīng ma?** = *Can you see the words on the blackboard?*

hěn 很 (彳 9) ADVERB = very

■ 这里春天天气很好，秋天天气不好。**Zhèli chūntiān tiānqì hěn hǎo, qiūtiān tiānqì bù hǎo.** = *Here, the spring weather is good, and the autumn weather is not very good.*

■ 我很喜欢这个歌。**Wǒ hěn xǐhuan zhège gē.** = *I like this song very much.*

NOTE: When used as predicates, Chinese adjectives normally require an adverbial. For example, 天气好 **Tiānqì hǎo** would sound unnatural, while 天气很好 **Tiānqì hěn hǎo**, 天气不好 **Tiānqì bù hǎo** and 天气非常好 **Tiānqì fēicháng hǎo** are normal sentences. The adverbial 很 **hěn** is often used as a default adverbial before an adjective. In such cases the meaning of 很 **hěn** as "very" is very weak. In colloquial Chinese, 挺 **tǐng** is sometimes used instead of 很 **hěn**.

hóng 红 (纟 6) [纟 sign + 工 phon **gōng**] Trad 紅 ADJECTIVE = red

■ 苹果红红的，已经熟了。**Píngguǒ hónghóng de, yǐjīng shú le.** = *The apples are red. They're ripe.*

H

■ 红花绿树，你的花园真好看！ **Hóng huā lǜ shù, nǐ de huāyuán zhēn hǎokàn!** = *With red flowers and green trees, your garden is really beautiful.*

hóngbāo 红包 = a red envelope (with money in it)

■ 去年春节，小明收到很多红包。 **Qù nián chūnjié, Xiǎo Míng shōudao hěn duō hóngbāo.** = *Xiao Ming got much gift money last Chinese New Year.*

> NOTE: In Chinese tradition, red is an auspicious color, used on celebrations and festive occasions such as weddings or New Year's Day.

hòu 后 (厂 6) Trad **後** NOUN = back, rear (antonym 前 **qián**, 先 **xiān**)

■ 请用后门。 **Qǐng yòng hòu mén.** = *Please use the rear door.*

hòubian 后边 [modif: 后 *rear* + 边 *side*] NOUN = back, rear

■ 我家的后边有一条小河。 **Wǒ jiā de hòubian yǒu yì tiáo xiǎo hé.** = *There's a stream behind my house.*

■ 来得晚的人只能坐在后边。 **Lái de wǎn de rén zhǐ néng zuò zài hòubian.** = *Latecomers can only sit in the rear.*

■ 后边的同学，你们听得清吗？ **Hòubian de tóngxué, nǐmen tīng de qīng ma?** = *Can the students sitting in the back hear clearly?*

hòu 候 (亻 10) VERB = wait (See 时候 **shíhou**, 有时候 **yǒushíhou**.)

hū 忽 (心 11)

hūrán 忽然 [suffix: 忽 *sudden* + 然 adverbial suffix] ADVERB = suddenly

■ 刚才还天晴，忽然下大雨了。 **Gāngcái hái tiān qíng, hūrán xià dà yǔ le.** = *It was fine just a moment ago. Suddenly it's raining hard.*

hú 湖 (氵 12) [氵 sign + 胡 phon **hú**] NOUN = lake

■ 这个湖很大，从南到北有二十公里。 **Zhège hú hěn dà, cóng nán dào běi yǒu èrshí gōnglǐ.** = *This lake is very big. It's twenty kilometres from the south to the north.*

húbiān 湖边 = lakeside

■ 湖边的房子很贵。 **Húbiān de fángzi hěn guì.** = *Houses on the lakeside are expensive.*

hù 互 (一 4) ADJECTIVE = reciprocal

hùxiāng 互相 [compound: 互 *reciprocal* + 相 *each other*] ADVERB = each other, one another

■ 我们有困难的时候，应该互相帮助。 **Wǒmen yǒu kùnnan de shíhou, yīnggāi hùxiāng bāngzhù.** = *When we're in difficulty, we should help each other.*

hù 户 (户 4) NOUN = door (See 窗户 **chuānghu**.)

huā 花 (艹 7) [艹 sign + 化 phon **huà**]

1 NOUN = flower

■ 这些花真美！ **Zhèxiē huā zhēn měi!** = *How beautiful these flowers are!*

■ 她生日那天，她的朋友送给她很多花。 **Tā shēngrì nà tiān, tā de péngyou sòng gei tā hěn duō huā.** =

H

On her birthday her friends gave her lots of flowers.

zhòng huā 种花 = grow flowers, gardening, be engaged in horticulture
■ "你喜欢种花吗?" "很喜欢，可是没有时间。" **"Nǐ xǐhuan zhòng huā ma?" "Hěn xǐhuan, kěshì méiyǒu shíjiān."** = *"Do you like gardening?" "Yes, I do, but I don't have the time."*

huāyuán 花园 = garden

2 VERB = spend (time or money)
■ 去年他花了三百块钱买书。**Qùnián tā huāle sānbǎi kuài qián mǎi shū.** = *Last year he spent three hundred dollars on books.*
■ 做这个作业要花多少时间? **Zuò zhège zuòyè yào huā duōshǎo shíjiān?** = *How much time will this assignment take?*

huà 化 (亻 4) VERB = transform (See 变化 **biànhuà**, 文化 **wénhuà**.)

huà 划 (戈 6) Trad 劃 VERB = plan (See 计划 **jìhuà**.)

huà 画 (凵 8) Trad 畫 VERB = paint, draw
■ 你会画画儿吗? **Nǐ huì huà huàr ma?** = *Can you draw* (or *paint*)?

huàr 画儿 [suffix: 画 *picture* + 儿 nominal suffix] NOUN = picture, painting, drawing (张 **zhāng**)
■ 这张画儿画得真好! **Zhè zhāng huàr huà de zhēn hǎo!** = *This picture is painted really well.*
■ 墙上挂着两张画儿。**Qiáng shang guàzhe liǎng zhāng huàr.** = *Two paintings are hanging on the wall.*

huà 话 (讠 8) [讠 sign + 舌 sign] Trad 話 NOUN = speech, what is said, words (句 **jù**)
■ 你这句话很有道理。**Nǐ zhè jù huà hěn yǒu dàolǐ.** = *What you said is very true.*
■ 别忘了我的话。**Bié wàngle wǒ de huà.** = *Don't forget what I told you.*

huài 坏 (土 7) Trad 壞 ADJECTIVE = bad; out of order (antonym 好 **hǎo**)
■ 今天早上天气坏极了，又刮风，又下雨。**Jīntiān zǎoshang tiānqì huài jíle, yòu guāfēng, yòu xià yǔ.** = *The weather was extremely bad this morning; it was windy and wet.*
■ 我的自行车坏了，只能走回家。**Wǒ de zìxíngchē huài le, zhǐ néng zǒu huí jiā.** = *My bike broke down. I've got to walk home.*

huān 欢 (又 6) Trad 歡 ADJECTIVE = joyful

huānyíng 欢迎 [modif: 欢 *joyfully* + 迎 *meet*] VERB = welcome
■ 我们欢迎您来我们学校参观。**Wǒmen huānyíng nín lái wǒmen xuéxiào cānguān.** = *You're welcome to come and visit our school.*

huán 还 (辶 7) Trad 還 VERB = return (what was borrowed)

huángěi 还给 = return to
■ 这本书明天一定要还给图书馆。**Zhè běn shū míngtiān yídìng yào huángěi túshūguǎn.** = *This book must be returned to the library tomorrow.*

huàn 换 (扌 10) [扌 sign + 奂 phon **huān**] Trad 換 VERB = exchange, replace
■ 这双鞋太小了，能不能换一双大一点儿的？ **Zhè shuāng xié tài xiǎo le, néng bu néng huàn yì shuāng dà yìdiǎnr de?** = *This pair of shoes is too small. May I exchange them for a bigger pair?*

huáng 黄 (艹 11) ADJECTIVE = yellow
■ 香蕉和桔子都是黄的。**Xiāngjiāo hé júzi dōu shì huáng de.** = *Bananas and tangerines are yellow.*

huángyóu 黄油 [modif: 黄 *yellow* + 油 *oil*] NOUN = butter
■ 黄油吃完了，明天别忘了去买。**Huángyóu chī wán le, míngtiān bié wàngle qù mǎi.** = *We've run out of butter. Don't forget to buy some tomorrow.*
■ 我不吃黄油，只要面包就行了。**Wǒ bù chī huángyóu, zhí yào miànbāo jiù xíng le.** = *I don't eat butter. Just bread will do.*

huí 回 (口 6)
1 VERB = return (to a place), go back
■ 时间不早了，回家吧。**Shíjiān bù zǎo le, huí jiā ba.** = *It's quite late. Let's go back home.*
huílai 回来 = return to a place (close to the speaker)
■ 妈，我回来了！ **Mā, wǒ huílai le.** = *Mum, I'm home!*
huíqu 回去 = return to a place (away from the speaker)
■ 张先生已经回去了，你明天来找他吧。**Zhāng xiānsheng yǐjīng huíqu le, nǐ míngtiān lái zhǎo tā ba.** = *Mr Zhang has gone back home. Come and see him tomorrow.*
2 MEASURE WORD = number of times
■ 我说了好几回了，你就是不听。**Wǒ shuōle hǎo jǐ huí le, nǐ jiùshì bù tīng.** = *I've said it several times, but you just won't listen.*
■ 他去过中国两回，对中国有些了解。**Tā qùguo Zhōngguó liǎng huí, duì Zhōngguó yǒuxiē liáojiě.** = *He's been to China twice. He has some knowledge of China.*

huì 会 (人 6) Trad 會
1 MODAL VERB = know how to, can
■ 你会游泳吗？ **Nǐ huì yǒuyǒng ma?** = *Can you swim?*
2 MODAL VERB = probably, will
■ 我看今天夜里会下雨。**Wǒ kàn jīntiān yèli huì xià yǔ.** = *I think it'll rain tonight.*
3 VERB = have ability or knowledge (e.g. of a language)
■ 我不会日文，我会一点儿中文。**Wǒ bú huì Rìwén, wǒ huì yìdiǎnr Zhōngwén.** = *I don't know Japanese. I know a little Chinese.*

NOTE: Both 会 **huì** and 能 **néng** are often glossed as "can," but they have different meanings. 会 **huì** means "know how to do," while 能 **néng** means "be able to do." For example: 我会游泳，但是今天不能游泳。**Wǒ huì yóuyǒng, dànshi jīntiān bù néng yóuyǒng.** = *I know how to swim, but I am not able to today [because I'm unwell, or too busy etc.].*

H

4 NOUN = assembly, meeting; association
■ 今天的会非常重要，请您一定要参加。**Jīntiān de huì fēicháng zhòngyào, qǐng nín yídìng yào cānjiā.** = *Today's meeting is very important. Please attend it.*
■ 王先生在开会，您有什么事情可以跟我说。**Wáng xiānsheng zài kāihuì, nín yǒu shénme shìqing kěyǐ gēn wǒ shuō.** = *Mr Wang's at a meeting. You could talk to me instead.*
kāihuì 开会 = have a meeting
■ 我们每星期一上午都要开会。**Wǒmen měi Xīngqīyī shàngwǔ dōu yào kāihuì.** = *We have a meeting every Monday morning.*

huìhuà 会话 [modif: 会 *assemble* + 话 *speech*]
1 VERB = talk, have a conversation
■ 我们什么时候能用中文会话？**Wǒmen shénme shíhou néng yòng Zhōngwén huìhuà?** = *When can we have a conversation in Chinese?*
hé/gēn ... huìhuà 和 / 跟…会话 = have a conversation with …
2 NOUN = conversation, dialogue
■ 这课会话我还念不好。**Zhè kè huìhuà wǒ hái niàn bù hǎo.** = *I still can't read this dialogue (in a textbook) very well.*
huìhuà shū 会话书 = conversation book
huìhuà kè 会话课 = conversation class

hūn 婚 (女 11) [女 sign + 昏 phon **hūn**] VERB = marry (See 结婚 **jiēhūn**.)

huó 活 (氵 9) [氵 sign + 舌 sign] Trad 活 VERB = be alive, living (antonym 死 **sǐ**)
■ 这条鱼还活着呢！**Zhè tiáo yú hái huózhe ne!** = *This fish is still alive!*

huór 活儿 [suffix: 活 *manual work* + 儿 nominal suffix] NOUN = (manual) work, job
■ 这活儿不容易，你干得了吗？**Zhè huór bù róngyì, nǐ gàn de liǎo ma?** = *This job is not easy. Are you able to do it?*
■ 现在没活儿干，你可以休息一会儿。**Xiànzài méi huór gàn, nǐ kěyǐ xiūxi yíhuìr.** *There's nothing to do now. You can take a break.*
gàn huór 干活儿 = (colloquial) work, do manual work

huódòng 活动 [compound: 活 *alive* + 动 *move*]
1 VERB = do physical exercise
■ 你别老是坐在屋里看电视，得出去活动活动。**Nǐ bié lǎoshì zuò zài wūli kàn diànshì, děi chūqu huódòng-huódòng.** = *You shouldn't sit in the house watching TV all the time. You must exercise outdoors.*
2 NOUN = activity
■ 他喜欢体育活动，他妹妹喜欢文艺活动。**Tā xǐhuan tǐyù huódòng, tā mèimei xǐhuan wényì huódòng.** = *He likes sports, and his sister likes the performing arts.*

huǒ 火 (火 4) NOUN = fire

huǒchē 火车 [modif: 火 *fire* + 车 *vehicle*] NOUN = train (辆 **liàng**)
■ 北京来的火车什么时候到？**Běijīng lái de huǒchē shénme shíhou dào?** = *When does the train from Beijing arrive?*

■ 我爸爸坐火车上班。**Wǒ bāba zuò huǒchē shàngbān.** = *My daddy goes to work by train.*
huǒchē zhàn 火车站 = railway station
huǒchē piào 火车票 = train ticket

huò 或 (戈 8) CONJUNCTION = or

huòzhě 或者 CONJUNCTION = or, otherwise
■ 我今天晚上或者明天早上打电话给你。**Wǒ jīntiān wǎnshang huòzhě míngtiān zǎoshang dǎ diànhuà gei nǐ.** = *I'll ring you this evening or early tomorrow morning.*

J

jī 基 (土 11) [其 phon **qí** + 土 sign] NOUN = (earthen) foundation

jīběn 基本 [compound: 基 *(earthen) foundation* + 本 *root*] ADJECTIVE = fundamental, basic
■ 这件事的基本情况我已经知道了。**Zhè jiàn shì de jīběn qíngkuàng wǒ yǐjīng zhīdào le.** = *I've learned the basic facts of this matter.*

jīchǔ 基础 [compound: 基 *foundation* + 础 *base*] NOUN = foundation, base
■ 你想建一座高楼，就要先打好基础。**Nǐ xiǎng jiàn yí zuò gāo lóu, jiùyào xiān dǎ hǎo jīchǔ.** = *If you want to erect a high building, you must first of all lay a good foundation.*

jī 机 (木 6) [木 sign + 几 phon **jǐ**] Trad 機 NOUN = machine

jīchǎng 机场 [modif: 机 *airplane* + 场 *ground, field*] NOUN = airport
■ "机场离这里远不远?" "不远，大概十公里。" **"Jīchǎng lí zhèli yuǎn bu yuǎn?" "Bù yuǎn, dàgài shí gōnglǐ."** = *"Is the airport far from here?" "Not very far. About ten kilometers."*
■ 下午我要去机场接一个朋友。**Xiàwǔ wǒ yào qù jīchǎng jiē yí ge péngyou.** = *I'm going to the airport this afternoon to meet a friend.*

jīhuì 机会 [compound: 机 *opportunity* + 会 *by chance*] NOUN = opportunity, chance
■ 这个机会很难得，不要错过。**Zhège jīhuì hěn nándé, bú yào cuòguò.** = *This is a rare opportunity. Don't miss it.*
■ 你有没有机会去北京学中文? **Nǐ yǒu méiyǒu jīhuì qù Běijīng xué Zhōngwén?** = *Do you have any chance of going to Beijing to learn Chinese?*

jīqì 机器 [compound: 机 *machine* + 器 *utensil*] NOUN = machine, machinery
■ 这种机器很有用。**Zhè zhǒng jīqì hěn yǒuyòng.** = *This kind of machine is very useful.*
■ 你会不会用这个机器? **Nǐ huì bu huì yòng zhè ge jīqì?** = *Do you know how to use this machine?*

jī 鸡 (鸟 7) [又 symb + 鸟 sign] Trad 雞 NOUN = chicken, hen, rooster (只 **zhī**)

■ 我们晚饭吃鸡，好吗？ **Wǒmen wǎnfàn chī jī, hǎoma?** = *We'll have chicken tonight, OK?* (→ *Shall we have chicken tonight?*)

gōngjī 公鸡 = rooster
mǔjī 母鸡 = hen
xiǎojī 小鸡 = chick

NOTE: 鸡 **jī** may denote a rooster, a hen or a chick, though they may be specified by 公鸡 **gōngjī** = *rooster*, 母鸡 **mǔjī** = *hen* and 小鸡 **xiǎojī** = *chick*. As food, it is always 鸡 **jī**.

jīdàn 鸡蛋 [modif: 鸡 *hen* + 蛋 *egg*] NOUN = hen's egg (只 **zhī**, 个 **gè**)
■ 妈妈每星期买两公斤鸡蛋。**Māma měi xīngqī mǎi liǎng gōngjīn jīdàn.** = *Mum buys two kilograms of eggs every week.*

jí 级 (纟 6) Trad 級 NOUN = grade, level (See 年级 **niánjí**.)

jí 极 (木 7) [木 symb + 及 phon **jí**] Trad 極 NOUN = extremity

jíle 极了 ADVERB = extremely, very
■ 这两天我忙极了。**Zhè liǎng tiān wǒ máng jí le.** = *I'm extremely busy these days.*

NOTE: 极了 **jíle** is used after adjectives or some verbs to mean "extremely..." or "very...," e.g. 好极了 **hǎo jí le** = *extremely good.*

jí 急 (心 9) [刍 symb + 心 sign] ADJECTIVE = anxious; urgent
■ 他心里很急。**Tā xīn li hěn jí.** = *He's very anxious.*
■ 这件事很急。**Zhè jiàn shì hěn jí.** = *This is an urgent matter.*
■ 他家里有急事，今天没来上班。**Tā jiā li yǒu jíshì, jīntiān méi lái shàngbān.** = *He has an urgent family matter* [*to attend to*] *and did not come to work today.*

jíxìngzi 急性子 = an impatient/impetuous person
■ 我妈妈是个急性子，我爸爸是个慢性子，但是他们俩好象很合得来。**Wǒ māma shì ge jíxìngzi, wǒ bàba shì ge mànxìngzi, dànshì tāmen liǎ hǎoxiàng hěn hédelái.** = *My mother is an impatient person while my father moves slowly. However, they seem to get along quite well.*

jí 集 (隹 12) VERB = assemble

jíhé 集合 [compound: 集 *assemble* + 合 *combine*] VERB = gather together, assemble
■ 我们明天上午十点钟在火车站集合。**Wǒmen míngtiān shàngwǔ shí diǎnzhōng zài huǒchēzhàn jíhé.** = *We'll assemble at the railway station at ten o'clock tomorrow morning.*

jǐ 几 (几 2) Trad 幾 PRONOUN
1 = several
■ 我上星期买了几本书。**Wǒ shàng xīngqī mǎile jǐ běn shū.** = *I bought several books last week.*
2 = how many
■ 你上星期买了几本书？ **Nǐ shàng xīngqī mǎile jǐ běn shū?** = *How many books did you buy last week?*

J

> NOTE: When 几 **jǐ** is used in a question to mean "how many," it is presumed that the answer will be a number less than ten. Otherwise 多少 **duōshǎo** should be used instead. Compare:
> ■ 你有几个哥哥？ **Nǐ yǒu jǐ ge gēge?** = *How many elder brothers do you have?*
> ■ 你们学校有多少学生？ **Nǐmen xuēxiào yǒu duōshǎo xúesheng?** = *How many students are there in your school?*

jǐ 己 (己 3) PRONOUN = self (See 自己 **zìjǐ**.)

jǐ 挤 (扌 9) [扌 sign + 齐 phon **qí**]
Trad 擠 PRONOUN = self
1 VERB = squeeze, crowd
■ 你会挤牛奶吗？ **Nǐ huì jǐ niúnǎi ma?** = *Do you know how to milk cows?*
2 ADJECTIVE = crowded
■ 圣诞节前几天商店很挤。**Shèngdànjié qián jǐ tiān shāngdiàn hěn jǐ.** = *Stores are crowded days before Christmas.*

J

jì 计 (讠 4) [讠 sign + 十 symb]
Trad 計 VERB = plan

jìhuà 计划 [compound: 计 *plan* + 划 *plan*]
1 NOUN = plan
■ 这个计划不可行。**Zhège jìhuà bù kě xíng.** = *This plan is not feasible.*
■ 你明年有什么计划？ **Nǐ míngnián yǒu shénme jìhuà?** = *What's your plan for next year?*
2 VERB = plan
■ 我计划明年去美国旅行。**Wǒ jìhuà míngnián qù Měiguó lǚxíng.** = *I plan to make a trip to the States next year.*

jì 记 (讠 5) [讠 sign + 己 phon **jǐ**]
Trad 記 VERB = record, remember, bear in mind
■ 你说得慢一点儿，我把它记下来。**Nǐ shuō de màn yìdiǎnr, wǒ bǎ tā jì xiàlai.** = *Speak slowly. I'll write it down.*
■ 你要记住我的话，别忘了! **Nǐ yào jìzhù wǒ de huà, bié wàng le.** = *You should bear in mind what I said. Don't forget it.*

jìdē 记得 = recall, remember
■ 我们第一次是在什么地方见面的，你还记得吗？ **Wǒmen dì-yī cì shì zài shénme dìfang jiànmiàn de, nǐ hái jìdē ma?** = *Do you still remember where we first met?*

jì bu dē 记不得 = cannot recall, cannot remember

jì 纪 (纟 6) Trad 紀 NOUN = age (See 年纪 **niánjì**.)

jì 技 (扌 7) [扌 sign + 支 symb]
NOUN = skill

jìshù 技术 [compound: 技 *skill* + 术 *craft*] NOUN = technique, technology, skill
■ 这个技术很有用。**Zhège jìshù hěn yǒuyòng.** = *This technology is very useful.*
■ 你得学点技术，走到那儿都有用。**Nǐ děi xúe diǎn jìshù, zǒu dào nǎr dōu**

yǒuyòng. = *You've got to learn some skills, which will be useful whenever you go.*

jìshù gōngrén 技术工人 = skilled worker

jì 济 (氵 9) [氵 sign + 齐 phon **qí**] Trad 濟 VERB = bring relief to (See 经济 **jīngjì**.)

jì 继 (纟 10) Trad 繼

jìxù 继续 [compound: 继 *continue* + 续 *keep on*] VERB = continue
■ 我们吃午饭吧，下午继续开会。**Wǒmen chī wǔfàn ba, xiàwǔ jìxù kāihuì.** = *Let's have lunch. The meeting will continue in the afternoon.*

jì 寄 (宀 11) [宀 sign + 奇 phon **qí**] VERB = send by mail, post
■ 我要寄这封信去香港。**Wǒ yào jì zhè fēng xìn qù Xiāngkǎng.** = *I want to post this letter to Hong Kong.*

jì 绩 (纟 11) Trad 績 NOUN = achievement (See 成绩 **chéngjì**.)

jiā 加 (力 5) [力 sign + 口 symb] VERB = add, plus
■ 二加三是五。**Èr jiā sān shì wǔ.** = *Two plus three is five.*

Jiānádà 加拿大 NOUN = Canada

jiā 家 (宀 10) [宀 sign + 豕 symb]
1 NOUN = family, household, home
■ 我家有四口人：父亲、母亲、姐姐和我。**Wǒ jiā yǒu sì kǒu rén: fùqin, mǔqin, jiějie hé wǒ.** = *There're four people in my family: my father, my mother, my sister and I.*
■ 下课以后我就回家。**Xià kè yǐhòu, wǒ jiù huí jiā.** = *I go home as soon as school is over.*
2 MEASURE WORD = for families or businesses
■ 四家人家 **sì jiā rénjiā** = *four families*
■ 一家商店 **yì jiā shāngdiàn** = *a store*
■ 两家工厂 **liǎng jiā gōngchǎng** = *two factories*
3 SUFFIX = (added to a noun or verb to indicate the person is a specialist)
huàjiā 画家 = painter, artist
jiàoyùjiā 教育家 = educator
kēxuéjiā 科学家 = scientist

jiātíng 家庭 [compound: 家 *home, family* + 庭 *courtyard*] NOUN = family (个 **gè**)
■ 他的家庭很幸福。**Tā de jiātíng hěn xìngfú.** = *He has a happy family.*
■ 她在这里没有家庭，也没有朋友。**Tā zài zhèlǐ méiyǒu jiātíng, yě méiyǒu péngyou.** = *She has neither family nor friends here.*

> NOTE: 家 **jiā** has more meanings than 家庭 **jiātíng**. While 家庭 **jiātíng** only means "family," 家 **jiā** may mean "family," "household" or "home."

jià 价 (亻 6) Trad 價 NOUN = price

jiàqián 价钱 [compound: 价 *price* + 钱 *money*] NOUN = price
■ 价钱太贵，还是不要买吧。**Jiàqián tài guì, háishì bú yào mǎi ba.** = *The price is too high. Don't buy it.*

J

■ 他只是问一下价钱，没有打算买。 **Tā zhǐshì wèn yíxia jiàqián, méiyǒu dǎsuàn mǎi.** = *He only asked the price, he didn't intend to buy it.*

jià 驾 (马 8) [加 phon **jiā** + 马 sign] Trad 駕 See 劳驾 **láojià**.

jià 假 (亻 11) NOUN = holiday

jiàqī 假期 [modif: 假 *holiday* + 期 *period*] NOUN = holiday period
■ 假期你想做什么？ **Jiàqī nǐ xiǎng zuò shénme?** = *What do you plan to do during the holidays?*

jiān 坚 (土 7) Trad 堅 ADJECTIVE = hard, firm

jiānchí 坚持 [modif: 坚 *firm, firmly* + 持 *hold*] VERB = uphold, persist (in)
■ 不管刮风下雨，他坚持每天跑步。 **Bùguǎn guāfēng xiàyǔ, tā jiānchí měitiān pǎobù.** *He persists in jogging every day, no matter how wet or windy it is.*

J

jiān 间 (门 7) [门 sign + 日 symb] Trad 間
1 NOUN = See 房间 **fángjiān**.
2 MEASURE WORD = (for rooms)
■ 这间办公室很大。 **Zhè jiān bàngōngshì hěn dà.** = *This office is very big.*

jiǎn 检 (木 11) Trad 檢

jiǎnchá 检查 [compound: 检 *examine* + 查 *inspect, check*] VERB = examine, inspect, check
■ 先生，我要检查一下你的行李。 **Xiānsheng, wǒ yào jiǎnchá yíxia nǐ de xíngli.** = *I want to check your luggage, sir.*

jiǎn 简 (竹 13)

jiǎndān 简单 [compound: 简 *simple* + 单 *single*] ADJECTIVE = simple (antonym 复杂 **fùzá**)
■ 这个问题不简单，要好好想一想。 **Zhège wèntí bù jiǎndān, yào hǎohǎo xiǎng yi xiǎng.** = *This question is not a simple one; it needs careful consideration.*

jiàn 见 (见 4) Trad 見 VERB = see, perceive
■ 我能不能见一下王先生？ **Wǒ néng bu néng jiàn yíxia Wáng xiānsheng?** = *May I see Mr Wang?*

jiànmiàn 见面 [v+obj: 见 *see* + 面 *face*] VERB = meet
■ "我们以前见过面吗？" "见过一次。" **"Wǒmen yǐqián jiànguo miàn ma?" "Jiànguo yí cì."** = *"Have we met before?" "Yes, once."*

jiàn 件 (亻 6) MEASURE WORD = (for things, affairs, clothes or furniture)
■ 一件东西 **yí jiàn dōngxi** = *a thing, something*
■ 我有一件东西忘在机场了。 **Wǒ yǒu yí jiàn dōngxi wàng zài jīchǎng le.** = *I've left something in the airport.*
■ 一件事情 **yí jiàn shìqing** = *a matter*
■ 我有几件事情要跟你谈。 **Wǒ yǒu jǐ jiàn shìqing yào gēn nǐ tán.** = *I've a few things to discuss with you.*

■ 一件衣服 **yí jiàn yīfu** – *a piece of clothing (e.g. a jacket, a dress)*
■ 她上星期买了三件衣服。**Tā shàng xīngqī mǎile sān jiàn yīfu.** = *She bought three pieces of clothing last week.*

jiàn 建 (廴 8) VERB = build, construct

jiànshè 建设 [compound: 建 *build* + 设 *install*]
1 VERB = build, construct
■ 我们努力工作，建设自己的国家。**Wǒmen nǔlì gōngzuò, jiànshè zìjǐ de guójiā.** = *We work hard to build up our country.*
2 NOUN = building up, construction activity, installing

jiàn 健 (亻 10) [亻 sign + 建 phon **jiàn**] ADJECTIVE = strong

jiànkāng 健康 [compound: 健 *energetic* + 康 *good health*]
1 NOUN = health
■ 母亲很关心孩子的健康。**Mǔqin hěn guānxīn háizi de jiànkāng.** = *Mothers are very concerned for their children's health.*
2 ADJECTIVE = healthy, in good health
■ 这位老人身体很健康。**Zhè wèi lǎorén shēntǐ hěn jiànkāng.** = *This old person is in good health.*
■ 祝您健康! (or 祝您身体健康!) **Zhù nín jiànkāng!** (or **Zhù nín shēntǐ jiànkāng!**) = *I wish you good health!*

jiàn 践 (足 12) [足 sign + 戋 phon] Trad 踐 VERB = carry out (See 实践 **shíjiàn**.)

jiāng 江 (氵 6) [氵 sign + 工 phon **gōng**] NOUN = river (条 **tiáo**)
■ 这条江从西向东流。**Zhè tiáo jiāng cóng xī xiàng dōng liú.** = *This river flows from west to east.*
■ 你能游过江吗? **Nǐ néng yóuguò jiāng ma?** = *Can you swim across the river?*

NOTE: The most famous 江 **jiāng** in China is 长江 **Chángjiāng**, the longest river in China, which literally means "long river." 长江 **Chángjiāng** is also known as the Yangtze River. In modern Chinese, 江 **jiāng** and 河 **hé** both mean "river." Usually (not always) rivers in the south are known as 江 **jiāng** and rivers in the north are 河 **hé**.

jiāng 将 (丬 9) Trad 將 ADVERB = shall, will

jiānglái 将来 [modif: 将 *shall, will* + 来 *come*] NOUN = future, in the future
■ 我现在看不懂中文报纸，将来一定看得懂。**Wǒ xiànzài kàn bu dǒng Zhōngwén bàozhǐ, jiānglái yídìng kàn de dǒng.** = *I can't read Chinese newspapers now, but I'll certainly be able to in the future.*

jiǎng 讲 (讠 6) [讠 sign + 井 symb] Trad 講 VERB = talk
■ 别讲了，这些事我都知道。**Bié jiǎng le, zhè xiē shì wǒ dōu zhīdào.** = *Say no more. I know all about these matters.*

jiǎng dàolǐ 讲道理 = See 道理 **dàolǐ**.
jiǎng gùshi 讲故事 = See 故事 **gùshi**.

J

jiāo 交 (亠 6) VERB
1 = hand over
■ 这件事交给我办吧。**Zhè jiàn shì jiāo gei wǒ bàn ba.** = *Hand this matter over to me.* (→ *Let me deal with this matter.*)
2 = pay (bills, fees)
■ 你的学费交了吗？ **Nǐ de xuéfèi jiāo le ma?** = *Have you paid your tuition fee?*

jiāo 教 (攵 10) VERB = teach
■ 张小姐教我们中文。**Zhāng xiǎojiě jiāo wǒmen Zhōngwén.** = *Miss Zhang teaches us Chinese.*

jiāo 蕉 (艹 14) [艹 sign + 焦 phon **jiāo**] NOUN = banana (See 香蕉 **xiāngjiāo**.)

jiǎo 角 (角 7) MEASURE WORD
= (Chinese currency 0.1 *yuan* or 10 *fen*), ten cents, a dime
■ 两角钱 **liǎng jiǎo qiān** = *two jiao; twenty cents*
■ 八块九角五分 **bā kuài jiǔ jiǎo wǔ fēn** = *eight yuan nine jiao and five fen; eight dollars and ninety-five cents*

jiǎo 饺 (饣 9) [饣 sign + 交 phon **jiāo**] Trad 餃 NOUN = same as 饺子 **jiǎozi**

jiǎozi 饺子 [suffix: 饺 *dumpling* + 子 nominal suffix] NOUN = stuffed dumpling, *jiaozi*
■ 李太太做的饺子真好吃！ **Lǐ tàitai zuò de jiǎozi zhēn hǎochī!** = *The dumplings made by Mrs Li are really delicious.*
■ 你晚饭吃了多少个饺子？ **Nǐ wǎnfàn chīle duōshǎo ge jiǎozi?** = *How many dumplings did you eat for supper?*

jiǎo 脚 (月 10) [月 sign + 却 symb] NOUN = foot (只 **zhī**)
■ 我的脚很大，穿不下这双鞋。**Wǒ de jiǎo hěn dà, chuān bú xià zhè shuāng xié.** = *My feet are big. This pair of shoes doesn't fit.*

jiào 叫 (口 5) [口 sign + symb]
1 VERB = call, shout, cry out
■ 大家都叫他小王。**Dàjiā dōu jiào tā Xiǎo Wáng.** = *Everybody calls him Xiao Wang.*
■ 外面有人叫你。**Wàimiàn yǒu rén jiào nǐ.** = *Someone's shouting for you outside.*
2 PREPOSITION = same as 被 **bèi**

jiào 教 (攵 10) NOUN = teaching

jiàoshì 教室 [modif: 教 *teaching* + 室 *room*] NOUN = classroom (间 **jiān**)
■ "你们的教室在哪里？" "在二楼，二二三房间。" **"Nǐmen de jiàoshì zài nǎlǐ?" "Zài èrlóu, èr-èr-sān fángjiān."** = *"Where is your classroom?" "It's on the second floor, Room 223."*
■ 我们在那间教室上数学课。**Wǒmen zài nà jiān jiàoshì shàng shùxué kè.** = *We have our mathematics class in that classroom.*

jiàoyù 教育 [compound: 教 *teach* + 育 *nurture*]
1 VERB = educate

J

■ 父母应该教育自己的孩子。**Fùmǔ yīnggāi jiàoyù zìjǐ de háizi.** = *Parents should educate their children.*

2 NOUN = education

■ 教育关系到国家的将来。**Jiàoyù guānxì dào gúojiā de jiānglái.** = *Education has an important bearing on the future of a country.*

■ 我姐姐在大学里念教育。**Wǒ jiějie zài dàxuě li niàn jiàoyù.** *My elder sister studies education at university.*

jiē 接 (扌 11) [扌 sign + 妾 symb] VERB = receive (a letter, a telephone call); meet and greet (a visitor)

■ 我昨天接到一封信、两个传真和八个电子邮件。**Wǒ zuótiān jiēdao yì fēng xìn, liǎng ge chuánzhēn hé bā ge diànzǐ yóujiàn.** = *Yesterday I received a letter, two faxes and eight e-mail messages.*

■ 王先生是第一次到这里来，你应该去机场接他。**Wáng xiānsheng shì dì-yī cì dào zhèli lái, nǐ yīnggāi qù jīchǎng jiē tā.** = *This is the first time that Mr Wang's coming here. You should meet him at the airport.*

jiēzhe 接着 CONJUNCTION = and immediately, then, at the heels of (a previous action or event)

■ 我先听到有人叫我，接着小王跑了进来。**Wǒ xiān tīngdao yǒu rén jiào wǒ, jiēzhe Xiǎo Wáng pǎole jìnlai.** = *I first heard someone calling me, then Xiao Wang came running in.*

jiē 街 (彳 12) [彳 sign + 圭 symb + 亍 sign] NOUN = street (条 **tiáo**)

■ 我家前边的那条街总是很安静。**Wǒ jiā qiánbian de nà tiáo jiē zǒngshì hěn ānjìng.** = *The street in front of my home is always quiet.*

jiē shang 街上 = on the street

■ 街上人很多。**Jiē shang rén hěn duō.** = *There are many people on the street.*

dàjiē 大街 = main street in a town or city (usually busy commercial centre)

jié 节 (艹 5) Trad 節

1 NOUN = festival

■ 这个节我过得很愉快。**Zhège jié wǒ guò de hěn yúkuài.** = *I had a very happy festival.*

■ 这个地方一年有好几个节。**Zhège dìfang yì nián yǒu hǎo jǐ ge jié.** = *There're quite a number of festivals in this area.*

guò jié 过节 = observe a festival, celebrate a festival.

chūnjié 春节 = Spring Festival (Chinese New Year)

zhōngqiūjié 中秋节 = Mid-Autumn Festival (the Moon Festival)

shèngdànjié 圣诞节 = Christmas

2 MEASURE WORD = (a period of time)

■ 一节课 **yì jié kè** = *a period of class*

jiémù 节目 [compound: 节 *section* + 目 *item*] NOUN = program

■ 昨天的电视节目很精彩。**Zuótiān de diànshì jiémù hěn jīngcǎi.** = *The TV program yesterday was wonderful!*

■ 我不喜欢这个节目。**Wǒ bù xǐhuan zhège jiémù.** = *I don't like this program.*

xīnwén jiémù 新闻节目 = news program (on TV or radio)

wényì jiémù 文艺节目 = theatrical program

tǐyù jiémù 体育节目 = sports program

jiérì 节日 [modif: 节 *festival* + 日 *day*] NOUN = festival day
■ 中国人最重要的节日是春节，也就是中国人的新年。**Zhōngguórén zuì zhòngyào de jiérì shì chūnjié, yě jiùshì Zhōngguó rén de xīnnián.** = *The most important festival for the Chinese is the Spring festival, which is the Chinese New Year.*

jié 结 (纟 9) [纟 sign + 吉 phon **jí**] Trad 結 VERB = tie, bear (fruit)

jiéguǒ 结果 [v+obj: 结 *bear* + 果 *fruit*] CONJUNCTION = finally, in the end
■ 我们找了他半天，结果在图书馆找到了他。**Wǒmen zhǎole tā bàntiān, jiéguǒ zài túshūguǎn zhǎodàole tā.** = *We looked for him for a long time and finally found him in the library.*

jiéhūn 结婚 [v+obj: 结 *tie* + 婚 *marriage*] VERB = marry
■ 他们明年春节结婚。**Tāmen míngnián chūnjié jiéhūn.** = *They'll marry at the Spring Festival next year.*
hé/gēn ... jiéhūn 和 / 跟…结婚 = marry (somebody), be married to...
■ 他和他中学时的情人结婚了。**Tā hé tā zhōngxué shí de qíngrén jiéhūn le.** = *He married his high school sweetheart.*

jiéshù 结束 [compound: 结 *tie* + 束 *knot*] VERB = end, terminate (antonym 开始 **kāishǐ**)
■ 电影什么时候结束？ **Diànyǐng shénme shíhou jiéshù?** = *When does the movie end?*

jiě 姐 (女 8) [女 sign + 且 symb] NOUN = same as 姐姐 **jiějie**

jiějie 姐姐 NOUN = elder sister
■ 我姐姐对我很好。**Wǒ jiějie duì wǒ hěn hǎo.** = *My elder sister is very nice to me.*
■ 你有没有姐姐？ **Nǐ yǒu méiyǒu jiějie?** = *Do you have an elder sister?*

jiě 解 (角 13) [角 sign + 刀 sign + 牛 sign] VERB = divide, separate

jiějué 解决 [compound: 解 *dissect* + 决 *finalize*] VERB = solve (a problem), settle (an issue)
■ 这个问题还没有解决。**Zhège wèntí hái méiyǒu jiějué.** = *This problem has not been solved yet.*

jiè 介 (人 4) VERB = intervene

jièshào 介绍 [compound: 介 *intervene* + 绍 *connect*] VERB
1 = introduce
■ 我来介绍一下，这位是李先生，这位是王小姐。**Wǒ lái jièshào yíxià, zhè wèi shì Lǐ xiānsheng, zhè wèi shì Wáng xiǎojiě.** = *Let me introduce* [*the people here*]. *This is Mr Li. This is Miss Wang.*
2 = give a briefing on
■ 你刚从中国回来，请你介绍一下中国最近的情况。**Nǐ gāng cóng Zhōngguó huílai, qǐng nǐ jièshào yíxià Zhōngguó zuìjìn de qíngkuàng.** = *As you've just come back from China, please tell us something about the latest situation in China.*

jiè 界 (田 9) [田 sign + 介 phon **jiè**] NOUN = boundary (See 世界 **shìjiè**.)

jiè 借 (亻 10) VERB = borrow, lend
■ 他借给我一百元。**Tā jiè gei wǒ yìbǎi yuán.** = *He lent me one hundred dollars.*
■ 我向他借了一百元。**Wǒ xiàng tā jièle yìbǎi yuán.** = *I borrowed one hundred dollars from him.*

NOTE: This verb may mean either "borrow" or " lend," depending on the patterns in which it occurs:
■ A 借给 B ... **A jiè gei B ...** = *A lends B...*
■ A 向 B 借... **A xiàng B jiè ...** = *A borrows ... from B*

jīn 斤 (斤 4) MEASURE WORD = *jin* (unit of weight, equivalent to half a kilogram)
■ 这条鱼重八斤。**Zhè tiáo yú zhòng bā jīn.** = *This fish weighs eight jin.*
■ 妈妈买了两斤肉。**Māma mǎile liǎng jīn ròu.** = *Mum bought two jin of meat.*

jīn 今 (人 4) NOUN = now, the present

jīnnián 今年 [modif: 今 *now* + 年 *year*] NOUN = this year
■ 今年是二〇〇五年。**Jīnnián shì èrlínglíngwǔ nián.** = *This year is the year 2005.*
■ 我祖父今年八十岁了。**Wǒ zǔfù jīnnián bāshí suì le.** = *My grandfather is eighty years old this year.*

jīntiān 今天 [modif: 今 *now* + 天 *day*] NOUN = today
■ 今天天气很好。**Jīntiān tiānqì hěn hǎo.** = *The weather's fine today.*
■ 我今天要上五节课。**Wǒ jīntiān yào shàng wǔ jié kè.** = *I have five classes today.*

jǐn 紧 (纟 10) Trad 緊 ADJECTIVE = tight, taut
■ 今天的活动安排得比较紧。**Jīntiān de huódòng ānpái de bǐjiào jǐn.** = *Today's activities are scheduled rather tightly.* (→ *We're on a tight schedule today.*)

jǐnzhāng 紧张 [compound: 紧 *tight* + 张 *tense*] ADJECTIVE = tense, nervous
■ 明天要考试了，我没有很好准备，心里真紧张。**Míngtiān yào kǎoshì le, wǒ méiyǒu hěn hǎo zhǔnbèi, xīn li zhēn jǐnzhāng.** = *We're having an examination tomorrow. I'm not well prepared, and feel really nervous.*

jìn 进 (辶 7) [辶 sign + 井 phon **jǐng**] Trad 進 VERB = move forward, enter
■ 请进！**Qǐng jìn!** = *Please come in!* (or *Please go in!*)
jìnlai 进来 = come in, come into
■ 进来吧，我们在等你呢！**Jìnlai ba, wǒmen zài děng nǐ ne.** = *Please come in, we've been waiting for you.*
jìnqu 进去 = go in, go into
■ 他们在开会，请不要进去。**Tāmen zài kāihuì, qǐng bú yào jìnqu.** = *They're having a meeting. Please don't go in.*

jìnxíng 进行 [compound: 进 *enter* + 行 *walk*] VERB = conduct, carry out
■ 孩子做错了事，应该进行教育。

J

Háizi zuò cuò le shì, yīnggāi jìnxíng jiàoyù. = *When a child makes a mistake, he should be educated.* (→ *When a child makes a mistake, he should be taught what's right.*)

jìn 近 (辶 7) [辶 sign + 斤 phon **jīn**] ADJECTIVE = close to, close by (antonym 远 **yuǎn**)

lí ... jìn 离 … 近 = be close to…

■ 爸爸的办公室离家很近。**Bàba de bàngōngshì lí jiā hěn jìn.** = *Father's office is close to home.*

jīng 京 (亠 8) NOUN = capital city (See 北京 **Běijīng**.)

jīng 经 (纟 9) Trad 經

jīngcháng 经常 [compound: 经 *constant* + 常 *often*] ADVERB = often

■ 你经常迟到，这样不好。**Nǐ jīngcháng chídào, zhèyàng bù hǎo.** = *You're often late, which is not good.*

jīngguò 经过 [compound: 经 *go through* + 过 *pass*]

1 VERB = go through, pass

■ 我到学校去的路上，要经过一座公园。**Wǒ dào xuéxiào qù de lù shang, yào jīngguò yí zuò gōngyuán.** = *I pass by a park on my way to school.*

2 PREPOSITION = through, after

■ 经过这件事，他变得聪明了。**Jīngguò zhè jiàn shì, tā biàn de cōngmíng le.** = *He was more sensible after this incident.*

jīngjì 经济 [compound: 经 *govern* + 济 *bring relief to*] NOUN = economy

■ 这个国家的经济不太好。**Zhège guójiā de jīngjì bú tài hǎo.** = *The economy of this country is not in good shape.*

■ 每个国家都在发展自己的经济。**Měi ge guójiā dōu zài fāzhǎn zìjǐ de jīngjì.** = *Every country is working to develop its economy.*

jīngyàn 经验 [compound: 经 *go through* + 验 *test*] NOUN = experience

■ 这个经验对我非常重要。**Zhège jīngyàn duì wǒ fēicháng zhòngyào.** = *This experience is very important to me.*

yǒu jīngyàn de 有经验的 = experienced

■ 她是一位有经验的老师。**Tā shì yí wèi yǒu jīngyàn de lǎoshī.** = *She's an experienced teacher.*

jīng 睛 (目 13) [目 sign + 青 phon **qīng**] NOUN = the pupil of the eye (See 眼睛 **yǎnjing**.)

jīng 精 (米 14) ADJECTIVE = choice, essence

jīngcǎi 精彩 [compound: 精 *choice* + 彩 *colorful, brilliant*] ADJECTIVE = (of a theatrical performance or sports event) brilliant, thrilling, wonderful

■ 昨天的足球比赛真精彩啊！**Zuótiān de zúqiú bǐsài zhēn jīngcǎi a!** = *The football match yesterday was really wonderful!*

jīngshén 精神 [compound: 精 *essence* + 神 *spirit*] NOUN = vigor, vitality

J

■ 这位老人八十多岁了，但是精神很好。**Zhè wèi lǎorén bāshí duō suì le, dànshì jīngshén hěn hǎo.** = *This old person is over eighty, but is energetic and alert.*

■ 不知道为什么，我今天没有精神。**Bù zhīdào wèishénme, wǒ jīntiān méiyǒu jīngshen.** = *I don't know why, but I'm in low spirits today.*

jīngshénbìng 精神病 = mental illness

jìng 净 (氵 8) ADJECTIVE = clean (See 干净 **gānjìng**.)

jiū 究 (穴 7) [穴 sign + 九 phon **jiǔ**] VERB = investigate (See 研究 **yánjiū**.)

jiǔ 九 (丿 2) NUMERAL = nine

■ 九千九百九十九 **jiǔqiān jiǔbǎi jiǔshíjiǔ** = *nine thousand, nine hundred and ninety-nine*

■ 九九 八十一 **jiǔjiǔ bāshíyī** = *Nine times nine is eighty-one.*

jiǔ 久 (丿 3) ADJECTIVE = for a long time

■ 时间太久了，我记不清了。**Shíjiān tài jiǔ le, wǒ jì bu qīng le.** = *It was too long ago. I can't remember clearly.*

■ 我等你等了很久了。**Wǒ děng nǐ děngle hěn jiǔ le.** = *I've been waiting for you for a long time.*

jiǔ 酒 (氵 10) [氵 sign + 酉 sign] NOUN = alcoholic beverage (种 **zhǒng**, 瓶 **píng**)

■ 这种酒，我不喜欢喝。**Zhè zhǒng jiǔ, wǒ bù xǐhuan hē.** = *I don't like this kind of alcoholic drink.*

■ 我不喝酒，我还要开车。**Wǒ bù hē jiǔ, wǒ háiyào kāichē.** = *No alcoholic drinks for me. I'll be driving.*

huángjiǔ 黄酒 = yellow rice wine

báijiǔ 白酒 = colorless spirit distilled from grains

jiù 旧 (日 5) Trad 舊 ADJECTIVE = (of things) old, secondhand (antonym 新 **xīn**)

■ 这件衣服不太旧，还可以穿。**Zhè jiàn yīfu bú tài jiù, hái kěyǐ chuān.** = *This jacket is not too old. It can still be worn.*

■ 他把旧车卖了一千块钱。**Tā bǎ jiù chē màile yìqiān kuài qián.** = *He sold his old car for one thousand dollars.*

jiù 就 (亠 12)

1 ADVERB = as early as ..., as soon as ... (used before a verb to emphasize that the action takes place very early, very quickly or only for a very short period of time)

■ 他今天早上六点钟就起床了。**Tā jīntiān zǎoshang liù diǎnzhōng jiù qǐchuáng le.** = *He got up as early as six o'clock this morning.*

■ 我马上就来。**Wǒ mǎshàng jiù lái.** = *I'll come immediately.* (→ *I'm coming.*)

yī … jiù 一 … 就 = as soon as ...

■ 妈妈一回家就做晚饭。**Māma yì huíjiā jiù zuò wǎnfàn.** = *Mom prepared supper once she got home.*

2 CONJUNCTION = even if

■ 我就是不睡觉，也要做完这个作业。**Wǒ jiùshì bú shuìjiào, yě yào zuò wán zhè ge zuòyè.** = *Even if I don't sleep, I must finish this assignment.*

J

jú 局 (尸 7) NOUN = office (See 邮局 **yóujú**.)

jú 橘 (木 16) [木 sign + symb] NOUN = tangerine

júzi 橘子 [suffix: 橘 *tangerine* + 子 nominal suffix] NOUN = tangerine (只 **zhī**)
■ 苹果、香蕉、橘子，我都爱吃。**Píngguǒ, xiāngjiāo, júzi, wǒ dōu ài chī.** = *I like apples, bananas and tangerines.*
■ 你会画橘子吗？ **Nǐ huì huà jǔzi ma?** = *Can you draw a tangerine?*

NOTE: 橘子 **júzi** can also be written as 桔子 **júzi**.

jǔ 举 (丶 9) Trad 舉 VERB = hold high, raise, lift
■ 谁同意，请举手！ **Shéi tóngyì, qǐng jǔ shǒu!** = *Those in favor [of the motion], please raise your hands.*

jù 句 (勹 5) [勹 symb + 口 sign] MEASURE WORD = (for sentences)
■ 一句话 **yí jù huà** = *one sentence*
■ 这句话 **zhè jù huà** = *this sentence*

jùzi 句子 [suffix: 句 *sentence* + 子 nominal suffix] NOUN = sentence (句 **jù**, 个 **ge**)
■ 张老师，这句句子什么意思？ 我看不懂。**Zhāng lǎoshī, zhè jù jùzi shénme yìsi? Wǒ kàn bu dǒng.** = *Teacher Zhang, what is the meaning of this sentence? I don't understand it.*
■ 请你把这个句子再说一遍。**Qǐng nǐ bǎ zhège jùzi zài shuō yí biàn.** = *Please say this sentence again.*

jué 觉 (见 9) Trad 覺 VERB = feel

juéde 觉得 VERB = feel, find, think
■ 我觉得你说的话很有道理。**Wǒ juéde nǐ shuō de huà hěn yǒu dàolǐ.** = *I think what you said is quite true* (or *reasonable*).

jué 决 (冫 6) VERB = decide

juédìng 决定 [compound: 决 *decide* + 定 *decide*]
1 VERB = decide, determine, make up one's mind
■ 你有没有决定买哪一辆汽车？ **Nǐ yǒu méiyǒu juédìng mǎi nǎ yí liàng qìchē?** = *Have you decided which car to buy?*
2 NOUN = decision
■ 你们的决定是错误的。**Nǐmen de juédìng shì cuòwù de.** = *You've made the wrong decision.*
zuò juédìng 做决定 = make a decision
■ 买哪一座房子，他们还没有做决定。**Mǎi nǎ yí zuò fángzi, tāmen hái méiyǒu zuò juédìng.** = *They haven't decided which house to buy.*

K

kāfēi 咖啡 NOUN = coffee (杯 **bēi**)
■ 这种咖啡很好喝。**Zhè zhǒng kāfēi hěn hǎohē.** = *This kind of coffee tastes good.*
■ 我爸爸每天喝三杯咖啡。**Wǒ bāba měi tiān hē sān bēi kāfēi.** = *My father drinks three cups of coffee every day.*

> NOTE: 咖啡 **kāfēi** is one of the few transliterations (音译词 **yīnyìcí**) in Chinese vocabulary, as it represents more or less the sound of "coffee."

kǎ 卡 (卜 5) NOUN = card

kǎchē 卡车 NOUN = lorry, truck (辆 **liàng**)
■ 开过来了一辆卡车。**Kāi guò láile yí liàng kǎchē.** = *A truck is coming.*
■ 我没有开过卡车，你开过吗？**Wǒ méiyǒu kāiguo kǎchē, nǐ kāiguo ma?** = *I've never driven a truck. Have you?*

> NOTE: The composition of 卡车 **kǎchē** is semi-transliteration (半音译词 **bàn yīnyìcí**): 卡 **kǎ** represents the sound of the English word "car" and 车 **chē** means "vehicle." (See 咖啡 **kāfēi** for an example of transliteration.)

kāi 开 (廾 4) Trad **開** VERB
1 = open
■ 开门！ **Kāi mén!** = *Open the door, please!*
2 = turn on
■ 天黑了，开灯吧。**Tiān hēi le, kāi dēng ba.** = *It's dark. Let's turn on the light.*
3 = drive (a vehicle), pilot (a plane)
■ 我会开汽车，不会开飞机。**Wǒ huì kāi qìchē, bú huì kāi fēijī.** = *I can drive a car, but I can't pilot a plane.*
kāiguān 开关 = switch
■ 这个机器的开关坏了。**Zhège jīqì de kāiguān huài le.** = *The switch of this machine is out of order.*
kāimén 开门 = open for business
■ "这里的商店什么时候开门？" "九点钟开门。" **"Zhèli de shāngdiàn shénme shíhou kāimén?" "Jiǔ diǎnzhōng kāimén."** = *"When do the stores here open for business?" "Nine o'clock."*
kāixué 开学 = begin (school term)
■ 中国的学校每年九月一日开学。**Zhōngguó de xuéxiào meǐ nián Jiǔyuè yírì kāixué.** = *In China, schools begin on September 1 every year.*
kāi yèchē 开夜车 = burn the midnight oil
■ 明天要交作业，今天晚上我得开夜车。**Míngtiān yào jiāo zuòyè, jīntiān wǎnshang wǒ děi kāi yèchē.** = *I must hand in my assignment tomorrow. I'll have to burn the midnight oil tonight.*

kāishǐ 开始 [compound: 开 *open* + 始 *begin*]
1 VERB = begin, commence (antonym 结束 **jiéshù**)
■ 我从明年一月一日开始每天跑步半小时！ **Wǒ cóng míngnián Yí yuè yírì kāishǐ měi tiān pǎobù bàn xiǎoshí!** = *I'll begin jogging half an hour every day from January 1 next year.*
2 NOUN = beginning, start
■ 开始的时候我觉得中文非常难，现在觉得不太难了。**Wǒ kāishǐ juéde Zhōngwén fēicháng nán, xiànzài júede bú tài nái le.** = *At the beginning I found Chinese very difficult, but now I think it's not too difficult.*

kāi wánxiào 开玩笑 VERB = play a joke

■ 别开玩笑了! **Bié kāi wánxiào le!** = *Stop joking!*

gēn/hé ... kāi wánxiào 跟 / 和…开玩笑 = play a joke on... , make fun of ...
■ 他常常跟妹妹开玩笑。**Tā chángcháng gēn mèimei kāi wánxiào.** = *He often makes fun of his younger sister.*

kàn 看 (目 9) [手 sign + 目 sign] VERB = look, watch; read
■ 我看看你的新衣服。**Wǒ kànkan nǐ de xīn yīfu.** = *Let me have a look at your new clothes.*
■ "你每天看报吗?" "我不每天看报。" **"Nǐ měi tiān kàn bào ma?" "Wǒ bù měi tiān kàn bào."** = *"Do you read the newspapers every day?" "No."*

kàn diànyǐng 看电影 = watch a film

kàn tǐyù bǐsài 看体育比赛 = watch a sports event

kànbìng 看病 [v+obj: 看 *see* + 病 *illness*] VERB = see a doctor
■ 你不舒服好几天了, 应该去看病。**Nǐ bù shūfu hǎo jǐ tiān le, yīnggāi qù kànbìng.** = *You've been unwell for a couple of days. You should go and see a doctor.*

kànjiàn 看见 [v+comp: 看 *look* + 见 *see*] VERB = catch sight of, see
■ 我朝山上看了很久, 才看见一个人在爬山。**Wǒ cháo shān shang kànle hěn jiǔ, cái kànjiàn yí ge rén zài pá shān.** = *I looked at the hills for a long time before I saw a man climbing.*

kàn de jiàn 看得见 = can see

kàn bu jiàn 看不见 = cannot see
■ "山上的人, 你看得见吗?" "看不见。" **"Shān shang de rén, nǐ kàn de jiàn ma?" "Kàn bu jiàn."** = *"Can you see the person* (or *people*) *on the hill?" "No, I can't."*

méi kànjiàn 没看见 = fail to see
■ 我没看见山上的人。**Wǒ méi kànjiàn shān shang de rén.** = *I did not see the person (or people) on the hill.*

kāng 康 (广 11) NOUN = good health
(See 健康 **jiànkāng**.)

kǎo 考 (老 6) VERB = examine

kǎoshì 考试 [compound: 考 *examine, inquire* + 试 *test*]
1 VERB = examine, test
■ 我们明天考试。**Wǒmen míngtiān kǎoshì.** = *We're having an examination tomorrow.*

kǎoshì kǎo de hǎo 考试考得好 = do well in an examination

kǎoshì kǎo de bù hǎo 考试考得不好 = do poorly in an examination
■ 我去年中文考得不好。**Wǒ qùnián Zhōngwén kǎo de bù hǎo.** = *I did not do well in the Chinese examination last year.*

2 NOUN = examination, test (次 **cì**)
■ 这次考试太难了! **Zhè cì kǎoshì tài nán le!** = *This test was really difficult!*
■ "你怕考试吗?" "准备好了就不怕, 没准备好就怕。" **"Nǐ pà kǎoshì ma?" "Zhǔnbèi hǎo le jiù bú pà, méi zhǔnbèi hǎo jiù pà."** = *"Are you afraid of examinations?" "Not when I'm prepared; if I weren't prepared, I'd be afraid."*

kē 科 (禾 9) NOUN = classification

kēxué 科学 [modif: 科 *classification* + 学 *study*] NOUN = science
■ 科学能解决世界上所有的问题吗？ **Kēxué néng jiějué shìjiè shang suǒyǒu de wèntí ma?** = *Can science solve all the problems in the world?*
■ 我丈夫学科学，我学语言。 **Wǒ zhàngfu xué kēxué, wǒ xué yǔyán.** = *My husband studies science, and I study language.*
kēxuéjiā 科学家 = scientist
kēxué yánjiū 科学研究 = scientific research

kē 棵 (木 12) [木 sign + 果 phon **guǒ**] MEASURE WORD = (for trees)
■ 三棵树 **sān kē shù** = *three trees*

ké 咳 (口 9) [口 sign + 亥 symb] VERB = cough

késou 咳嗽 [compound: 咳 *cough* + 嗽 *cough up*] VERB = cough
■ 这个病人每天夜里都咳。 **Zhège bìngrén měi tiān yèli dōu késou.** = *The patient coughs every night.*

kě 可 (一 5) MODAL VERB = may

kěnéng 可能 [compound: 可 *may* + 能 *can*]
1 MODAL VERB = may, possible, possibly
■ 他两天没来上课，可能病了。 **Tā liǎng tiān méi lái shàngkè, kěnéng bìng le.** = *He's been absent from class for two days. He may be ill.*
2 NOUN = possibility
■ 这种可能是有的。 **Zhè zhǒng kěnéng shì yǒu de.** = *This is possible.*
(méi)yǒu kěnéng (没)有可能 = (im)possible, (im)possibly
■ "这件事有解决的可能吗？" "有可能。" **"Zhè jiàn shì yǒu jiějué de kěnéng ma?" "Yǒu kěnéng."** = *"Is it possible to resolve this matter?" "Yes."*

kěkǒukělè 可口可乐 NOUN = Coca-Cola (瓶 **píng**)
■ 可口可乐有吗？ **Kěkǒukělè yǒu ma?** = *Do you have Coca-Cola?*
■ 我很渴，我想喝一瓶可口可乐。 **Wǒ hěn kě, wǒ xiǎng hē yì píng kěkǒukělè.** = *I'm thirsty. I want to drink a bottle of Coca-Cola.*

NOTE: 可口可乐 **kěkǒukělè** is a transliteration of "Coca-Cola." It can be shortened to 可乐 **kělè**.

kěyǐ 可以 MODAL VERB = giving permission, may
■ "我可以走了吗？" "可以。" **"Wǒ kěyǐ zǒu le ma?" "Kěyǐ."** = *"May I leave now?" "Yes, you may."*

kě 渴 (氵 12) [氵 sign + 曷 symb] ADJECTIVE = thirsty
kǒu kě 口渴 = thirsty
■ 你口渴吗？ 这里有水。 **Nǐ kǒu kě ma? Zhèli yǒu shuǐ.** = *Are you thirsty? Here's some water.*

kè 克 (十 7) MEASURE WORD = gram
■ 五百克 **wǔ bǎi kè** = *500 grams*

kè 刻 (刂 8) MEASURE WORD = quarter of an hour
■ 一刻钟 **yí kè zhōng** = *a quarter of an hour (= 15 minutes)*
■ 三点一刻 **sān diǎn yí kè** = *a quarter past three*

kè 客 (宀 9) NOUN = guest

kèqi 客气 [modif: 客 *guest* + 气 *manner*] ADJECTIVE
1 = polite; stand on ceremony
■ 您跟我们一起吃午饭吧，别客气。**Nín gēn wǒmen yìqǐ chī wǔfàn ba, bié kèqi.** = *Have lunch with us. Don't stand on ceremony.*
2 = modest
■ 你唱歌唱得这么好，还说不好，太客气了。**Nǐ chànggē chàng de zhème hǎo, hái shuō bù hǎo, tài kèqi le.** = *You sing so well but you still say you don't sing well. You're too modest.*

kè 课 (讠 10) [讠 sign + 果 phon **guǒ**] Trad 課 NOUN = lesson, class, lecture
■ 今天的课你听懂没有？ **Jīntiān de kè nǐ tīngdǒng méiyǒu?** = *Do you understand today's lesson?*
shàng kè 上课 = go to class
xià kè 下课 = finish class

kèběn 课本 NOUN = textbook, course book (本 **běn**)
■ 你知不知道哪一本中文课本比较好？ **Nǐ zhī bu zhīdào nǎ yì běn Zhōngwén kèběn bǐjiào hǎo?** = *Do you know which Chinese textbook is relatively good?* (→ *Do you know of a good Chinese textbook?*)

kèwén 课文 [modif: 课 *lesson* + 文 *writing*] NOUN = text (篇 **piān**)
■ 这篇课文写得真好。**Zhè piān kèwén xiě de zhēn hǎo.** = *This text is really well written.*
■ 我要多念几遍课文。**Wǒ yào duō niàn jǐ biàn kèwén.** = *I should read the text a few more times.*

kōngqì 空气 [modif: 空 *empty* + 气 *air*] NOUN = air
■ 这里的空气真好！ **Zhèli de kōngqì zhēn hǎo!** = *The air here is really fresh.*

kòng 空 (穴 8) [穴 sign + 工 phon **gōng**] NOUN = free time
■ "你今天晚上有空吗？""我今天晚上没有空，明天晚上有空。" **"Nǐ jīntiān wǎnshang yǒu kòng ma?" "Wǒ jīntiān wǎnshang méiyǒu kòng, míngtiān wǎnshang yǒu kòng."** = *"Are you free this evening?" "No, I'm not. I'll be free tomorrow evening."*

kǒu 口 (口 3)
1 NOUN = mouth
lùkǒu 路口 = crossroads, road intersection
2 MEASURE WORD = for members of a family
■ 我家有四口人。**Wǒ jiā yǒu sì kǒu rén.** = *There're four people in my family.*

kǒuyǔ 口语 [modif: 口 *mouth* + 语 *speech*] NOUN = spoken language, speech
■ 我中文口语不行，很多话不会说。**Wǒ Zhōngwén kǒuyǔ bù xíng, hěn duō huà bú huì shuō.** = *My oral Chinese is rather poor. There're many things I can't express.*
■ 要学好口语，就要多听、多说。**Yào xué hǎo kǒuyǔ, jiù yào duō tīng, duō shuō.** = *To learn the spoken*

language well, one should listen a lot and speak a lot. (→*To learn the spoken language well, one needs to hear it often and speak it often.*)

kū 哭 (犬 10) VERB = cry, weep, sob (antonym 笑 **xiào**)
■ 别哭了，有话好好说。**Bié kū le, yǒu huà hǎohǎo shuō.** = *Don't cry. Speak up if you've something to say.*

kǔ 苦 (艹 8) [艹 sign + 古 phon **gǔ**]
ADJECTIVE
1 = bitter
■ 这杯咖啡太苦了，要放点儿糖。**Zhè bēi kāfēi tài kǔ le, yào fàng diǎnr táng.** = *This coffee is too bitter. Put a bit of sugar in it.*
2 = (of life) hard, miserable
■ 经济不好，不少人生活很苦。**Jīngjì bù hǎo, bù shǎo rén shēnghuó hěn kǔ.** = *As the economy is not in good shape, many people's lives are very hard.*

kù 裤 (衤 12) [衤 sign + 库 phon **kù**]
Trad 褲 NOUN = trousers

kùzi 裤子 [suffix: 裤 *trousers* + 子 nominal suffix] NOUN = trousers (条 **tiáo**)
■ 这条裤子短了一点儿。**Zhè tiáo kùzi duǎn le yì diǎnr.** = *This pair of trousers is a bit too short.*
■ 这个小孩会脱裤子，但还不会穿裤子。**Zhège xiǎohái huì tuō kùzi, dànshì hái bú huì chuān kùzi.** = *This child can take off his trousers, but still can't put them on.*

kuài 块 (土 7) [土 sign + phon **kuài**]
Trad 塊 MEASURE WORD = (for things that can be broken into lumps or chunks; for money), *yuan*, dollar
■ 一块蛋糕 **yí kuài dàngāo** = *a piece/slice of cake*
■ 两块面包 **liǎng kuài miànbāo** = *two pieces of bread*
■ 三块钱 **sān kuài qián** = *three yuan* (or *dollars*)

kuài 快 (忄 7) [忄 sign + phon]
ADJECTIVE = quick, fast (antonym 慢 **màn**)
■ 快，车来了! **Kuài, chē láile!** = *Quick, the bus is coming!*
■ 他跑得很快。**Tā pǎo de hěn kuài.** = *He runs very fast.*

kuài 筷 (竹 13) [竹 sign + 快 phon **kuài**]

kuàizi 筷子 [suffix] 筷 *chopstick* + 子 nominal suffix] NOUN = chopsticks (双 **shuāng**)
■ 你会用筷子吃东西吗? **Nǐ huì yòng kuàizi chī dōngxi ma?** = *Can you eat with chopsticks?*

kuàng 况 (冫 7) NOUN = situation (See 情况 **qíngkuàng**.)

kùn 困 (口 7) [口 sign + 木 symb]
VERB = be stranded

kùnnan 困难 [compound: 困 *be stranded* + 难 *difficult*]
1 NOUN = difficulty
■ 困难是有的，但是没有关系。**Kùnnan shì yǒu de, dànshì méiyǒu**

K

guānxi. = *There are difficulties, but it doesn't matter.*

■ 你不要怕困难，你要想一想怎么办。**Nǐ bú yào pà kùnnan, nǐ yào xiǎng yì xiǎng zěnme bàn.** = *You mustn't be afraid of difficulties. You should think of what to do.*

2 ADJECTIVE = difficult

■ 我们现在的情况比较困难。**Wǒmen xiànzài de qíngkuàng bǐjiào kùnnan.** = *Our situation is rather difficult.*

L

lā 拉 (扌 8) [扌 sign + 立 symb] VERB = pull

■ 请你拉这个门，别推这个门。**Qǐng nǐ lā zhège mén, bié tuī zhège mén.** = *Please pull this door, not push it.*

la 啦 (口 11) [口 sign + 拉 phon **lā**] PARTICLE = (an exclamation indicating completion of an action and/or emergence of a new situation)

■ 我做完作业啦！ **Wǒ zuòwán zuòyè la!** = *I've finished my assignment!*

NOTE: 啦 **la** is a combination of the two words 了 **le** and 啊 **a**. It has the meanings of both words. It is only used in spoken Chinese.

lái 来 (一 7) Trad **來** VERB = come, come to; move toward the speaker

■ 王先生来了没有？ **Wáng xiānsheng láile méiyǒu?** = *Has Mr Wang come?*

■ 他是三年前来这座城市的。**Tā shì sān nián qián lái zhè zuò chéngshì de.** = *He came to this city three years ago.*

lán 兰 (八 4) Trad **蘭** NOUN = orchid (See 新西兰 **Xīnxīlán**.)

lán 蓝 (艹 13) [艹 sign + 监 phon] Trad **藍** ADJECTIVE = blue

■ 天很蓝，因为空气很干净。**Tiān hěn lán, yīnwèi kōngqì hěn gānjìng.** = *The sky is blue because the air is clean.*

■ 蓝天白云，美极了。**Lántiān báiyún, měi jíle.** = *A blue sky and white clouds, how very beautiful.*

lán 篮 (丿 16) Trad **籃** NOUN = basket

lánqiú 篮球 [modif: 篮 *basket* + 球 *ball*] NOUN = basketball

dǎ lánqiú 打篮球 = play basketball

■ 他们在打篮球。**Tāmen zài dǎ lánqiú.** = *They're playing basketball.*

lánqiú bǐsài 篮球比赛 = basketball match

lǎn 览 (见 9) [symb + 见 sign] Trad **覽** VERB = view (See 展览 **zhǎnlǎn**.)

láo 劳 (力 7) [symb + 力 sign] Trad **勞** VERB = toil

láodòng 劳动 [compound: 劳 *toil* + 动 *move*] VERB = do manual labor

■ 他夏天在父亲的农场劳动。**Tā xiàtiān zài fùqin de nóngchǎng láodòng.** = *In summer he works on his father's farm.*

láojià 劳驾 IDIOM = May I trouble you…, Would you mind (doing … for me)
■ 劳驾，请您让一下。**Láojià, qǐng nín ràng yíxià.** = *Excuse me, could you please make way?*

lǎo 老 (老 6)
1 ADJECTIVE = old, elderly; long-standing
■ 爸爸老了，不能在农场劳动了。**Bāba lǎo le, bù néng zài nóngchǎng láodòng le.** = *Father's old and can't work on the farm.*
■ 他在帮一位老太太过马路。**Tā zài bāng yí wèi lǎo tàitai guò mǎlù.** = *He's helping an old lady cross the street.*
lǎo péngyou 老朋友 = long-standing friend
■ 我们在小学的时候就认识了，是老朋友。**Wǒmen zài xiǎoxué de shíhòu jiù rènshi le, shì lǎo péngyou.** = *We've known each other since primary school days. We're old friends.*
lǎo xiānsheng 老先生 = old gentleman, old man
lǎo tàitai 老太太 = old lady, old woman

NOTE: Chinese tradition values and respects old age. Today people still attach 老 **lǎo** to a family name as a form of address showing respect and friendliness to a person older than oneself, e.g. 老李 **Lǎo Lǐ**, 老王 **Lǎo Wáng**.

2 PREFIX = (added to numerals to indicate seniority among siblings)
■ 老大 **lǎo dà** = *the eldest child/brother/sister*
■ 老二 **lǎo èr** = *the second child/brother/sister*

lǎoshī 老师 [modif: 老 *aged* + 师 *teacher*] NOUN = teacher (位 **wèi**)
■ 我的中文老师是北京人。**Wǒ de Zhōngwén lǎoshī shì Běijīng rén.** = *My Chinese teacher is from Beijing.*
■ 我要问老师几个问题。**Wǒ yào wèn lǎoshī jǐ ge wèntí.** = *I want to ask the teacher some questions.*

NOTE: 老师 **lǎoshī**, usually prefixed by a family name, is the standard form of address to a teacher, e.g. 王老师 **Wáng Lǎoshī**. There is no equivalent of 王老师 **Wáng Lǎoshī** in English; this dictionary uses the literal translation "Teacher Wang."

lè 乐 (丿 5) Trad 樂 ADJECTIVE = joyful (See 可口可乐 **kěkǒukělè**.)

le 了 (乙 2) PARTICLE
1 = (used after a verb to indicate the completion of an action)
■ 我昨天写了三封信。**Wǒ zuótiān xiěle sān fēng xìn.** = *I wrote three letters yesterday.*
■ 他做了作业就睡觉。**Tā zuòle zuòyè jiù shuìjiào.** = *He went to bed after doing his assignment.*
2 = (used at the end of a sentence to indicate the emergence of a new situation)
■ 天晴了。**Tiān qíng le.** = *The weather's clearing up.*
■ 我懂了。**Wǒ dǒng le.** = *I understand.*
■ 我会说一点儿中文了。**Wǒ huì shuō yìdiǎnr Zhōngwén le.** = *I can speak a bit of Chinese now.*

lèi 累 (田 11) [田 sign + 糸 symb]
ADJECTIVE = exhausted, tired
■ 你劳动了半天，累不累？ **Nǐ láodòngle bàntiān, lèi bú lèi?** = *You've labored for a long time, are you tired?*

lěng 冷 (冫 7) [冫 sign + 令 phon **lìng**] ADJECTIVE = cold (antonym 热 **rè**)
■ 今天很冷。**Jīntiān hěn lěng.** = *It's cold today.*
■ 他每天都洗冷水澡。**Tā měi tiān dōu xǐ lěngshuǐ zǎo.** = *He takes a cold bath every day.*

lí 离 (亠 10) Trad **離**
1 VERB = depart, leave
■ 他每天很早就离家，很晚才回家。**Tā měi tiān hěn zǎo jiù lí jiā, hěn wǎn cái huí jiā.** = *He leaves home early and returns home late every day.*
2 PREPOSITION = (indicating distance in space or time) away from, from
■ 新西兰离英国很远，离澳大利亚比较近。**Xīnxīlán lí Yīngguó hěn yuǎn, lí Àodàlìyà bǐjiào jìn.** = *New Zealand is far away from Britain, and relatively close to Australia.*
■ 现在离寒假只有两个星期了。**Xiànzài lí hánjià zhǐ yǒu liǎng ge xīngqī le.** = *There're only two weeks left before the winter holiday.*
lí ... yuǎn 离…远 = far away from …
lí ... jìn 离…近 = close to ...

L

líkāi 离开 [compound: 离 *leave* + 开 *away from*] VERB = depart, leave
■ 他十八岁的时候离开父母，到美国去念书。**Tā shíbā suì de shíhou líkāi fùmǔ, dào Měiguó qù niànshū.** = *When he was eighteen he left his parents and went to America to study.*
■ 我离开一会儿，马上就回来。**Wǒ líkāi yíhuìr, mǎshàng jiù huílai.** = *Excuse me for a minute. I'll be back soon.*

lǐ 礼 (礻 5) [礻 sign + 乙 symb] Trad **禮**
NOUN = gift

lǐwù 礼物 [modif: 礼 *gift* + 物 *thing*]
NOUN = gift, present (件 **jiàn**)
■ 这件小小的礼物，请您收下。**Zhè jiàn xiǎoxiǎo de lǐwù, qǐng nín shōuxia. = Please accept this small present.**
■ 今天是你的生日，我送你一件小礼物。**Jīngtiān shì nǐ de shēngrì, wǒ sòng nǐ yí jiàn xiǎo lǐwù.** = *Today's your birthday. I'll give you a little gift.*
shēngrì lǐwù 生日礼物 = birthday present
xīnnián lǐwù 新年礼物 = New Year present

NOTE: Chinese modesty requires that you belittle your present, describing it as 一件小礼物 **yí jiàn xiǎo lǐwù.** Upon receiving a present, it is bad manners to open it immediately. Instead, the recipient is first supposed to say 不用不用 **búyòng, búyòng** = *You didn't have to* and then express thanks for the gift, describing it as 这么好的礼物 **zhème hǎo de lǐwù** = *such a good present*, e.g. 谢谢，谢谢你送给我这么好的礼物。**Xièxie, xièxie nǐ sòng gei wǒ zhème hǎo de lǐwù** = *Thank you! Thank you for giving me such a good present.*

lǐ 里 (里 7) Trad 裏
1 NOUN = inside (antonym 外 **wài**)
■ 房间里没有人。**Fángjiān li méiyǒu rén.** = *There's no one in the room.*
2 MEASURE WORD = (a Chinese unit of length, equivalent to 0.5 kilometers)
■ 从学校到飞机场有二十里，也就是十公里。**Cóng xuéxiào dào fēijīchǎng yǒu èrshí lǐ, yě jiùshì shí gōnglǐ.** = *From the school to the airport it's twenty li, or ten kilometers.*

lǐbian 里边 [modif: 里 *inner* + 边 *side*] NOUN = inside, in (antonym 外边 **wàibian**)
■ 房子外边不好看，里边很舒服。**Fángzi wàibian bù hǎokàn, lǐbian hěn shūfu.** = *The outside of the house is not very attractive, but inside is very comfortable.*

Lǐ 李 (木 7) NOUN = a common family name

NOTE: According to the latest census, 李 **Lǐ** is the most common family name in China.

lǐ 理 (王 11) [王 sign + 里 phon **lǐ**] NOUN = pattern, reason (See 道理 **dàolǐ**, 物理 **wùlǐ**.)

lì 力 (力 2) NOUN = strength, power (See 努力 **nǔlì**.)

lì 历 (厂 4) Trad 歷 NOUN = past experience

lìshǐ 历史 [compound: 历 *past experience* + 史 *recording*] NOUN = history
■ 中国的历史非常长，有三千多年。**Zhōngguó de lìshǐ fēicháng cháng, yǒu sānqiān duō nián.** = *China has a very long history of over three thousand years.*
■ 你知道这个城市的历史吗？ **Nǐ zhīdào zhège chéngshì de lìshǐ ma?** = *Do you know the history of this city?*

lì 立 (立 5) ADVERB = immediately

lìkè 立刻 [compound: 立 *immediately* + 刻 *a brief time*] ADVERB = at once, immediately
■ 我接到你的电话，立刻就来了。**Wǒ jiēdào nǐ de diànhuà, lìkè jiù lái le.** = *I came immediately after getting your call.*

lì 利 (刂 7) [禾 symb + 刂 sign] NOUN = benefit

lìyòng 利用 [compound: 利 *benefit from* + 用 *use*] VERB = make use of, benefit from
■ 你应该好好利用时间。**Nǐ yīnggāi hǎohǎo lìyòng shíjiān.** = *You should make good use of your time.*

lì 例 (亻 8) NOUN = example

lìrú 例如 [compound: 例 *example* + 如 *same as*] CONJUNCTION = for example, such as
■ 有些汉字，例如"日"、"月"、"山"，是从图画变来的。**Yǒu xiē hànzì, lìrú rì, yuè, shān, shì cóng túhuà biànlai de.** *Some Chinese characters, such as* 日, 月, 山 *are derived from pictures.*

liǎ 俩 (亻 9) [亻 sign + 两 word *two*]
Trad 倆 NUMERAL = two people
■ 他们俩是好朋友，经常在一起玩。**Tāmen liǎ shì hǎo péngyou, jīngcháng zài yìqǐ wán.** = *They two are good friends; they often play together.*

lián 连 (辶 7) Trad 連 ADVERB = even

lián...dōu... 连…都… IDIOM = even
■ 啊，你连中文报纸都会看了！**À, nǐ lián Zhōngwén bàozhǐ dōu huì kàn le!** = *Oh, you can even read Chinese language newspapers!*

> NOTE: 连…都… **lián...dōu...** is an emphatic expression. It is used to emphasize the word after 连 **lián**. 都 **dōu** may be replaced by 也 **yě**; 连…也… **lián...yě...** is the same as 连…都… **lián...dōu...**.

lián 联 (耳 12) Trad 聯 VERB = connect

liánxì 联系 [compound: 联 *connect* + 系 *tie, knot*]
1 VERB = get in touch, contact
hé/gēn ... liánxi 和 / 跟…联系 = get in touch with …
■ 你有什么事，可以和张小姐联系。**Nǐ yǒu shénme shì, kěyǐ hé Zhāng xiǎojiě liánxì.** = *You can contact Miss Zhang if you've any business.*
2 NOUN = connection, being related
■ 这两件事有什么联系？ **Zhè liǎng jiàn shì yǒu shénme liánxì?** = *What do these two matters have to do with each other?*

liǎn 脸 (月 11) [月 sign + 佥 symb]
Trad 臉 NOUN = face (张 **zhāng**)
■ 我每天早上用冷水洗脸。**Wǒ měi tiān zǎoshang yòng lěngshuǐ xǐ liǎn.** = *I wash my face in cold water every morning.*

liàn 练 (纟 8) Trad 練 VERB = drill, train

liànxí 练习 [compound: 练 *drill, train* + 习 *practice*]
1 VERB = exercise, train, drill
■ 你常常练习汉语口语吗？ **Nǐ chángcháng liànxí Hànyǔ kǒuyǔ ma?** = *Do you often practice oral Chinese?*
2 NOUN = exercise (道 **dào**)
■ 我数学练习做好了，还有三道英文练习没有做。**Wǒ shùxué liànxí zuòhǎo le, hái yǒu sān dào Yīngwén liànxí méiyǒu zuò.** = *I've finished my mathematics exercises, and haven't done the three English exercises.*

liàn 炼 (火 9) [火 sign + phon **liàn**]
Trad 煉 VERB = smelt (See 锻炼 **duànliàn**.)

liáng 凉 (冫 10) [冫 sign + 京 symb]
ADJECTIVE = cool (of temperature)

liángkuai 凉快 [compound: 凉 *cool* + 快 *pleasant*] ADJECTIVE = pleasantly cool
■ 今天很热，但是树下比较凉快。**Jīntiān hěn rè, dànshì shù xia bǐjiào liángkuài.** = *It's hot today but it's rather cool under the tree.*

L

liǎng 两 (一 7) Trad 兩 NUMERAL = two
■ 两个人 **liǎng ge rén** = *two people*
■ 两本书 **liǎng běn shū** = *two books*

NOTE: Both 两 **liǎng** and 二 **èr** may mean "two," but are used differently. 二 **èr** must be used in mathematics or when saying the number 2 in isolation, e.g.
■ 一、二、三、四… **yī, èr, sān, sì...** = *1, 2, 3, 4...*
■ 二加三是五 **Èr jiā sān shì wǔ.** = 2 plus 3 is 5.
两 **liǎng** must be used when referring to "two something," e.g.
■ 两张桌子 **liǎng zhāng zhōuzi** = *two tables*
■ 两个小时 **liǎng ge xiǎoshí** = *two hours*

liàng 亮 (亠 9) ADJECTIVE = bright
■ 天亮了！ **Tiān liàng le!** = *Day is breaking!*
■ 这个灯不太亮。**Zhège dēng bú tài liàng.** = *This lamp is not very bright.*

liàng 谅 (讠 10) Trad 諒 VERB = forgive (See 原谅 **yuánliàng**.)

liàng 辆 (车 11) [车 sign + 两 phon **liǎng**] Trad 輛 MEASURE WORD = (for vehicles)
■ 一辆汽车 **yí liàng qìchē** = *a car*
■ 两辆自行车 **liǎng liàng zìxíngchē** = *two bicycles*

liǎo 了 (乙 2) VERB = finish, be done with
■ 这么多工作，一星期也做不了。**Zhème duō gōngzuò, yì xīngqī yě zuò bu liǎo.** = *So much work can't be finished even in a week.*

liǎojiě 了解 [compound: (here) 了 see through + 解 analyze, comprehend] VERB = know, understand
■ 我和他是老朋友，我很了解他。**Wǒ hé tā shì lǎo péngyou, wǒ hěn liǎojiě tā.** = *He and I are old friends. I know him very well.*

líng 零 (雨 13) NUMERAL = zero
■ 一百零二 **yìbǎi líng èr** = *102*
■ 四千零五 **sìqiān líng wǔ** = *4005*

lǐng 领 (页 11) VERB = lead

lǐngdǎo 领导 [compound: 领 *lead* + 导 *guide*]
1 VERB = lead, provide leadership
■ 政府领导人民发展经济。**Zhèngfǔ lǐngdǎo rénmín fāzhǎn jīngjì.** = *The government provides leadership to the people in developing the economy.*
2 NOUN = leader, the person in charge
■ 领导不在，你有什么事请跟我说。**Lǐngdǎo bú zài, nǐ yǒu shénme shì qǐng gen wǒ shuō.** = *The person in charge is not in. Please talk to me if you've any business.*
■ 我要找你们的领导。**Wǒ yào zhǎo nǐmen de lǐngdǎo.** = *I want to see the person in charge here.*

NOTE: 领导 **lǐngdǎo** as a verb is a somewhat pompous word, appropriate only in grand cases. As a noun 领导 **lǐngdǎo** is no longer very popular in China and never has been so in other Chinese-speaking communities. To refer to the "person in charge," many Chinese use 老板 **lǎobǎn** = *boss* or a specific term such as 厂长 **chǎngzhǎng** = *factory manager* or 校长 **xiàozhǎng** = *headmaster, school principal, university president.*

liú 留 (田 10) VERB = remain (in the same place), stay behind
■ 你们先回家吧，我再留一会儿做完这件事。**Nǐmen xiān huíjiā ba, wǒ zài liú yīhuìr zuò wán zhè jiàn shì.** = *You go home first. I'll stay behind for a while to finish this job.*

liúxué 留学 [compound: 留 *stay* + 学 *study*] VERB = study abroad
■ 很多亚洲学生在美国留学。**Hěn duō Yàzhōu xuésheng zài Měiguó liúxué.** = *Many Asian students are studying in America.*
liúxuéshēng 留学生 = international students (especially in a university)
■ 不少留学生星期日也在图书馆学习。**Bùshǎo liúxuéshēng Xīngqīrì yě zài túshūguǎn xuéxí.** = *Even on Sundays, quite a few international students study in the library.*

liú 流 (氵 10) [氵 sign + symb] VERB = flow
■ 河水慢慢地向东流去。**Héshuǐ mànman de xiàng dōng liúqù.** = *The river flows slowly to the east.*

liù 六 (亠 4) NUMERAL = six
■ 六十六 **liùshí liù** = *sixty-six*
■ 六十五岁 **liùshí wǔ suì** = *sixty-five years of age*

lóu 楼 (木 13) [木 sign + 娄 phon **lóu**] Trad 樓 NOUN
1 = building with two or more stories (座 **zuò**)
■ 这座楼是去年建的。**Zhè zuò lóu shì qùnián jiàn de.** = *This building was built last year.*
■ 她住在那座白色的大楼里。**Tā zhù zài nà zuò báisè de dàlóu lǐ.** = *She lives in that white building.*
2 = floor (层 **céng**)
■ 这一层楼有多少房间？ **Zhè yì céng lóu yǒu duōshǎo fángjiān?** = *How many rooms are there on this floor?*
■ 老师的办公室在三楼。**Lǎoshī de bàngōngshì zài sānlóu.** = *Teachers' offices are on the third floor.*
dàlóu 大楼 = a big building (especially a high-rise building)
lóufáng 楼房 = multi-storied building (compare 平房 **píngfáng** = one-story building, bungalow)
gāolóu 高楼 = high-rise
lóushàng 楼上 = upstairs
lóuxià 楼下 = downstairs

NOTE: In naming floors, the Chinese system is the same as the American system and different from the British one, i.e. 一楼 **yīlóu** is the American "first floor" and the British "ground floor."

lù 录 (彐 8) Trad 錄 VERB = record

lùyīn 录音 [v+obj: 录 *record* + 音 *sound*]
1 VERB = make a recording of sounds (e.g. music, reading)

L

■ 这里在录音，请安静！ **Zhèli zài lùyīn, qǐng ānjìng!** = *Recording is in progress. Please be quiet.*

2 NOUN = recording of sounds (e.g. music, reading)

■ 你有没有听过王老师读这篇课文的录音？ **Nǐ yǒu méiyǒu tīngguo Wáng lǎoshī dú zhè piān kèwén de lùyīn?** = *Have you listened to the recording of Teacher Wang's reading of this text?*

lù 路 (足 13) [足 sign + 各 symb] NOUN = road (条 **tiáo**)

■ 这条路很长，一直通到山里。 **Zhè tiáo lù hěn cháng, yìzhí tōngdao shān lǐ.** = *This road is very long and leads all the way into the hills.*

■ 你认识去大学的路吗？ **Nǐ rènshi qù dàxué de lù ma?** = *Do you know the way to the university?*

lǚ 旅 (方 10) VERB = travel

lǚxíng 旅行 [compound: 旅 *travel* + 行 *walk, go*] VERB = travel

■ 我在中国旅行的时候，学到不少知识。 **Wǒ zài Zhōngguó lǚxíng de shíhou, xuédao bùshǎo zhīshi.** = *I gained a lot of knowledge when I traveled in China.*

lǚxíngshè 旅行社 = travel agency

■ 我要去旅行社买去英国的飞机票。 **Wǒ yào qù lǚxíngshè mǎi qù Yīngguó de fēijī piào.** = *I'll go to the travel agency to buy an air ticket to Britain.*

> NOTE: While 旅行 **lǚxíng** means "travel," the word 旅游 **lǚyóu** refers to "travel for pleasure, sightseeing." For example:
>
> ■ 我有了钱，就到国外去旅游。 **Wǒ yǒule qián, jiù dào guówài qù lǚyóu.** = *When I've got the money, I'll go sightseeing overseas.*

lǜ 绿 (纟 11) Trad 綠 ADJECTIVE = green

■ 春天到了，树木都绿了。 **Chūntiān dào le, shùmù dōu lǜ le.** = *Spring has come; all the trees are green.*

■ 红花绿树，美极了！ **Hónghuā lǜshù, měi jíle!** = *Red flowers and green trees—they're so beautiful!*

luàn 乱 (舌 7) Trad 亂 ADJECTIVE = disorderly, chaotic (antonym 整齐 **zhěngqí**)

■ 我的房间很乱，要收拾一下。 **Wǒ de fángjiān hěn luàn, yào shōushi yíxià.** = *My room is messy and needs tidying up.*

lùn 论 (讠 6) [讠 sign + 仑 phon **lún**] Trad 論 VERB = discuss (See 讨论 **tǎolùn**.)

M

mā 妈 (女 6) [女 sign + 马 phon **mǎ**] Trad 媽 NOUN = ma, mom

māma 妈妈 NOUN = mom, mommy

■ 妈妈在辅导妹妹做作业。 **Māma zài fǔdǎo mèimei zuò zuòyè.** = *Mom is tutoring sister in her homework.*

■ 我想每个人都爱自己的妈妈。 **Wǒ xiǎng měi ge rén dōu ài zìjǐ de māma.** = *I think everyone loves their mom.*

má 麻 (麻 11) NOUN = hemp

máfan 麻烦 [idiom]

1 VERB = bother

■ 这封信我能翻译，不用麻烦陈先生了。**Zhè fēng xìn wǒ néng fānyì, búyòng máfan Chén xiānsheng le.** = *I can translate this letter. We don't have to bother Mr Chen.*

2 ADJECTIVE = troublesome (antonym 方便 **fāngbiàn**)

■ 这件事很麻烦，我不一定能做好。**Zhè jiàn shì hěn máfan, wǒ bù yídìng néng zuò hǎo.** = *This matter is complicated. I'm not sure I can get it done well.*

mǎ 马 (马 3) Trad 馬 NOUN = horse

■ 你会骑马吗？ **Nǐ huì qí mǎ ma?** = *Can you ride a horse?*

■ 马跑得快，还是狗跑得快？ **Mǎ pǎo de kuài, háishì gǒu pǎo de kuài?** = *Which runs faster—the horse or the dog?*

mǎlù 马路 [modif: 马 *horse* + 路 *road*] NOUN = street, avenue (条 **tiáo**)

■ 这条马路从早到晚车很多。**Zhè tiáo mǎlù cóng-zǎo-dà-wǎn chē hěn duō.** = *This street has lots of traffic from morning till night.*

mǎlù shang 马路上 = in the street, on the road

■ 你不能把车停在马路上。**Nǐ bù néng bǎ chē tíng zài mǎlù shang.** = *You can't park the car in the street.*

chuān mǎlù 穿马路 = walk across a street

■ 穿马路要特别小心。**Chuān mǎlù yào tèbié xiǎoxīn.** = *One should be especially careful when crossing a street.*

mǎshàng 马上 [idiom] ADVERB = at once, immediately

■ 好，我马上来！ **Hǎo, wǒ mǎshàng lái!** = *OK, I'm coming!*

ma 吗 (口 6) [口 sign + 马 phon **mǎ**] Trad 嗎 PARTICLE = (used at the end of a sentence to turn it into a "yes/no" question)

■ 你是上海人吗？ **Nǐ shì Shànghǎi rén ma?** = *Are you from Shanghai?*

■ 你会说中文吗？ **Nǐ huì shuō Zhōngwén ma?** = *Do you speak Chinese?*

ma 嘛 (口 14) [口 sign + 麻 phon **má**] PARTICLE = (used at the end of a sentence to indicate that the truth of the statement is obvious) surely, that goes without saying

■ 农村的空气就是比城市干净嘛！ **Nóngcūn de kōngqì jiùshì bǐ chéngshì gānjìng ma!** = *The air in rural areas is surely cleaner than that in cities.*

mǎi 买 (大 6) Trad 買 VERB = buy

■ 我要买一双鞋。**Wǒ yào mǎi yì shuāng xié.** = *I want to buy a pair of shoes.*

mài 卖 (十 8) Trad 賣 VERB = sell

■ 你们这里卖水果吗？ **Nǐmen zhèli mài shuǐguǒ ma?** = Do *you sell fruit here?*

mǎimai 买卖 = business (especially small business)

■ 他在城里有个小买卖。**Tā zài chéngli yǒu ge xiǎo mǎimai.** = *He has a small business in town.*

zuò mǎimai 做买卖 = do business
■ 我想跟中国做买卖。**Wǒ xiǎng gēn Zhōngguó zuò mǎimai.** = *I want to do business with China.*

mǎn 满 (氵 13) [氵 sign + symb]
ADJECTIVE = full, full to the brim
■ 碗里的水满了。**Wǎn li de shuǐ mǎn le.** = *The bowl is full of water.*

mǎnyì 满意 [v+obj: 满 *make full* + 意 *wish, desire*] ADJECTIVE = satisfied, satisfactory
■ 我对你们的服务很不满意。**Wǒ duì nǐmen de fúwù hěn bù mǎnyì.** = *I'm very dissatisfied with your service.*
duì...mǎnyì 对…满意 = be satisfied with ...

màn 慢 (忄 14) [忄 sign + 曼 phon **màn**] ADJECTIVE = slow (antonym 快 **kuài**)
■ 我的表慢了五分钟。**Wǒ de biǎo mànle wǔ fēnzhōng.** = *My watch is five minutes slow.*
■ 别着急，慢慢地说。**Bié zháojí, mànman de shuō.** = *Don't be too excited. (→ Take it easy.) Speak slowly.*
■ 你说得慢，我就听得懂。**Nǐ shuō de màn, wǒ jiù tīng de dǒng.** = *If you speak slowly, I can understand you.*

máng 忙 (忄 6) [忄 sign + 亡 phon **wáng**] ADJECTIVE = busy
■ 我最近很忙，没有空儿跟你去看电影。**Wǒ zuìjìn hěn máng, méiyǒu kòngr gēn nǐ qù kàn diànyǐng.** = *I'm busy these days, and don't have time to go to the movies with you.*

NOTE: When friends meet in China, a common conversation opener is 你最近忙吗？ **Nǐ zuìjìn máng ma?** = *Have you been busy lately?*

māo 猫 (犭 11) [犭 symb + 苗 phon **miáo**] Trad 貓 NOUN = cat (只 **zhī**)
■ 我家有一只小白猫。**Wǒ jiā yǒu yì zhī xiǎo bái māo.** = *We have a white kitten at home.*

máo 毛 (毛 4)
1 MEASURE WORD = (a Chinese money unit, colloquialism for 角 **jiǎo** = 0.1 元 **yuán** or 10 分 **fēn**)
2 NOUN = hair
yángmáo 羊毛 = wool
máoyī 毛衣 = woolen sweater

mào 冒 (目 9) See 感冒 **gǎnmào**.

mào 帽 (巾 12) [巾 sign + 冒 phon **mào**]

màozi 帽子 [suffix: 帽 *hat, cap* + 子 nominal suffix] NOUN = hat, cap
■ 你这个帽子很漂亮，在哪里买的？ **Nǐ zhège màozi hěn piàoliang, zài nǎli mǎi de?** = *Your hat is beautiful. Where did you buy it?*
dài màizi 戴帽子 = put on/wear a hat (or a cap)
■ 今天外面很冷，你要戴帽子。**Jīntiān wàimiàn hěn lěng, nǐ yào dài màozi.** = *It's very cold outside. You'd better wear a hat.*
tuō màozi 脱帽子 = take off a hat (or a cap)

me 么 (丿 3) Trad **麼** PARTICLE = (used to form certain words) (See 多么 **duōme**, 那么 **nàme**, 什么 **shénme**, 为什么 **wèishénme**, 怎么 **zěnme**, 这么 **zhème**.)

méi 没 (氵 7) Same as 没有 **méiyǒu**.

méi(yǒu) guānxi 没(有)关系 = see 关系 **guānxi**

méi(yǒu) yìsi 没(有)意思 = see 意思 **yìsi**

méiyǒu 没有 ADVERB = did not, have/has not (indicating negation of past experiences, usually used before a verb or at the end of a question)

■ 我没有学过这个字。**Wǒ méiyǒu xuéguo zhège zì.** = *I haven't learnt this Chinese character.*

hái méiyǒu 还没有 = not yet

■ "你去过中国没有?" "还没有。" **"Nǐ qùguo Zhōngguó méiyǒu?" "Hái méiyǒu."** = *"Have you ever been to China?" "Not yet."*

NOTE: Colloquially, 没有 **méiyǒu** is often contracted to 没 **méi**. However, when 没有 **méiyǒu** is used at the end of a question, as in 你去过中国没有? **Nǐ qùguo Zhōngguó méiyǒu?** = *Have you ever been to China?* it cannot be replaced by 没 **méi**.

měi 每 (母 7) PRONOUN = every, each

■ 你每天都看电视新闻吗? **Nǐ měi tiān dōu kàn diànshì xīnwén ma?** = *Do you watch TV news every day?*

■ 这条街每座房子前面都有一个小花园。**Zhè tiáo jiē měi zuò fángzi qiánmian dōu yǒu yí ge xiǎo huāyuán.** = *There is a small garden in front of every house in this street.*

NOTE: Usage in Chinese requires that 每 **měi** is followed by 都 **dōu** = *all, without exception.*

měi 美 (羊 9) ADJECTIVE = pretty

■ 这花儿真美啊! **Zhè huār zhēn měi a!** = *This flower is so pretty!*

Měiguó 美国 NOUN = America, the USA

■ 中国和美国离得很远。**Zhōngguó hé Měiguó lí de hěn yuǎn.** = *China and the US are far apart.*

mèi 妹 (女 8) [女 sign + 未 phon **wèi**] NOUN = younger sister

mèimei 妹妹 NOUN = younger sister

■ 我妹妹还在念小学呢。**Wǒ mèimei hái zài niàn xiǎoxué ne.** = *My younger sister is still in primary school.*

■ 去年夏天我教妹妹游泳。**Qùnián xiàtiān wǒ jiāo mèimei yóuyǒng.** = *I taught my younger sister to swim last summer.*

mén 门 (门 3) Trad **門** NOUN = door, gate

■ 我们学校的大门正对汽车站。**Wǒmen xuéxiào de dàmén zhèng duì qìchē zhàn.** = *There is a bus stop directly opposite the gate of our school.*

■ 你家的狗会看门吗? **Nǐ jiā de gǒu huì kān mén ma?** = *Can your dog guard the gate?*

ménkǒu 门口 = doorway

■ 他站在门口等一个朋友。**Tā zhàn**

M

zài ménkǒu děng yí ge péngyou. = *He's standing by the door, waiting for a friend.*

men 们 (亻 5) [亻 sign + 门 phon **mén**] Trad **們** SUFFIX = (indicating plural number)
■ 学生们都很喜欢这位新老师。**Xuéshengmen dōu hěn xǐhuān zhè wèi xīn lǎoshī.** = *All the students like this new teacher.*

> NOTE: As a plural number marker, 们 **men** is only used with nouns denoting people. It is not used when there are words indicating plurality, such as numerals or words like 一些 **yīxiē** = *several*, 很多 **hěnduō** = *many*. In many cases, the plural number of a personal number is implicit without the use of 们 **men**: in the example sentence, 们 **men** is not obligatory; i.e. 学生都很喜欢这位新老师。**Xuēsheng dōu hěn xǐhuān zhè wèi xīn lǎoshī**. is correct and idiomatic.

mǐ 米 (米 6)
1 MEASURE WORD = meter
■ 一米 **yì mǐ** = *one meter*
■ 三米半 **sān mǐ bàn** = *three and half meters*

> NOTE: The formal word for "meter" is 公尺 **gōngchǐ** (compare with 公斤 **gōngjīn** = *kilogram*, 公里 **gōnglǐ** = *kilometer*).

2 NOUN = rice, paddy rice
■ 在中国南方，很多农民种米。**Zài Zhōngguó nánfāng, hěn duō nóngmín zhòng mǐ.** = *In South China many farmers grow rice.*

mǐfàn 米饭 [compound: 米 *rice* + 饭 *meal*] NOUN = cooked rice (碗 **wǎn**)
■ 米饭好了，菜还没有做好。**Mǐfàn hǎo le, cài hái méiyǒu zuòhǎo.** = *The rice is cooked, but the dishes are not ready yet.*
■ 王家是南方人，每天都吃米饭。**Wáng jiā shì nánfāng rén, měitiān dōu chī mǐfàn.** = *The Wangs are southerners. They eat rice every day.*

> NOTE: The staple food for Southern Chinese (Chinese living south of the Yangtze River) is 米饭 **mǐfàn**, while Northern Chinese mainly eat 面食 **miànshí** = *food made of wheat flour* such as 面条儿 **miàntiáor** = *noodles.*

miàn 面 (一 9) Trad **麵** NOUN = wheat

miànbāo 面包 [modif: 面 *wheat flour* + 包 *lump*] NOUN = bread (只 **zhī**, 条 **tiáo**)
■ 新做的面包特别香。**Xīn zuò de miànbāo tèbié xiāng.** = *Freshly baked bread smells particularly good.*

miàntiáor 面条儿 NOUN = noodles (碗 **wǎn**)
■ 面条儿要热的才好吃。**Miàntiáor yào rè de cái hǎochī.** = *Noodles must be eaten hot.*
■ 她是北方人，面条儿做得好，米饭做得不好。**Tā shì běifāng rén, miàntiáor zuò de hǎo, mǐfàn zuò de bù hǎo.** = *She's a northerner. She makes good noodle meals, but doesn't cook rice well.*

mín 民 (乙 5) NOUN = people

mínzú 民族 [compound: 民 *people* + 族 *clan*] NOUN = ethnic group, nationality
■ 汉民族是中国最大的民族。**Hàn mínzú shì Zhōngguó zuì dà de mínzú.** = *The Hans are the biggest ethnic group in China.*
■ 你们国家有多少个民族? **Nǐmen guójiā yǒu duōshǎo ge mínzú?** = *How many ethnic groups are there in your country?*
shǎoshù mínzù 少数民族 = minority ethnic group, national minority
duō mínzú wénhuà 多民族文化 = multiculturalism

míng 明 (日 8) [日 sign + 月 sign]

míngnián 明年 [modif: 明 (in this context) *next* + 年 *year*] NOUN = next year
■ 明年我二十一岁了! **Míngnián wǒ èrshíyī suì le!** = *I'll be 21 next year!*

míngtiān 明天 [modif: 明 (in this context) *next* + 天 *day*] NOUN = tomorrow
■ "明天几月几号?" "明天六月二十一号。" **"Míngtiān jǐ yuè jǐ hào?" "Míngtiān Liù yuè èrshíyī hào."** = *"What date is tomorrow?" "It's June 21st."*
■ 我想睡觉了, 这些作业明天再做吧。**Wǒ xiǎng shuìjiào le, zhèxiē zuòyè míngtiān zài zuò ba.** = *I want to go to bed. I'll do the assignment tomorrow.*

míng 名 (夕 6) NOUN = given name

míngzì 名字 [compound: 名 *given name* + 字 *courtesy name*] NOUN = name, given name
■ 我的名字叫王小明。**Wǒ de míngzì jiào Wáng Xiǎomíng.** = *My name is Wang Xiaoming.*
■ "你知道他的名字吗?" "不知道。" **"Nǐ zhīdào tā de míngzi ma?" "Bù zhīdào."** = *"Do you know his name?" "No."*

NOTE: To be exact, 名字 **míngzi** only means "given name," but in informal usage 名字 **míngzi** may also mean "full name" (family name + given name). The formal word for "full name" is 姓名 **xìngmíng**. See note on 姓 **xìng**.

mǔ 母 (母 5) NOUN = mother

mǔqin 母亲 [modif: 母 *mother* + 亲 *parent*] NOUN = mother
■ 母亲在家照顾孩子。**Mǔqin zài jiā zhàogù háizi.** = *Mother takes care of her children at home.*
■ 你常常给母亲打电话吗? **Nǐ chángcháng gěi mǔqin dǎ diànhuà ma?** = *Do you often give mother a call?*
mǔqin jié 母亲节 = Mother's Day

mù 目 (目 5) NOUN = eye

mùqián 目前 [modif: 目 *eye* + 前 *in front of*] NOUN = present time, at present
■ 我们目前有很多困难。**Wǒmen mùqián yǒu hěn duō kùnnan.** = *We're having many difficulties at present.*

■ 目前的情况怎么样? **Mùqián de qíngkuàng zěnmeyàng?** = *What's the situation at present?*

N

ná 拿 (人 10) [合 symb + 手 sign]
VERB = hold, carry in hand
■ 我手里拿着很多书，不能开门，请你帮帮我。**Wǒ shǒu li názhe hěn duō shū, bù néng kāi mén, qǐng nǐ bāngbang wǒ.** = *I'm holding lots of books and can't open the door. Please help me.*

nǎ 哪 (口 9) [口 sign + 那 phon **nà**]
PRONOUN = which
■ 哪辆自行车是你的? **Nǎ liàng zìxíngchē shì nǐ de?** = *Which bike is yours?*

NOTE: 哪 **nǎ** may also be pronounced **něi**, e.g. 哪辆自行车是你的? **Neǐ liàng zìxíngchē shì nǐ de?** = *Which bike is yours?*

nǎli 哪里 [modif: 哪 *which* + 里 *place*] PRONOUN = where
■ 你住在哪里? **Nǐ zhù zai nǎli?** = *Where do you live?*

NOTE: 哪儿 **nǎr** has the same meaning and use as 哪里 **nǎli** = *where*. 哪儿 **nǎr** sounds more colloquial than 哪里 **nǎli**. In 哪里 **nǎli** and 哪儿 **nǎr**, 哪 cannot be pronounced **něi**; it must be pronounced **nǎ**.

nà 那 (阝 6)
1 PRONOUN = that
■ 这辆自行车是我的，那辆自行车是我弟弟的。= **Zhè liàng zìxíngchē shì wǒ de, nà liàng zìxíngchē shì wǒ dìdi de.** = *This bike is mine. That one is my younger brother's.*
2 CONJUNCTION = same as 那么 **nàme** 2 CONJUNCTION

NOTE: 那 may also be pronounced **nèi**, e.g. 那个 **nèige**, 那里 **nèilǐ**.

nàge 那个 [modif: 那 *that* + 个 *one*]
PRONOUN = that one
■ 那个不是我的。我的在这里。**Nàge bú shì wǒ de. Wǒ de zài zhèlǐ.** = *That one is not mine. Mine's here.*

nàli 那里 [modif: 那 *that* + 里 *place*]
PRONOUN = there, over there
■ 他在那里工作。**Tā zài nàli gōngzuò.** = *He works there.*
■ 那里就是图书馆。**Nàli jiù shì túshūguǎn.** = *Over there is the library.*

NOTE: In spoken Chinese 那里 **nàli** can be replaced by 那儿 **nàr**.

nàme 那么
1 PRONOUN = like that, in that manner, so
■ 上海没有北京那么冷。**Shànghǎi méiyǒu Běijīng nàme lěng.** = *Shanghai is not as cold as Beijing.*
■ 你那么做，她会不高兴。**Nǐ nàme zuò, tā huì bù gāoxìng.** = *If you behave like that, she'll be unhappy.*
2 CONJUNCTION = in that case, then
■ 你不喜欢吃米饭，那么吃面包吧。**Nǐ bù xǐhuān chī mǐfàn, nàme chī miànbāo ba.** = *You don't like rice; in*

N

that case eat bread. (→ *Since you don't like rice, have bread instead.*)

NOTE: Although 那么 **nàme** as a conjunction is glossed as "in that case," "then," Chinese speakers tend to use it much more than English speakers use "in that case" or "then." In colloquial Chinese 那么 **nàme** is often shortened to 那 **nà**, e.g.
■ 你不喜欢吃米饭，那吃面包吧。**Nǐ bù xǐhuān chī mǐfàn, nà chī miànbāo ba.** = *You don't like rice; in that case eat bread.*

nàxiē 那些 PRONOUN = those
■ 这些是中文书，那些是英文书。**Zhèxiē shì Zhōngwén shū, nàxiē shì Yīngwén shū.** = *These are Chinese books. Those are English books.*

nàyàng 那样 Same as 那么 **nàme** 1 PRONOUN

na 哪 (口 9) [口 sign + 那 phon **nà**] Same as 啊 **ā** 2 (used when the character preceding it ends with **n** or **ng**)
■ 这花真好看哪！ **Zhè huār zhēn hǎokàn na!** = *How beautiful this flower is!*

nán 南 (十 9) NOUN = south (antonym 北 **běi**)
■ 很多老年人喜欢住在南方。**Hěn duō lǎonián rén xǐhuan zhù zai nánfāng.** = *Many aged people like to live in the south.*

nánbian 南边 [modif: 南 *south* + 边 *side*] NOUN = south side, to the south, in the south
■ "新西兰的南边还有什么国家吗？" "没有了。" **"Xīngxīlán de nánbian hái yǒu shénme guójiā ma?" "Méiyǒu le."** = *"Is there any country to the south of New Zealand?" "No, there isn't."*

nán 男 (田 7) [田 sign + 力 sign] ADJECTIVE = (of humans) male (antonym 女 **nǚ**)
■ 那个男孩子是王先生的小儿子。**Nàge nán háizi shì Wáng xiānsheng de xiǎo érzi.** = *That boy is Mr Wang's youngest son.*

nánrén 男人 = man, men
■ 男人能做的事，女人也能做。**Nánrén néng zuò de shì, nǚrén yě néng zuò.** = *What men can do, women also can.*

nán qīngnián 男青年 = young man
■ 昨天有一个男青年来找你。**Zuótiān yǒu yí ge nán qīngnián lái zhǎo nǐ.** = *A young man came to see you yesterday.*

nán háizi 男孩子 = boy

nánshēng 男生 = male student/pupil

nán 难 (又 10) Trad 難 ADJECTIVE = difficult (antonym 容易 **róngyì**)
■ 这道练习太难了，我不会做。**Zhè dào liànxí tài nán le, wǒ bú huì zuò.** = *This exercise is too difficult. I can't do it.*

nǎo 脑 (月 10) [月 sign + phon] Trad 腦 NOUN = brain (See 电脑 **diànnǎo**.)

ne 呢 (口 8) [口 sign + 尼 phon **ní**] PARTICLE = (used at the end of a question to soften the tone of enquiry)

N

■ 你打算明年做什么呢？ **Nǐ dǎsuàn míngnián zuò shénme ne?** = *What do you intend to do next year?*

nèi 内 (冂 4) NOUN = inside, within
■ 这些书只能在图书馆内看。**Zhè xiē shū zhǐnéng zài túshūguǎn nèi kàn.** = *These books can only be read within the library.*

nèiróng 内容 [modif: 内 *inside* + 容 *contain*] NOUN = content, substance
■ 这本书的内容很丰富。**Zhè běn shū de nèiróng hěn fēngfù.** = *This book is rich in content.*
■ 他说了半天，但是没有什么内容。**Tā shuōle bàntiān, dànshì méiyǒu shénme nèiróng.** = *He talked for a long time but there wasn't much substance.*

néng 能 (厶 10) MODAL VERB = can, be able to
■ 我今天不舒服，不能去上班。**Wǒ jīntiān bù shūfu, bù néng qù shàngbān.** = *I'm unwell today and won't be able to go to work.*

NOTE: See note after 会 **huì** 1 MODAL VERB.

nénggòu 能够 Same as 能 **néng**.

ng 嗯 (口 13) [口 sign + 恩 phon **ēn**] INTERJECTION = (used after a question to reinforce the questioning), eh
■ 你把自行车借给谁了，嗯？ **Nǐ bǎ zìxíngchē jiègěi shuíle, ng?** = *Who did you lend your bike to, eh?*

nǐ 你 (亻 7) [亻 sign + 尔 symb] PRONOUN = you (singular)
■ 你是谁？ **Nǐ shì shuí?** = *Who're you?*
■ 我不认识你。**Wǒ bú rènshi nǐ.** = *I don't know you.*

nǐmen 你们 [suffix: 你 *you* (singular) + 们 (suffix denoting a plural number)] PRONOUN = you (plural)
■ 你们都是我的朋友。**Nǐmen dōu shì wǒ de péngyou.** = *You all are my friends.*
■ 我告诉你们一个好消息。**Wǒ gàosu nǐmen yí ge hǎo xiāoxi.** = *I'll tell you a piece of good news.*

nián 年 (丿 6) NOUN = year (no measure word required)
■ 一年有十二个月。**Yì nián yǒu shí'èr ge yuè.** = *There're twelve months in a year.*
■ 我在美国住了两年。**Wǒ zài Měiguó zhùle liǎng nián.** = *I lived in the States for two years.*
jīnnián 今年 = this year
qùnián 去年 = last year
míngnián 明年 = next year

niánjí 年级 [compound: 年 *year* + 级 *grade*] NOUN = grade (in school)
■ 这个年级有多少学生？ **Zhège niánjí yǒu duōshǎo xuésheng?** = *How many students are there in this grade?*
■ 他们的孩子刚念一年级。**Tāmen de háizi gāng niàn yì niánjí.** = *Their child is only a Grade One pupil.*

niánjì 年纪 [compound: 年 *year* + 纪 *number*] NOUN = age

■ “老先生，您多大年纪了？”“七十了。” **“Lǎoxiānsheng, nín duōdà niánjì le?” “Qīshí le.”** = *“How old are you, sir?” “Seventy.”*
■ 他虽然年纪小，但是很懂事。**Tā suírán niánjì xiǎo, dànshì hěn dǒngshì.** = *Although he's very young, he's very sensible.*

NOTE: 您多大年纪了？ **Nín duōdà niánjì le?** is an appropriate way to ask the age of an elderly person. To ask a young child his/her age, the question should be 你几岁了？ **Nǐ jǐ suì le?** For people who are neither children nor old the question to use is 你多大岁数？ **Nǐ duō dà suìshu?**

niánqīng 年轻 [modif: 年 *age* + 轻 *light*] ADJECTIVE = young
■ 你还年轻，有些事你还不大懂。**Nǐ hái niánqīng, yǒuxiē shì nǐ hái bú dà dǒng.** = *You're still young, and there are matters you don't really understand yet.* (→*You're still too young to understand some matters.*)
■ 他喜欢和年轻人交朋友。**Tā xǐhuan hé niánqīng rén jiāo péngyou.** = *He likes to make friends with young people.*
niánqīng rén 年轻人 = young person (from late teens to late twenties)

niàn 念 (心 8) VERB
1 = read, read aloud
■ 你每天念中文课文吗？ **Nǐ měi tiān niàn Zhōngwén kèwén ma?** = *Do you read [your] Chinese lessons every day?*
2 = study (in a school)
■ 他们的大儿子在英国念大学，他念数学。**Tāmen de dà érzi zài Yīngguó niàn dàxué, tā niàn shùxué.** = *Their eldest son is studying in a university in the UK; he studies mathematics.*

niáng 娘 (女 10) [女 sign + 良 phon **liáng**] NOUN = woman (See 姑娘 **gūniang**.)

niǎo 鸟(鸟 5) NOUN = bird (只 **zhī**)
■ 我多么希望能像鸟儿一样飞。**Wǒ duōme xīwàng néng xiàng niǎor yíyàng fēi.** = *How I wish I could fly like a bird.*

NOTE: 鸟 **niǎo** is seldom used alone in everyday Chinese. Instead, 鸟儿 **niǎor** or 小鸟 **xiǎoniǎo** is used.

nín 您 (心 11) [你 *you* + 心 sign] PRONOUN = you (honorific)

NOTE: 您 **nín** is the honorific form of 你 **nǐ**. You should use 您 **nín** when respect or deference is called for. Normally 您 **nín** does not have a plural form. 您们 **nínmen** is absolutely unacceptable in spoken Chinese, and only marginally so in written Chinese. If you want to politely address more than one person, you can say 您两位 **nín liǎng wèi** (for two people), 您三位 **nín sān wèi** (for three people), or 您几位 **nín jǐ wèi** (for a few/several people).

niú 牛 (牛 4) NOUN = cattle, ox, cow, calf, buffalo (头 **tóu**)

■ 牛在草地上吃草。**Niú zài cǎodì shang chī cǎo.** = *The cattle are grazing in the field.*
■ 人们用狗放羊放牛，所以狗是人们最好的朋友。**Rénmen yòng gǒu fàng yáng fàng niú, suǒyǐ gǒu shì rénmen zuì haǒ de péngyou.** = *People use dogs to herd sheep and cattle; that's why the dog is man's best friend.*

nǎiniú 奶牛 = cow
gōngniú 公牛 = bull
shuǐniú 水牛 = buffalo
huángniú 黄牛 = ox
xiǎoniú 小牛 = calf
niúnǎi 牛奶 = cow's milk, milk
niúròu 牛肉 = beef

NOTE: In the Chinese context, the ox (黄牛 **huángniú**) and the water buffalo (水牛 **shuǐniú**) are more important than the milk cow (奶牛 **nǎiniú**).

nóng 农 (冖 6) Trad 農 NOUN = farming

nóngchǎng 农场 [modif: 农 *farming* + 场 *field, ground*] NOUN = farm
■ 这个农场真大！ **Zhège nóngchǎng zhēn dà!** = *How big this farm is!*
■ 外国人可以在这里买农场吗？ **Wàiguórén kěyǐ zài zhèli mǎi nóngchǎng ma?** = *Can a foreigner buy a farm here?*

nóngcūn 农村 [modif: 农 *farming* + 村 *village*] NOUN = farming area, rural area, country (antonym 城市 **chéngshì**)
■ 农村人口比较少，生活不太方便。**Nóngcūn rénkǒu bǐjiào shǎo, shēnghuó bú tài fāngbiàn.** = *In rural areas, the population is small and life is not very convenient.* (→*In rural areas, there are fewer people and life is not very easy.*)
■ 农村生活很有趣。**Nóngcūn shēnghuó hěn yǒuqù.** = *Rural life is very interesting.*

nóngmín 农民 [modif: 农 *farming* + 民 *people*] NOUN = farmer, peasant
■ 农民都很关心天气。**Nóngmín dōu hěn guānxīn tiānqì.** = *All farmers are concerned about the weather.*
■ 她十年前和一位农民结婚，以后一直住在农村。**Tā shí nián qián hé yí wèi nóngmín jiéhūn, yǐhòu yìzhí zhù zai nóngcūn.** = *She married a farmer ten years ago and has since lived in rural areas.*

nóngyè 农业 [modif: 农 *farming* + 业 *industry*] NOUN = agriculture
■ 农业十分重要。**Nóngyè shífēn zhòngyào.** = *Agriculture is of great importance.*
■ 我们必须努力发展农业。**Wǒmen bìxū nǔlì fāzhǎn nóngyè.** = *We must strive to develop agriculture.*

nǔ 努 (力 7) [奴 phon **nú** + 力 sign]

nǔlì 努力 [compound: 努 *physical effort* + 力 *strength*] ADJECTIVE = making great efforts
■ 她是个很努力的学生，考试一定能取得好成绩。**Tā shì ge hěn nǔlì de xuésheng, kǎoshì yídìng néng qǔdé hǎo chéngjì.** = *She's a hardworking student, and will definitely get good results in the examinations.*

N

■ 我们大家为了更好的明天努力工作。**Wǒmen dàjiā wèile gèng hǎo de míngtiān nǔlì gōngzuò.** = *We all work hard for a better tomorrow.*
■ 他中文学习得很努力。**Tā Zhōngwén xuéxí de hěn nǔlì.** = *He studies Chinese very hard.*

nǚ 女 (女 3) ADJECTIVE = (female of humans) (antonym 男 **nán**)
■ 请问，女洗手间在哪里? **Qǐngwèn, nǚ xǐshǒujiān zài nǎli?** = *Excuse me, where's the women's toilet?*
nǚrén 女人 = woman
nǚ qīngnián 女青年 = young woman
nǚ háizi 女孩子 = girl
nǚshēng 女生 = female student/pupil
nǚ'ér 女儿 = daughter
■ 他们的三个孩子都是女儿，没有儿子。**Tāmen de sān ge háizi dōu shì nǚ'ér, méiyǒu érzi.** = *All their three children are daughters; they don't have a son.*

nuǎn 暖 (日 13) [日 sign + 爰 symb] ADJECTIVE = warm

nuǎnhuo 暖和 [compound: 暖 *warm* + 和 *mild*] ADJECTIVE = (of weather) warm
■ 春天的太阳不太热，很暖和。**Chūntiān de tàiyang bú tài rè, hěn nuǎnhuo.** = *The sunshine in spring is not hot; it's warm.*

NOTE: The pronunciation of 和 in 暖和 **nuǎnhuo** is **huō**, not **hé** as in 我和他 **wǒ hé tā**.

P

pá 爬 (爪 8) [爪 symb + 巴 phon **bā**] VERB = crawl, climb
■ 他们的儿子才一岁，还不会走路，只会在地上爬。**Tāmen de érzi cái yí suì, hái bú huì zǒulù, zhǐhuì zài dì shang pá.** = *Their son is only a year old; he still can't walk, and can only crawl on the floor.*

pà 怕 (忄 8) [忄 sign + 白 phon **bái**] VERB = fear, be afraid
■ 一个人住这么大的房子，我有点儿怕。**Yí ge rén zhù zhème dà de fángzi, wǒ yǒudiǎnr pà.** = *I'm a bit afraid to live alone in such a big house.*

pāi 拍 (扌 8) [扌 sign + 白 phon **bái**] VERB = pat, clap
pāishǒu 拍手 = clap, applaud
■ 孩子们拍手欢迎新老师。**Háizimen pāishǒu huānyíng xīn lǎoshī.** = *The children clapped to welcome the new teacher.* (→ *The children gave the new teacher a big hand.*)

pái 排 (扌 11) [扌 sign + 非 symb] NOUN = row

páiqiú 排球 [modif: 排 *row* + 球 *ball*] NOUN = volleyball (只 **zhī**)
■ 夏天我们常常在海边打排球。**Xiàtiān wǒmen chángcháng zài hǎibiān dǎ páiqiú.** = *In summer we often play volleyball at the seaside.*

pāi 派 (氵 9)
1 VERB = dispatch, assign
■ 校长派她教三年级。**Xiàozhǎng pài tā jiāo sān niánjí.** = *The principal assigned her to teach third grade.*
2 NOUN = faction, school (of thought)
■ 在这个问题上有很多派。**Zài zhège wèntí shang yǒu hěn duō pài.** = *There're many schools of thought on this issue.*

páng 旁 (方 10) NOUN = aside

pángbiān 旁边 [modif: 旁 *aside* + 边 *side*] NOUN = side
■ 小河旁边有一个农场。**Xiǎohé pángbiān yǒu yí ge nóngchǎng.** = *There's a farm by the small river.*

pàng 胖 (月 9) ADJECTIVE = fat, overweight
■ 她觉得自己很胖，每天吃很少东西。**Tā juéde zìjǐ hěn pàng, měi tiān chī hěn shǎo dōngxi.** = *She thinks herself overweight and eats very little every day.*

pǎo 跑 (足 12) [足 sign + 包 phon **bāo**] VERB = run
■ 我们比一比，看谁跑得快。**Wǒmen bǐ yi bǐ, kàn shéi pǎo de kuài.** = *Let's compete and see who runs faster.*

pǎobù 跑步 [modif: 跑 *run* + 步 *steps*] VERB = jog
■ 早上很多人在公园里跑步。**Zǎoshang hěn duō rén zài gōngyuán lǐ pǎobù.** = *Early every morning, many people jog in the park.*

pēng 朋 (月 8) NOUN = companion

péngyou 朋友 [compound: 朋 *companion* + 友 *friend*] NOUN = friend
■ 朋友应该互相帮助。**Péngyou yīnggāi hùxiāng bāngzhù.** = *Friends should help one another.*
■ 他有很多朋友。**Tā yǒu hěn duō péngyou.** = *He has many friends.*
gēn/hé...jiāo péngyou 跟 / 和…交朋友 = make friends with ...
■ 他在中学的时候交了不少朋友。**Tā zài zhōngxué de shíhou jiāole bùshǎo péngyou.** = *He made quite a few friends in high school.*

pèng 碰 (石 13) VERB = bump into, touch
■ 别碰我，我手里拿着水呢！ **Bié pèng wǒ, wǒ shǒu li názhe shuǐ ne!** = *Don't bump into me, I'm carrying water.*
pèngdao 碰到 = meet unexpectedly, run into, come across
■ 我昨天在城里碰到一个老同学。**Wǒ zuótiān zài chéng lǐ pèngdào yí ge lǎo tóngxué.** = *I ran into an old classmate of mine in town yesterday.*

pī 批 (扌 7) [扌 sign + 比 phon **bǐ**] VERB = criticize

pīpíng 批评 [compound: 批 *criticism* + 评 *comment*]
1 VERB = criticize, scold (antonym 表扬 **biǎoyáng**)
■ 老师批评他上课常常迟到。**Lǎoshī pīpíng tā shàngkè chángcháng chídào.** = *The teacher criticized him for being often late for class.*

2 NOUN = criticism
■ 你对他的批评很正确。**Nǐ duì tā de pīpíng hěn zhèngquè.** = *Your criticism of him is correct.*
■ 我不同意你对他的批评。**Wǒ bù tóngyì nǐ duì tā de pīpíng.** = *I don't agree with your criticism of him.*

pí 啤 (口 11) [口 sign + 卑 phon **bì**]

píjiǔ 啤酒 NOUN = beer (瓶 **píng**, 杯 **bēi**)
■ 这种啤酒很好喝。**Zhě zhǒng píjiǔ hěn hǎohē.** = *This beer is tastes good.*
■ 爸爸每星期五买很多啤酒。**Bāba měi Xīngqīwǔ mǎi hěn duō píjiǔ.** = *Daddy buys lots of beer every Friday.*

NOTE: 啤酒 **píjiǔ** is an example of semi-transliteration: 啤 **pí** represents the sound of the English word "beer" and 酒 **jiǔ** means "alcoholic drink."

piān 篇 (竹 15) [竹 sign + 扁 phon **biǎn**] MEASURE WORD = for a piece of writing
■ 一篇文章 **yì piān wénzhāng** = *an article/essay*

pián 便 (亻 9) ADJECTIVE = comfortable

piányi 便宜 [idiom] ADJECTIVE = inexpensive, cheap (antonym 贵 **guì**)
■ 这家商店东西很便宜。**Zhè jiā shāngdiàn dōngxi hěn piányi.** = *Things are cheap in this store.*
■ 我想买便宜一点儿的衣服。**Wǒ xiǎng mǎi piányi yìdiǎnr de yīfu.** = *I want to buy clothes that are less expensive.*

piàn 片 (片 4)
1 NOUN = thin and flat piece, slice
■ 王太太做的肉片特别好吃。**Wáng tàitai zuò de ròupiàn tèbié hǎochī.** = *The meat slices cooked by Mrs Wang are particularly delicious.*
2 MEASURE WORD = (for thin, flat pieces)
■ 一片面包 **yípiàn miànbāo** = *a slice of bread*

piào 票 (西 11) NOUN = ticket (张 **zhāng**)
■ 这场电影的票全卖完了。**Zhè chǎng diànyǐng de piào quán màiwán le.** = *Tickets for this movie are sold out.*
■ 我买两张去香港的飞机票。**Wǒ mǎi liǎng zhāng qù Xiānggǎng de fēijīpiào.** = *I want to buy two air tickets to Hong Kong.*
fēijī piào 飞机票 = air ticket
huǒchē piào 火车票 = train ticket
qìchē piào 汽车票 = bus/coach ticket
diànyǐng piào 电影票 = movie ticket
ménpiào 门票 = admission ticket (to a show, sporting event, etc.)

piāo 漂 (氵 14) ADJECTIVE = pretty

piàoliang 漂亮 [idiom] ADJECTIVE = pretty, good-looking
■ 这个小女孩真漂亮！ **Zhège xiǎo nǚhái zhēn piàoliang!** = *This little girl is really pretty!* (→ *What a pretty little girl!*)
■ 你的汉字写得很漂亮。**Nǐ de hànzì xiě de hěn piàoliang.** = *Your Chinese characters are beautifully written.*

píng 平 (一 5) ADJECTIVE = flat, level (See 水平 **shuǐpíng**.)

píng 评 (讠7) [讠 sign + 平 phon **píng**] Trad 評 VERB = comment (See 批评 **pīpíng**.)

píng 苹 (艹 8) [艹 sign + 平 phon **píng**] Trad 蘋 NOUN = apple

píngguǒ 苹果 [modif: 苹 *apple* + 果 *fruit*] NOUN = apple (个 **gè**)
■ 这种苹果多少钱一公斤？ **Zhè zhǒng píngguǒ duōshǎo qián yì gōngjīn?** = *How much is a kilo of these apples?*
■ 我喜欢吃新西兰苹果。**Wǒ xǐhuan chī Xīnxīlán píngguǒ.** = *I like New Zealand apples.*

píng 瓶 (瓦 10) [并 phon **bìng** + 瓦 symb]
1 NOUN = bottle (个 **ge**)
■ 给我一个空瓶子。**Gěi wǒ yí ge kōng píngzi.** = *Give me an empty bottle.*
píngzi 瓶子 = bottle
huāpíng 花瓶 = vase
2 MEASURE WORD = a bottle of
■ 一瓶啤酒 **yì píng píjiǔ** = *a bottle of beer*
■ 两瓶可口可乐 **liǎng píng kěkǒukělè** = *two bottles of Coca-Cola*

pō 坡 (土 8) NOUN = slope (See 新加坡 **Xīnjiāpō**.)

pò 破 (石 10)
1 VERB = break, damage
■ 你的衣服破了。**Nǐ de yīfu pò le.** = *Your clothes are torn.*
2 ADJECTIVE = torn, damaged
■ 这件破衣服不能穿了。**Zhè jiàn pò yīfu bù néng chuān le.** = *This torn clothing is no longer wearable.*
■ 花瓶打破了。**Huāpíng dǎpò le.** = *The vase is broken.*

Q

qī 七 (一 2) NUMERAL = seven
■ 七百七十七 **qībǎi qīshí qī** = *seven hundred and seventy-seven*
■ 七个小矮人 **qí ge xiǎo ǎirén** = *the seven dwarves*
■ 零零七 **líng líng qī** = *007*

qī 妻 (女 8) [symb + 女 sign] NOUN = wife

qīzi 妻子 [suffix: 妻 *wife* + 子 nominal suffix] NOUN = wife (antonym 丈夫 **zhàngfu**)
■ 他妻子对他照顾得很好。**Tā qīzi duì tā zhàogù de hěn hǎo.** = *His wife takes good care of him.*
■ 他对他妻子好吗？ **Tā duì tā qīzi hǎo ma?** = *Is he nice to his wife?*

qī 期 (月 12) [其 phon **qí** + 月 sign] NOUN = period (See 假期 **jiàqī**, 星期 **xīngqī**.)

qí 齐 (齐 6) Trad 齊 See 整齐 **zhěngqí**.

qí 其 (八 8) PRONOUN = this, that (See 尤其 **yóuqí**.)

qí 骑 (马, 11) [马 sign + 奇 phon **qí**] Trad **騎** VERB = ride (a horse, a bicycle, etc.)

qí mǎ 骑马 = ride a horse

qí zìxíngche 骑自行车 = ride a bicycle

■ 我每天骑自行车去上学。**Wǒ měitiān qí zìxíngchē qù shàngxué.** = *I go to school by bike every day.*

qǐ 起 (走 10) [走 sign + 已 phon **jǐ**] VERB = rise, get up

■ 快十点钟了，他还没起呢！ **Kuài shí diǎnzhōng le, tā hái méi qǐ ne!** = *It's almost ten o'clock and he still hasn't gotten up yet!*

qǐ chuáng 起床 = get up

qǐlai 起来 = rise, stand up

■ 校长走进教室，大家都站起来。 **Xiàozhǎng zǒujìn jiàoshì, dàjiā dōu zhàn qǐlai.** = *When the school principal entered the classroom, everybody stood up.*

NOTE: 起 **qǐ** is seldom used alone. To express "to get up," 起床 **qǐ chuáng** is more common than 起 **qǐ**. One can correctly say 快十点钟了，他还没起床呢！ **Kuài shí diǎnzhōng le, tā hái méi qǐ chuáng ne!** = *It's almost ten o'clock and he still hasn't gotten up yet!*

qì 气 (气 4) Trad **氣** NOUN = air (See 客气 **kèqi**, 空气 **kōngqì**.)

qì 汽 (氵 7) [氵 sign + 气 sign] NOUN = vapor, steam

qìchē 汽车 [modif: 汽 *vapor* + 车 *vehicle*] NOUN = automobile, car (辆 **liàng**)

■ 我的汽车坏了！ **Wǒ de qìchē huài le!** = *My car's broken down.*

kāi qìchē 开汽车 = drive a car

■ 你会开汽车吗？ **Nǐ huì kāi qìchē ma?** = *Can you drive a car?*

qìshuǐ 汽水 [modif: 汽 *vapor* + 水 *water*] NOUN = soft drink, soda water, soda, pop (瓶 **píng**，杯 **bēi**)

■ 这瓶汽水是给你的。**Zhè píng qìshuǐ shì gěi nǐ de.** = *This bottle of soda water is for you.*

■ 我不喝汽水，我喝水。 **Wǒ bù hē qìshuǐ, wǒ hē shuǐ.** = *I don't take soft drinks; I drink water.*

qì 器 (口 16) NOUN = utensil (See 机器 **jīqì**.)

qiān 铅 (钅 10) [钅 sign + symb] Trad **鉛** NOUN = lead

qiānbǐ 铅笔 [modif: 铅 *lead* + 笔 *pen*] NOUN = pencil (支 **zhī**)

■ 我的红铅笔哪里去了？ **Wǒ de hóng qiānbǐ nǎli qù le?** = *Where's my red pencil?*

■ 我可以用一下你的铅笔吗？ **Wǒ kěyǐ yòng yíxià nǐ de qiānbǐ ma?** = *May I use your pencil for a while?*

qiān 千 (丿 3) NUMERAL = thousand

■ 一千零一夜 **yìqiān líng yí yè** = *a thousand and one nights*

■ 四千五百八十 **sìqiān wǔbǎi bāshí** = *four thousand five hundred and eighty*

qián 前 (八 9) NOUN = front (antonym 后 **hòu**)
■ 房子前有一块草地。**Fángzi qián yǒu yí kuài cǎodì.** = *In front of the house there's a lawn.*
■ 中国人的姓名姓在前，名在后。**Zhōngguórén de xìngmíng xìng zài qián, míng zài hòu.** = *In a Chinese person's name, the family name is put before the given name.*

qiánbian 前边 [modif: 前 *front* + 边 *side*] NOUN = front (antonym 后边 **hòubiān**)
■ 房子前边有一块草地。**Fángzi qiánbian yǒu yí kuài cǎodì.** = *In front of the house there's a lawn.*
■ 中国人的姓名姓在前边，名在后边。**Zhōngguórén de xìngmíng xìng zài qiánbian, míng zài hòubiān.** = *In a Chinese person's name, the family name is put before the given name.*

NOTE: In Modern Standard Chinese, 前 **qián** is seldom used alone. Usually, it is better to use 前边 **qiánbiān**.

qián 钱 (钅 10) [钅 sign + 戋 phon **jiān**] Trad 錢 NOUN = money (笔 **bǐ**)
■ 钱很重要，但不是万能的。**Qián hěn zhòngyào, dàn bú shì wànnéng de.** = *Money is important, but it is not all-powerful.*
■ 他在银行里有一大笔钱。**Tā zài yínháng li yǒu yí dà bǐ qián.** = *He has a big sum of money in the bank.*

qiǎn 浅 (氵 8) [氵 sign + 戋 phon] Trad 淺 ADJECTIVE
1 = shallow (antonym 深 **shēn**)
■ 这条河很浅，可以走过去。**Zhè tiáo hé hěn qiǎn, kěyǐ zǒu guòqu.** = *This river is shallow; you can walk across it.*
2 = easy, of low standard (antonym 深 **shēn**)
■ 这本书太浅，你不用看。**Zhè běn shū tài qiǎn, nǐ búyòng kàn.** = *This book is too easy for you; you don't have to read it.*

qiáng 墙 (土 14) [土 sign + 啬 phon] Trad 牆 NOUN = wall (道 **dào**)
■ 墙上有一张世界地图。**Qiáng shang yǒu yì zhāng shìjiè dìtú.** = *There's a map of the world on the wall.*

qiáo 桥 (木 10) [木 sign + 乔 phon **qiáo**] Trad 橋 NOUN = bridge (座 **zuò**)
■ 这座石桥历史很久。**Zhè zuò shíqiáo lìshǐ hěn jiǔ.** = *This stone bridge has a long history.*
■ 长江上有很多大桥。**Chángjiāng shang yǒu hěn duō dàqiáo.** = *There're many big bridges across the Yangtze River.*

qiě 且 (丨 5) CONJUNCTION = moreover (See 而且 **érqie**.)

qiè 切 (刀 5) VERB = cut (See 一切 **yíqiè**.)

qīn 亲 (立 9) Trad 親 NOUN = blood relation (See 父亲 **fùqin**, 母亲 **mǔqin**.)

qīng 青 (青 8) ADJECTIVE = green

Q

qīngnián 青年 [modif: 青 *green* + 年 *year*] NOUN = young person, young people, youth (especially male) (位 **wèi,** 个 **ge**)
■ 那位青年是我姐姐的男朋友。**Nà wèi qīngnián shì wǒ jiějie de nánpéngyou.** = *That young man is my elder sister's boyfriend.*
■ 青年工人往往没有多少经验。**Qīngnián gōngrén wǎngwǎng méiyǒu duōshǎo jīngyàn.** = *Young workers often don't have much experience.*

qīng 轻 (车 9) ADJECTIVE = light (in weight) (antonym 重 **zhòng**)
■ 空气比水轻。**Kōngqì bǐ shuǐ qīng.** = *Air is lighter than water.*

qīng 清 (氵 11) [氵 sign + 青 phon **qīng**] ADJECTIVE = clear

qīngchu 清楚 [compound: 清 *clear* + 楚 *clear-cut*] ADJECTIVE = clear (of speech or image)
■ 你的意思很清楚，我明白。**Nǐ de yìsi hěn qīngchu, wǒ míngbai.** = *Your meaning is clear. I understand it.*
■ 老师，黑板上的字我看不清楚。**Lǎoshī, hēibǎn shang de zì wǒ kàn bu qīngchu.** = *Teacher, I can't see the words on the blackboard clearly.*

qíng 晴 (日 12) [日 sign + 青 phon **qīng**] ADJECTIVE = fine, clear (of weather)
■ 今天上午晴，中午以后开始下雨了。**Jīntiān shàngwǔ qíng, zhōngwǔ yǐhòu kāishǐ xià yǔ le.** = *It was fine this morning; it began raining in the afternoon.*
■ 晴天比雨天舒服。**Qíngtiān bǐ yǔtiān shūfu.** = *A fine day is more comfortable than a rainy day.*

qíng 情 (忄 11) [忄 sign + 青 phon **qīng**] NOUN = circumstance

qíngkuàng 情况 [compound: 情 *circumstance* + 况 *situation*] NOUN = situation, circumstance
■ 他生重病住院了，情况很不好。**Tā shēng zhòngbìng zhùyuàn le, qíngkuàng hěn bù hǎo.** = *He's seriously ill and hospitalized; things are very bad with him.*
■ 我不大了解这个国家的情况。**Wǒ bú dà liáojiě zhège guójiā de qíngkuàng.** = *I don't quite know the situation this country is in.*

qǐng 请 (讠 10) [讠 sign + 青 phon **qīng**] Trad 請 VERB = ask, request, invite
■ 学生请老师再说一遍。**Xuésheng qǐng lǎoshī zài shuō yí biàn.** = *The students asked the teacher to repeat it.*
■ 今天晚上我请你吃饭。**Jīntiān wǎnshang wǒ qǐng nǐ chīfàn.** = *I'll invite you to dinner tonight.*
qǐng jià 请假 = ask for leave
qǐng bìngjià 请病假 = ask for sick leave
qǐng shìjià 请事假 = ask for leave of absence
Qǐngwèn, ... 请问, ... = Excuse me, ...
■ 请问，您是上海来的张先生吗？**Qǐngwèn, nín shì Shànghǎi lái de Zhāng xiānsheng ma?** = *Excuse me, aren't you Mr Zhang from Shanghai?*

NOTE: 请 **qǐng** is used to start a polite request, equivalent to "Please...," e.g. ■ 请坐！ **Qǐng zuò!** = *Please sit down!* (→ *Please have a seat.*) ■ 请喝茶！ **Qǐng hē chá!** = *Please have some tea!*

qiū 秋 (禾 9) [禾 sign + 火 symb] NOUN = fall, autumn

qiūtiān 秋天 [modif: 秋 *autumn* + 天 *day*] NOUN = fall, autumn
■ 秋天不冷不热，十分舒服。 **Qiūtiān bù lěng bú rè, shífēn shūfu.** = *Autumn is neither hot nor cold; it's very comfortable.*

qiú 求 (一 7) VERB = request (See 要求 **yāoqiú**.)

qiú 球 (王 11) [王 sign + 求 phon **qiú**] NOUN = ball (只 **zhī**), ball game (场 **chǎng**)
■ 我们每星期六下午打一场球。 **Wǒmen měi Xīngqīliù xiàwǔ dǎ yì chǎng qiú.** = *We have a ball game every Saturday afternoon.*
lánqiú 篮球 = basketball
páiqiú 排球 = volleyball
zúqiú 足球 = football
dǎ qiú 打球 = play basketball or volleyball
tī qiú 踢球 = play football
bǐ qiú 比球 = have a ball match
kàn qiú 看球 = watch a ball game

qǔ 取 (耳 8) VERB = obtain

qǔdé 取得 [compound: 取 *obtain* + 得 *get*] VERB = obtain, achieve
■ 我们去年取得很大成绩。 **Wǒmen qùnián qiǔdé hěn dà chéngjì.** = *We made great achievements last year.*

qù 去 (去 5) VERB = leave for, go to
■ 你什么时候去中国？ **Nǐ shénme shíhou qù Zhōngguó?** = *When are you going to China?*

qùnián 去年 [modif: 去 *what has gone* + 年 *year*] NOUN = last year
■ 她去年才开始学中文。 **Tā qùnián cái kāishǐ xué Zhōngwén.** = *She began learning Chinese only last year.*

quán 全 (人 6) ADJECTIVE = whole, complete
■ 过圣诞节那天，全家人一块儿吃午饭。 **Guò Shèngdànjié nàtiān, quán jiā rén yíkuàir chī wǔfàn.** = *On Christmas Day the whole family has lunch together.*

quánbù 全部 [modif: 全 *whole* + 部 *part*] NOUN = all, without exception
■ 我爸爸全部的时间都放在工作上。 **Wǒ bàba quánbù de shíjiān dōu fàng zai gōngzuò shang.** = *My father devotes all his time to work.*

quántǐ 全体 [modif: 全 *whole* + 体 *body*] NOUN = (of a group of people) all, each and every one
■ 她代表全体学生向老师表示感谢。 **Tā dàibiǎo quántǐ xuésheng xiàng lǎoshī biǎoshì gǎnxiè.** = *On behalf of all the students she expressed gratitude to the teacher.*

què 确 (石 12) ADJECTIVE = certain
Trad 確

quèshí 确实 [compound: 确 *certain* + 实 *substantial*] ADJECTIVE = verified to be true; indeed
■ 这个消息不确实。**Zhè ge xiāoxi bú quèshí.** = *This news is not true.*
■ 你确实错了。**Nǐ quèshí cuò le.** = *You're indeed wrong.*

Q

R

rán 然 (灬 12) CONJUNCTION = however

ránhòu 然后 [idiom] CONJUNCTION = afterwards, and then
xiān... ránhòu... 先… 然后… = first ... and then ...
■ 他早上先跑步，然后吃早饭。**Tā zǎoshang xiān pǎobù, ránhòu chī zǎofàn.** = *Every morning he first jogs and then has breakfast.*

ràng 让 (讠5) Trad 讓 VERB = let, allow
■ 你应该让那辆车先行。**Nǐ yīnggāi ràng nà liàng chē xiān xíng.** = *You should let that vehicle go first.* (→ *You should give way to that vehicle.*)
■ 让我想一想。**Ràng wǒ xiǎng yi xiǎng.** = *Let me think.*

rè 热 (灬 10) [灬 sign + 执 symb] Trad 熱 ADJECTIVE = hot (antonym 冷 **lěng**)
■ 香港的夏天热得很。**Xiānggǎng de xiàtiān rè de hěn.** = *Summer in Hong Kong is very hot.*
■ 我想喝一杯热水，不要冷水。**Wǒ xiǎng hē yì bēi rè shuǐ, bú yào lěng shuǐ.** = *I want to drink a glass of hot water, not cold water.*

rèqíng 热情 [modif: 热 *hot* + 情 *emotion*] ADJECTIVE = enthusiastic, warmhearted
■ 她对人很热情。**Tā duì rén hěn rèqíng.** = *She's warmhearted towards people.*
■ 他常常热情地帮助朋友。**Tā chángcháng rèqíng de bāngzhù péngyou.** = *He often helps his friends enthusiastically.*

rén 人 (人 2) NOUN = human being, person
■ 人和人应该互相帮助。**Rén hé rén yīnggāi hùxiāng bāngzhù.** = *People should help each other.*
■ 你认识这个人吗？ **Nǐ rènshi zhège rén ma?** = *Do you know this person?*
rénmen 人们 = people (in general)
■ 人们都认为发展经济很重要。**Rénmen dōu rènwéi fāzhǎn jīngjì hěn zhòngyào.** = *People think it is important to develop the economy.*
rénkǒu 人口 = population
■ 这个国家有多少人口？ **Zhège guójiā yǒu duōshǎo rénkǒu?** = *What's the population of this country?*

rénmín 人民 [compound: 人 *human being* + 民 *the people*] NOUN = the people (of a state)
■ 人民是国家的主人。**Rénmín shì guójiā de zhǔrén.** = *The people are the masters of a country.*

■ 政府应该为人民服务的。**Zhèngfǔ yīnggāi wèi rénmín fúwù de.** = *The government should serve the people.*

rèn 认 (讠 4) VERB = recognize (Trad 認)

rènshi 认识 [compound: 认 *recognize* + 识 *know*] VERB = know, understand
■ 我不认识这个人。**Wǒ bú rènshi zhège rén.** = *I don't know this person.* (→ *I've never met this person before.*)
■ 你认识这个汉字吗？ **Nǐ rènshi zhège hànzì ma?** = *Do you know this Chinese character?*

rènwéi 认为 VERB = think, consider (normally followed by a clause)
■ 我认为你说得不对。**Wǒ rènwéi nǐ shuō de bú duì.** = *I think what you said is not correct.*

rènzhēn 认真 [v+comp: 认 *consider* + 真 *real*] ADJECTIVE = earnest, conscientious, serious
■ 他是在开玩笑，你不要太认真。**Tā shì zài kāiwánxiào, nǐ bú yào tài rènzhēn.** = *He's joking. Don't take it too seriously.*
■ 她是个认真的学生。**Tā shì ge rènzhēn de xuésheng.** = *She's a conscientious student.*

rèn 任 (亻 6) CONJUNCTION = no matter

rènhé 任何 [compound: 任 *no matter* + 何 *what*] PRONOUN = any, whatever
■ 你任何时候都可以来找我。**Nǐ rènhé shíhou dōu kěyǐ lái zhǎo wǒ.** = *You can come to see me at any time.*

rènhé rén 任何人 = anyone
■ 任何人都不可以那样做。**Rènhé rén dōu bù kěyǐ nàyàng zuò.** = *No one is allowed to do that.*

rènhé shì 任何事 = any matter, anything, everything
■ 他做任何事都挺认真。**Tā zuò rènhé shì dōu tǐng rènzhēn.** = *He does everything conscientiously.*

rì 日 (日 4) NOUN = date, day
■ 三月二十四日 **Sānyuè èrshísì rì** = *the twenty-fourth of March*
■ 九月一日 **Jiǔyuè yírì** = *the first of September*

NOTE: See note on 号 **hào**.

Rìběn 日本 NOUN = Japan
■ 日本在中国东边。**Rìběn zài Zhōngguó dōngbian.** = *Japan lies to the east of China.*
■ 你去过日本吗？ **Nǐ qùguo Rìběn ma?** = *Have you been to Japan?*

Rìwén 日文 [modif: 日 *Japanese* + 文 *writing*] NOUN = the Japanese language (especially Japanese writing)

Rìyǔ 日语 [modif: 日 *Japan* + 语 *speech*] NOUN = the Japanese language
■ 日语和汉语很不一样。**Rìyǔ hé Hànyǔ hěn bù yíyàng.** = *Japanese is very different from Chinese.*
■ 你们学校教日语吗？ **Nǐmen xuéxiào jiāo Rìyǔ ma?** = *Does your school teach Japanese?*

rìzi 日子 [suffix: 日 *day* + 子 nominal suffix] NOUN
1 = day, date
■ 今天这个日子对我来说特别重要。**Jīntiān zhège rìzi duì wǒ lái shuō tèbié zhòngyào.** = *Today is particularly important to me.*
■ 今天是什么日子？为什么街上这么多人？ **Jīntiān shì shénme rìzi? Wèi shénme jiēshang zhème duō rén?** = *What day is today? Why are there so many people in the street?*
■ 这些日子你在忙什么？ **Zhè xiē rìzi nǐ zài máng shénme?** = *What are you busy with these days?*
2 = life
■ 我们家的日子比过去好多了。**Wǒmen jiā de rìzi bǐ guòqù hǎo duō le.** = *The life of my family is much better than before.* (→ *My family is better off now.*)
■ 我只想安安静静地过日子。**Wǒ zhǐ xiǎng ānānjìngjìng de guò rìzi.** = *I only want to live a quiet and peaceful life.*

róng 容 (宀 10) [宀 sign + 谷 symb] VERB = tolerate

róngyì 容易 [compound: 容 *tolerant* + 易 *easy*] ADJECTIVE = easy, not difficult (antonym 难 **nán**)
■ 这件事很容易做。**Zhè jiàn shì hěn róngyì zuò.** = *This is easy to do.*
■ 这么容易的问题，你都不会回答？ **Zhème róngyì de wèntí, nǐ dōu bú huì huídá?** = *You even can't answer such an easy question?*

ròu 肉 (冂 6) NOUN = flesh, meat
■ 肉比鱼便宜。**Ròu bǐ yú piányi.** = *Pork is cheaper than fish.*
zhūròu 猪肉 = pork
níuròu 牛肉 = beef
jīyòu 鸡肉 = chicken meat
yúyòu 鱼肉 = fish meat
yángròu 羊肉 = mutton

NOTE: The most popular meat in China is pork. Unspecified, 肉 **ròu** often refers to "pork."

rú 如 (女 6) CONJUNCTION = if

rúguǒ 如果 CONJUNCTION = if
■ 如果明天下雨，我们就不去海边游泳。**Rúguǒ míngtiān xiàyǔ, wǒmen jìu bú qù hǎibiān yǒuyóng.** = *If it rains tomorrow, we won't go to the seaside to swim.*

S

sài 赛 (贝 14) Trad 賽 VERB = compete (See 比赛 **bǐsài**.)

sān 三 (一 3) NUMERAL = three
■ 十三 **shísān** = *thirteen*
■ 三十 **sānshí** = *thirty*

sàn 散 (攵 12)

sànbù 散步 [modif: 散 *random* + 步 *step*] VERB = take a short leisurely walk, stroll
■ 这位老人常常在公园散步。**Zhè wèi lǎorén chángcháng zài gōngyuán**

li sànbù. = *This old man often takes a walk in the park.*

sè 色 (色 6) NOUN = color (See 颜色 **yánsè.**)

shān 山 (山 3) NOUN = mountain, hill (座 **zuò**)

■ 这座山真高啊！ **Zhè zuò shān zhēn gāo a!** = *How high this mountain is!*

páshān 爬山 = mountain-climbing, mountaineering

■ 星期六我们去爬山吧！ **Xīngqīliù wǒmen qù páshān ba!** = *Let's go mountain-climbing this Saturday.*

shānshuǐ 山水 = landscape

■ 新西兰的山水很好看。**Xīngxīlán de shānshuǐ hěn hǎokàn.** = *The landscape of New Zealand is beautiful.*

yóu-shān-wán-shuǐ 游山玩水 = go sightseeing

■ 他有钱，又有时间，所以常常出国游山玩水。**Tā yǒu qián, yòu yǒu shíjiān, suóyǐ chángcháng chūguó yóu-shān-wán-shuǐ.** = *He's rich and he's got the time, so he often goes sightseeing overseas.*

shāng 商 (亠 11) NOUN = commerce

shāngdiàn 商店 NOUN = shop, store (家 **jiā**)

■ 这家商店是卖什么的？ **Zhè jiā shāngdiàn shì mài shénme de?** = *What does this store sell?*

■ 我常去那家商店买东西。**Wǒ cháng qù nà jiā shāngdiàn mǎi dōngxi.** = *I often shop in that store.*

shāngrén 商人 = businessman

shāngchǎng 商场 = shopping mall

shāngyè 商业 = commerce, business

shàng 上 (上 3)

1 PREPOSITION = on top of, on, above (antonym 下 **xià**)

■ 山上有一座白房子。**Shānshang yǒu yí zuò bái fángzi.** = *There's a white house on the hill.*

shànglai 上来 = come up

■ 楼上有空房间，快上来吧！ **Lóushang yǒu kòng fángjiān, kuài shànglai ba!** = *There's a vacant room upstairs, come on up!*

shàngqu 上去 = go up

■ 他们在楼上等你。快上去吧！ **Tāmen zài lóushang děng nǐ, kuài shàngqu ba!** = *They're waiting for you upstairs, go on up!*

2 VERB = attend (a school); enter a vehicle

shàngxué 上学 = go to school

■ 你弟弟上学了吗？ **Nǐ dìdi shàngxué le ma?** = *Has your younger brother started schooling?*

■ 我骑自行车上学。**Wǒ qí zìxíngchē shàngxué.** = *I go to school by bike.*

shàngkè 上课 = attend class, have class

■ 明天放假，不上课。**Míngtiān fàngjià, bú shàngkè.** = *Tomorrow's a holiday. There're no classes.*

shàngbān 上班 = go to work

■ 我母亲每天九点上班，五点下班。**Wǒ mǔqīn měitiān jiǔ diǎn shàngbān, wǔ diǎn xiàbān.** = *Every day my mother goes to work at nine and finishes at five.*

shàng fēijī 上飞机 = get on a plane

shàng chuán 上船 = board a ship

shàng chē 上车 = get in/on a vehicle
■ 火车来了，准备上车吧！ **Huǒchē lái le, zhǔnbèi shàng chē ba!** = *The train's coming. Let's get ready for boarding.*

Shànghǎi 上海 NOUN = Shanghai (the biggest city in China)

shàngbian 上边 [modif: 上 *top, upper* + 边 *side*] NOUN = above, high up (antonym 下边 **xiàbiān**)
■ 从那座大楼的上边可以看见飞机场。 **Cóng nà zuò dàlóu de shàngbian kěyǐ kànjiàn fēijīchǎng.** = *From the top of that high building, one can see the airport.*

S

shàngwǔ 上午 [modif: 上 *upper half* + 午 *noon*] NOUN = morning (usually from 8 a.m. to 12 noon) (antonym 下午 **xiàwǔ**)
■ 我们上午上三节课。 **Wǒmen shàngwǔ shàng sān jié kè.** = *We have three classes in the morning.*

NOTE: 上午 **shàngwǔ** does not mean the whole of "morning." It denotes the part of morning from about eight or nine o'clock to noon. The period before eight or nine o'clock is 早晨 **zǎochéng** or 早上 **zǎoshang**.

shāo 烧 (火 10) [火 sign + 尧 symb] Trad 燒 VERB = burn (See 发烧 **fāshāo**.)

shǎo 少 (小 4)
1 ADJECTIVE = small amount, few, little (antonym 多 **duō**)
■ 这个地方人很少。 **Zhège dìfang rén hěn shǎo.** = *This place has very few people.* (→ *This place is sparsely populated.*)
2 ADJECTIVE = not often, seldom
■ 我们虽然在同一个学校，但是很少见面。 **Wǒmen suírán zài tóng yī ge xuéxiào, dànshì hěn shǎo jiànmiàn.** = *Although we're in the same school, we seldom see each other.*
3 VERB = *be short, be missing*
■ 原来我有一百元，现在怎么少了二十元？ **Yuánlái wǒ yǒu yì bǎi yuán, xiànzài zénme shǎole èrshí yuán?** = *I originally had one hundred dollars. How is it that I have twenty dollars less now?*

shào 绍 (纟 8) VERB = connect (See 介绍 **jièshào**.)

shè 设 (讠 6) Trad 設 VERB = equip (See 建设 **jiànshè**.)

shè 社 (礻 7) [礻 sign + 土 sign] NOUN = association

shèhuì 社会 [compound: 社 *god of the earth* + 会 *gathering*] NOUN = society
■ 我们每个人都应该关心社会。 **Wǒmen měi ge rén dōu yīnggāi guānxīn shèhuì.** = *Every one of us should have concern for society.*

shè 舍 (人 8) NOUN = hut, shed (See 宿舍 **sùshè**.)

shēn 身 (身 7)

shēntǐ 身体 [compound: 身 *body* + 体 *physical*] NOUN = human body, health
■ 我爸爸年纪大了，但是身体还很好。**Wǒ bàba niánjì dà le, dànshì shēntǐ hái hěn hǎo.** = *My father's getting old, but is still in good health.*
■ 你要注意身体。**Nǐ yào zhùyì shēntǐ.** = *You should pay attention to your health.*

NOTE: Although its original meaning is "the body," 身体 **shēntǐ** is often used in colloquial Chinese to mean "health." Friends often ask about each other's health as greetings, e.g.
■ 你身体好吗？ **Nǐ shēntǐ hǎo ma?** = *How's your health? How're you?*
■ 你最近身体怎么样？ **Nǐ zuìjìn shēntǐ zěnmeyàng?** = *How's your health been recently?*

shēn 深 (氵 11) [氵 sign + symb] ADJECTIVE
1 = deep (antonym 浅 **qiǎn**)
■ 这条河深吗？ **Zhè tiáo hé shēn ma?** = *Is this river deep?*
2 = difficult to understand, profound (antonym 浅 **qiǎn**)
■ 这本书太深了，我看不懂。**Zhè běn shū tài shēn le, wǒ kàn bu dǒng.** = *This book is too difficult. I can't understand it.*

shén 什 (亻 4) PRONOUN = what

shénme 什么 [idiom] PRONOUN = what
■ 什么是语法？ **Shénme shì yǔfǎ?** = *What is grammar?*
■ 你要什么？ **Nǐ yào shénme?** = *What do you want?*
■ 你要什么菜？ **Nǐ yào shénme cài?** = *What dishes do you want? (→ What would you like to order?)*

shén 神 (礻 9) [礻 sign + 申 phon **shēn**] NOUN = god (See 精神 **jīngshén**.)

shēng 生 (丿 5) VERB = give birth to, grow

shēngchǎn 生产 [compound: 生 *grow* + 产 *produce*] VERB = produce, manufacture
■ 这家工厂去年生产一万辆汽车。**Zhè jiā gōngchǎng qùnián shēngchǎn yí wàn liàng qìchē.** = *This factory manufactured 10,000 automobiles last year.*

shēngcí 生词 [modif: 生 *unfamiliar* + 词 *word*] NOUN = new word (in a language lesson)
■ 这个句子里有一个生词，我不认识，也不会念。**Zhège jùzi lǐ yǒu yí ge shēngcí, wǒ bú rènshi, yě bú huì niàn.** = *There's a new word in the sentence. I don't know it, nor do I know how to say it.*
■ 这些生词你都记住了吗？ **Zhèxie shēngcí nǐ dōu jìzhu le ma?** = *Have you committed these new words to memory?*
jì shēngcí 记生词 = memorize new words

shēnghuó 生活 [compound: 生 *living* + 活 *alive*]

S

1 NOUN = life
■ 这位老人的生活很困难。**Zhè wèi lǎorén de shēnghuó hěn kùnnan.** = *This old man's life is difficult.*
■ 请您介绍一下中国大学生的生活。**Qǐng nín jièshào yíxià Zhōngguó dàxuéshēng de shēnghuó.** = *Please tell us something about the life of Chinese university students.*
2 VERB = live, lead (a life)
■ 我小时候生活得很愉快。**Wǒ xiǎo shíhou shēnghuó de hěn yúkuài.** = *I lived a happy life in childhood.* (→ *I had a happy childhood.*)

S

shēngrì 生日 [modif: 生 *birth* + 日 *day*] NOUN = birthday
■ 你的生日是哪一天？ **Nǐ de shēngrì shì nǎ yì tiān?** = *Which date is your birthday?* (→ *When is your birthday?*)
■ 啊呀！我忘了今天是我妻子的生日！ **Āyā! Wǒ wàngle jīntiān shì wǒ qīzi de shēngrì!** = *Oh, no! I forgot it's my wife's birthday today.*
■ 祝你生日快乐！ **Zhù nǐ shēngrì kuàilè!** = *I wish you a happy birthday.*
guò shēngrì 过生日 = celebrate a birthday
■ 你今年打算怎么过生日？ **Nǐ jīnnián dǎsuàn zěnme guò shēngrì?** = *How do you intend to celebrate your birthday this year?*

shēng 声 (士 7) Trad 聲 NOUN = sound, voice
■ 机器声很大，我听不清你说什么。**Jīqì shēng hěn dà, wǒ tīng bu qīng nǐ shuō shénme.** = *The noise from the machine is too loud; I can't hear what you're saying.*

shēngdiào 声调 [modif: 声 *voice* + 调 *tone*] NOUN = tone of a Chinese word
■ 汉语的声调确实比较难学。**Hànyǔ de shēngdiào quèshí bǐjiào nánxué.** = *The tones of Chinese are really rather difficult to learn.*
■ "这个字读哪个声调？" "这个字读第二声。" **"Zhège zì dú nǎ ge shēngdiào?" "Zhège zì dú dì-èr shēng."** = *"Which tone should this character be read with? (→ Which tone does this character have?)" "This character is read with the second tone."*

shēngyīn 声音 [compound: 声 *voice* + 音 *sound*] NOUN = voice, sound
■ 她的声音很好听。**Tā de shēngyīn hěn hǎotīng.** = *Her voice is pleasant.*
■ 我听见有人在楼下说话的声音。**Wǒ tīngjiàn yǒurén zài lóuxià shuōhuà de shēngyīn.** = *I heard the sounds of conversation downstairs.*

shěng 省 (小 9) NOUN = province
■ 中国有多少个省？ **Zhōngguó yǒu duōshǎo ge shěng?** = *How many provinces are there in China?*

shèng 胜 (月 9) [月 symb + 生 phon shēng] Trad 勝 VERB = triumph

shènglì 胜利 [compound: 胜 *triumph* + 利 *gain benefit*]
1 VERB = win victory
■ 那一场球赛，哪个队赢了？ **Nǎ yì chǎng qiúsài, nǎ ge duì yíng le?** = *Which team won that ball match?*

2 NOUN = victory
■ 我们的胜利来得不容易。**Wǒmen de shènglì lái de bù róngyì.** = *Our victory was hard-won.*

shèng 剩 (刂 12) [乘 phon **chéng** + 刂 sign] VERB = be left over, have as surplus
■ 我原来有五百块钱，用了四百块，还剩一百块。**Wǒ yuánlái yǒu wǔ bǎi kuài qián, yòngle sìbǎi kuài, hái shèng yìbǎi kuài.** = *I originally had five hundred dollars; I've used four hundred dollars and now have one hundred dollars left.*

shī 师 (丨 6) Trad 師 NOUN = master, teacher

shīfu 师傅 [compound: 师 *teacher* + 傅 *tutor*] NOUN = master worker (位 **wèi**)
■ 这位师傅技术很高。**Zhè wèi shīfu jìshù hěn gāo.** = *This master worker is highly skilled.*
■ 这个机器坏了，要请一位师傅来看看。**Zhège jīqì huài le, yào qǐng yí wèi shīfu lai kànkan.** = *This machine is not working properly. We need to ask a master worker to come and have a look.*

NOTE: 师傅 **shīfu** is often used as a polite form of address, especially to a worker. For example, you can address an electrician or mechanic as 师傅 **shīfu** or, if his family name is 李 **Lǐ**, 李师傅 **Lǐ shīfu**.

shí 十 (十 2) NUMERAL = ten
■ 十五 **shíwǔ** = *fifteen*
■ 五十 **wǔshí** = *fifty*

shífēn 十分 [modif: 十 *ten* + 分 *point*] ADVERB = one hundred percent, totally, fully
■ 我十分满意。**Wǒ shífēn mǎnyì.** = *I'm completely satisfied.*

shí 时 (日 7) [日 sign + 寸 symb] Trad 時 NOUN = time

shíhou 时候 [compound: 时 *time* + 候 *a certain point in time*] NOUN = a certain point in time, (the time) when
■ 飞机什么时候开？ **Fēijī shénme shíhou kāi?** = *When will the plane depart?*
■ 他来的时候，我正在打电话。**Tā lái de shíhou, wǒ zhèngzài dǎ diànhuà.** = *I was on the phone when he came.*

shíjiān 时间 [compound: 时 *time* + 间 *moment*] NOUN = a period of time
■ 时间不够，我没做完那道练习。**Shíjiān bú gòu, wǒ méi zuòwán nà dào liànxí.** = *As there wasn't enough time, I did not finish that exercise.*
■ 我没有时间写信。**Wǒ méiyǒu shíjiān xiě xìn.** = *I don't have time to write letters.*

shí 食 (食 9)

shítáng 食堂 [modif: 食 *food* + 堂 *hall*] NOUN = dining hall
■ 吃饭的时候，食堂里人很多。**Chīfàn de shíhou, shítáng li rén hěn**

S

duō. = *At mealtimes, there're many people in the dining hall.*

shí 识 (讠7) [讠 sign + 只 phon **zhī**] Trad **識** NOUN = understanding (See 认识 **rènshi**, 知识 **zhīshi**.)

shí 实 (宀 8) Trad **實** NOUN = fruit

shíjiàn 实践 [compound: 实 *fruit, fruition* + 践 *implement*]
1 VERB = put into practice, apply
■ 懂了这个道理，就要实践。 **Dǒngle zhège dàolǐ, jiù yào shíjiàn.** = *After you've understood this principle, you should put it into practice.*
2 NOUN = practice
■ 实践出真知。 **Shíjiàn chū zhēnzhī.** = *Practice leads to genuine knowledge.*

shíxiàn 实现 [compound: 实 *fruit, fruition* + 现 *materialize*] VERB = materialize, realize
■ 我一定要实现这个计划。 **Wǒ yídìng yào shíxiàn zhège jìhuà.** = *I must realize this plan.*

shí 拾 (扌9) [扌 sign + 合 symb] VERB = pick up (from the ground) (See 收拾 **shōushi**.)

shǐ 史 (口 5) NOUN = history (See 历史 **lìshǐ**.)

shǐ 使 (亻8) VERB = use, cause

shǐyòng 使用 [compound: 使 *use* + 用 *use*] VERB = use, apply
■ 你会使用这个电脑吗？ **Nǐ huì shǐyòng zhège diànnǎo ma?** = *Do you know how to use this computer?*

shǐ 始 (女 8) See 开始 **kāishǐ**.

shì 世 (一 4)

shìjiè 世界 [compound: 世 *world* + 界 *boundary*] NOUN = the world
■ 世界每天都在变。 **Shìjiè měi tiān dōu zài biàn.** = *The world is changing every day.*
■ 世界上的事情都很复杂。 **Shìjiè shang de shìqing dōu hěn fùzá.** = *Everything in the world is complicated.*
quán shìjiè 全世界 = the whole world

shì 示 (示 5) VERB = show, indicate (See 表示 **biǎoshì**.)

shì 市 (亠 5) NOUN = municipality, city; market
■ 下午我要到市里去。 **Xiàwǔ wǒ yào dào shìli qù.** = *I'm going to the city this afternoon.*
shìchǎng 市场 = marketplace, market

shì 试 (讠8) [讠 symb + 式 phon **shì**] Trad **試** VERB = test, try
■ 你的办法不行，试试我的办法。 **Nǐ de bànfǎ bùxíng, shìshi wǒ de bànfǎ.** = *Your method didn't work. Try my method.*
shìshi 试试 = have a try
shìyishì 试一试 = have a try
shìyixià 试一下 = have a try

S

shì 视 (礻 8) [礻 symb] + 见 sign]
Trad **視** VERB = see (See 电视 **diànshì**.)

shì 事 (一 8) NOUN = matter, affair

shìqing 事情 [compound: 事 *affair, matter* + 情 *emotion*] NOUN = affair, matter (件 **jiàn**)
■ 这件事情很重要，一定要办好。**Zhè jiàn shìqing hěn zhòngyào, yídìng yào bànhǎo.** = *This is an important matter and must be done well.*
■ 大家都很关心这件事情。**Dàjiā dōu hěn guānxīn zhè jiàn shìqing.** = *Everybody is concerned over this matter.*

NOTE: In many cases, as in the two examples above, 事情 **shìqing** may be replaced by 事 **shì**. 事 **shì** or 事情 **shìqing** is a noun that can be applied widely, denoting any affair, matter or business to be done or considered. More examples:
■ 今天晚上我没有事做。**Jīntiān wǎnshang wǒ méiyǒu shì zuò.** = *I've nothing to do this evening.*
■ 我跟你说一件事情。**Wǒ gēn nǐ shuō yí jiàn shì.** = *I want to tell you something.*
■ 他们在路上出事了。**Tāmen zài lùshang chūshì le.** = *They had an accident on the way.*

shì 是 (日 9) VERB = be; yes
■ 这是小王的房间。**Zhè shì Xiǎo Wáng de fángjiān.** = *This is Xiao Wang's room.*
■ "你是李老师吗？" "是，我是李老师。" **"Nǐ shì Lí lǎoshí ma?" "Shì, wǒ shì Lǐ lǎoshi."** = *"Are you Teacher Li?" "Yes, I am."*

shì 室 (宀 9) [宀 sign + 至 symb] NOUN = room (See 办公室 **bàngōngshì**, 教室 **jiàoshì**.)

shì 适 (辶 9) Trad **適** ADJECTIVE = suitable (See 合适 **héshì**.)

shōu 收 (攵 6) [symb + 攵 sign] VERB = receive, accept
shōudào 收到 = receive
■ 我昨天收到一封信。**Wǒ zuótiān shōudào yì fēng xìn.** = *I received a letter yesterday.*
shōuxia 收下 = accept
■ 请你收下这件小礼物。**Qǐng nǐ shōuxià zhè jiàn xiǎo lǐwù.** = *Please accept this small gift.*

shōushi 收拾 [compound: 收 *get* + 拾 *pick up*] VERB = put in order, tidy up
■ 桌子上的书和报纸很多，我要收拾一下。**Zhuōzi shang de shū he bàozhǐ hěn duō, wǒ yào shōushi yíxià.** = *There are many books and newspapers on the table. I'll tidy it up.*

shǒu 手 (手 4) NOUN = hand (只 **zhī**, 双 **shuāng**)
■ 我的手不很干净，要洗一下才能吃饭。**Wǒ de shǒu bù hěn gānjìng, yào xǐ yíxià cái néng chīfàn.** = *My hands aren't very clean. I have to wash them before eating my meal.*
zuǒshǒu 左手 = the left hand
yòushǒu 右手 = the right hand

S

shǒu li 手里 = in the hand
■ 他手里拿着一本书。**Tā shǒu li názhe yì běn shū.** = *He's holding a book in his hand.*

shǒubiǎo 手表 [modif: 手*hand* + 表 *watch*] NOUN = wrist watch (块 **kuài**)
■ 我的手表慢了，你的手表几点？ **Wǒ de shǒubiǎo màn le, nǐ de shǒubiǎo jǐ diǎn?** = *My watch is slow. What time is it by your watch?*

> NOTE: In everyday usage, 手表 **shǒubiǎo** is often shortened to 表 **biǎo**, for example:
> ■ 我的表慢了，你的表几点？ **Wǒ de biǎo màn le, nǐ de biǎo jǐ diǎn?** = *My watch is slow. What time is it by your watch?*

S

shǒu 首 (八 9) MEASURE WORD = (for songs and poems)
■ 他唱了一首中文歌。**Tā chàngle yì shǒu Zhōngwén gē.** = *He sang a Chinese song.*

shǒudū 首都 [modif: 首 *the head, first* + 都 *metropolis*] NOUN = capital city
■ 中国的首都是北京。**Zhōngguó de shǒudū shì Běijīng.** = *China's capital city is Beijing.*

shū 书 (丨 4) Trad 書 NOUN = book (本 **běn**)
■ 这本书很有意思，你看过没有？ **Zhè běn shū hěn yǒu yìsi, nǐ kànguo méiyǒu?** = *This book is very interesting. Have you read it?*
■ 她常常去图书馆借书。**Tā chángcháng qù túshūguǎn jiè shū.** = *She often goes to the library to borrow books.*

kànshū 看书 = read, do reading
■ 我喜欢看书。**Wǒ xǐhuan kànshū.** = *I like reading.*

shū 舒 (人 12) VERB = relax

shūfu 舒服 [compound: 舒*relax* + 服 *conceding*] ADJECTIVE = comfortable
■ 这把椅子很舒服，你坐下去就不想起来了。**Zhè bǎ yǐzi hěn shūfu, nǐ zuò xiàqu jiù bù xiǎng qǐlai le.** = *This chair is very comfortable. Sit on it and you don't want to get up.*

bù shūfu 不舒服 = (of a person) not very well, be under the weather
■ 我今天不舒服，想早点回家。**Wǒ jīntiān bù shūfu, xiǎng zǎo diǎnr huí jiā.** = *I'm unwell today. I want to go home early.*

shū 输 (车 13) Trad 輸 VERB = lose (a game, a bet) (antonym 赢 **yíng**)
■ 上回我们队输了，这回一定要赢！ **Shànghuí wǒmen duì shū le, zhèhuí yídìng yào yíng!** = *Our team lost the game the last time; this time we must win!*

shú 熟 (灬 15) [孰 phon **shū** + 灬 sign] ADJECTIVE = ripe, cooked; familiar with, know well
■ 苹果还没有熟，很酸。**Píngguǒ hái méiyǒu shú, hěn suān.** = *The apples are not yet ripe. They're sour.*
■ 肉熟了就可以吃饭。**Ròu shúle jiù kěyǐ chīfàn.** = *When the meat is done we can have our meal.*

■ 这个城市我不熟。**Zhège chéngshì wǒ bù shú.** = *I don't know this city very well.*

shǔ 数 (攵 13) Trad 數 VERB = count
■ 我来数一下，这里有多少人，一、二、三、… 。**Wǒ lái shǔ yíxia, zhèlǐ yǒu duōshǎo rén, yī, èr, sān, ...** = *Let me count to see how many people there are here. One, two, three, ...*

shù 术 (木 5) Trad 術 NOUN = craft, skill (See 技术 **jìshù**, 艺术 **yìshù**.)

shù 束 (束 7) NOUN = knot (See 结束 **jiéshù**.)

shù 树 (木 9) [木 sign + 对 symb] Trad 樹 NOUN = tree (棵 **kē**)
■ 这棵树又高又大，树下很凉快。**Zhè kē shù yòu gāo yòu dà, shùxia hěn liángkuài.** = *This tree is big and tall; it's cool under it.*
■ 我爸爸在花园里种了两棵树。**Wǒ bàba zài huāyuán li zhòngle liǎng kē shù.** = *My father planted two trees in the garden.*

shùxué 数学 [modif: 数 *number* + 学 *knowledge, study of*] NOUN = mathematics
■ 我看，数学和语文是学校里最重要的两门课。**Wǒ kàn, shùxué hé yǔwén shì xuéxiào li zuì zhòngyào de liǎng mén kè.** = *In my view, mathematics and language are the two most important subjects in school.*
■ 我们明天考数学。**Wǒmen míngtiān kǎo shùxué.** = *We're having a mathematics examination tomorrow.*

shuāng 双 (又 4) Trad 雙 MEASURE WORD = a pair of (shoes, chopsticks, etc.)
■ 一双鞋 **yì shuāng xié** = *a pair of shoes*
■ 两双筷子 **liǎng shuāng kuàizi** = *two pairs of chopsticks*

shuí, shéi 谁 (讠 10) Trad 誰 PRONOUN = who, whom
■ 谁是你们的中文老师？ **Shuí shì nǐmen de Zhōngwén lǎoshī?** = *Who's your Chinese teacher?*
■ 你在找谁？ **Nǐ zài zhǎo shéi?** = *For whom are you looking?*

shuǐ 水 (水 4) NOUN = water
■ 这里的水能喝吗？ **Zhèli de shuǐ néng hē ma?** = *Can the water here be drunk? (→ Is the water here potable?)*
■ 我口渴，我要喝水。**Wǒ kǒu kě, wǒ yào hē shuǐ.** = *I'm thirsty. I want to drink some water.*
zìláishuǐ 自来水 = running water, tap water
kāishuǐ 开水 = boiled water

shuǐguǒ 水果 [modif: 水 *water* + 果 *fruit*] NOUN = fruit
■ 水果人人都爱吃。**Shuǐguǒ rénrén dōu ài chī.** = *Everybody loves to eat fruit.*
■ 我要去商店买一些水果。**Wǒ yào qù shāngdiàn mǎi yìxiē shuǐguǒ.** = *I'm going to the store to buy some fruit.*
shuǐguǒ diàn 水果店 = fruit shop, fruiterer
shuǐguǒ dāo 水果刀 = penknife

shuǐpíng 水平 NOUN

1 = level, standard

■ 政府努力提高人民的生活水平。**Zhèngfǔ nǔlì tígāo rénmín de shēnghuó shuǐpíng.** = *The government is working hard to raise the people's living standard.*

2 = (language) proficiency

■ 我的中文水平不大高，请您多多帮助。**Wǒ de Zhōngwén shuǐpíng bú da gāo, qǐng nín duōduō bāngzhù.** = *My proficiency in Chinese is not very high. Please help me.*

tígāo shuǐpíng 提高水平 = raise the standard

shēnghuó shuǐpíng 生活水平 = living standard

wénhuà shuǐpíng 文化水平 = cultural level, educational experience

■ 这位老人文化水平不高，但是说的话总是很有道理。**Zhè wèi lǎorén wénhuà shuǐpíng bù gāo, dànshì shuō de huà zǒngshì hěn yǒu dàolǐ.** = *This old person is not very well educated, but what he/she says always has a lot of truth in it.*

shuì 睡 (目 13) [目 sign + 垂 phon **chuí**] VERB = sleep

■ 爸爸睡了，你明天再跟他说吧。**Bàba shuì le, nǐ míngtiān zài gēn tā shuō ba.** = *Daddy's sleeping. Talk to him tomorrow.*

shuìzháo 睡着 = fall asleep

■ 昨天我十点就睡了，到十二点钟才睡着。**Zuótiān wǒ shí diǎnzhōng jiù shuì le, dào shí'èr diǎnzhōng cái shuìzháo.** = *I went to bed at ten yesterday and didn't fall asleep until twelve o'clock.*

shuìyī 睡衣 = pajamas

shuìjiào 睡觉 [compound: 睡 *sleep* + 觉 (in this context) *sleep*] VERB = sleep, go to bed

■ "你每天什么时候睡觉?" "十点钟以后" **"Nǐ měi tiān shénme shíhou shuìjiào?" "Shí diǎnzhōng yǐhòu."** = *"When do you go to bed every day?" "After ten o'clock."*

> NOTE: 睡 **shuì** and 睡觉 **shuìjiào** are often interchangeable. Also note that 觉 is pronounced **jiào** in 睡觉 **shuìjiào**, but **jué** in 觉得 **juéde**.

shuō 说 (讠 9) [讠 sign + 兑 symb] Trad **說** VERB = say, speak

■ 他说今天晚上没有时间。**Tā shuō jīntiān wǎnshang méiyǒu shíjiān.** = *He said he did not have time this evening.*

shuōmíng 说明 [v+comp: 说 *say* + 明 *clear*]

1 VERB = explain

■ 我来说明一下，为什么我最近有时候迟到。**Wǒ lái shuōmíng yíxià, wèi shénme wǒ zuìjìn yǒu shíhou chídào.** = *Let me explain why recently I've been sometimes late.*

2 VERB = prove, show

■ 你考试取得了好成绩，这说明你学习很努力。**Nǐ kǎoshì qǔdéle hǎo chéngjì, zhè shuōmíng nǐ xuéxí hěn nǔlì.** = *You got a good grade at the examination. This shows you studied very hard.*

3 NOUN = explanation, manual

■ 这个电脑怎么用，我要看一下说明。**Zhège diànnǎo zěnme yòng, wǒ yào kàn yíxià shuōmíng.** = *As to how to use this computer, I need to read the manual.*

sī 思 (心 9) [田 symb + 心 sign] VERB
= think

sīxiǎng 思想 [compound: 思 *think* + 想 *think*] NOUN = thought, thinking
■ 人们的思想是什么决定的? **Rénmen de sīxiǎng shì shénme juédìng de?** = *What determines people's thought?*

sǐ 死 (歹 6) VERB = die (antonym 活 **huó**)
■ 我家的狗昨天死了。**Wǒ jiā de gǒu zuótiān sǐ le.** = *Our family dog died yesterday.*

NOTE: It would be rude to use 死 **sǐ** when someone you respect dies. The expression to use is 去世 **qùshì** = *leave the world*, e.g.
■ 我祖父上个月去世了。**Wǒ zǔfù shàng ge yuè qùshì le.** = *My grandfather passed away last month.*

sì 四 (口 5) NUMERAL = four
■ 四十四 **sìshí sì** = *forty-four*
■ 四海为家 **sì hǎi wéi jiā** = *Make the four seas one's home* (→ *Make one's home wherever one is.*)

sòng 送 (辶 9) VERB
1 = give as a gift
■ 去年圣诞节，爸爸送给他一辆自行车。**Qùnián shèngdànjié, bàba sòng gei tā yí liàng zìxíngchē.** = *Last Christmas his father gave him a bike.*
2 = deliver
■ 我们可以把洗衣机送到你家。**Wǒmen kěyǐ bǎ xǐyījī sòngdào nǐ jiā.** = *We can deliver the washing machine to your home.*

sòu 嗽 (口 14) [口 sign + symb] VERB
= cough up (See 咳嗽 **kēsou**.)

sù 诉 (讠 7) [讠 sign + 斥 symb]
Trad 訴 VERB = inform (See 告诉 **gàosu**.)

sù 宿 (宀 11) [宀 sign + 佰 symb] VERB
= stay overnight

sùshè 宿舍 [modif: 宿 *stay overnight* + 舍 *lodge*] NOUN = hostel, dormitory
■ 我的书忘在宿舍里了! **Wǒ de shū wàng zài sùshè li le.** = *I've left my book in the dormitory.*
xuéshēng sùshè 学生宿舍 = students' hostel (dormitory).

suān 酸 (酉 14) [酉 sign + symb]
ADJECTIVE = sour
■ 这种酒太酸了一点儿。**Zhè zhǒng jiǔ tài suān le yìdiǎnr.** = *This wine is a bit too sour.*
■ 我不喜欢吃酸的东西。**Wǒ bù xǐhuan chī suān de dōngxi.** = *I don't like to eat sour food.*

suàn 算 (竹 14) VERB = calculate
■ 我算一下这个星期花了多少钱。**Wǒ suàn yíxia zhège xīngqī huāle duōshǎo qián.** = *Let me calculate how much money I've spent this week.*

suī 虽 (口 9) Trad 雖 CONJUNCTION = although

suīrán 虽然 [suffix: 虽 *although* + 然 adjectival suffix] CONJUNCTION = although, though

S

■ 虽然我们球赛输了，但是大家都玩得很高兴。**Suīrán wǒmen qiúsài shū le, dànshì dàjiā dōu wán de hěn gāoxìng.** = *Although we lost the ball game, everybody had a good time.*

NOTE: 虽然 **suīrán** is often used in conjunction with 但是 **dànshì**: 虽然 ...，但是 ....。**suīrán..., dànshì... .** = *Although..., ...*

suì 岁 (山 6) Trad 歲 MEASURE WORD = year (of age)

■ 我小弟弟今年八岁。**Wǒ xiǎodìdi jīnnián bā suì.** = *My youngest brother is eight years old this year.*

NOTE: See note on 年纪 **niánjì**.

suǒ 所 (斤 8) CONJUNCTION = which

suǒyǐ 所以 [idiom] CONJUNCTION = therefore, so

■ 我上星期病了，所以没有来上班。**Wǒ shàng xīngqī bìng le, suǒyǐ méiyǒu lái shàngbān.** = *I was sick last week, therefore I did not come to work.*

suǒyǒu 所有 [idiom] ADJECTIVE = all

■ 所有的朋友都反对他的计划。**Suǒyǒu de péngyou dōu fǎnduì tā de jìhuà.** = *All his friends are opposed to his plan.*

NOTE: 所有 **suǒyǒu** is: (1) only used as an attribute, (2) always followed by 的 **de** and (3) often used together with 都 **dōu.**

T

tā 他 (亻 5) [亻 sign + 也 symb]

PRONOUN = he, him

■ “他是谁？” “他是我的同学。” **“Tā shì shéi?” “Tā shì wǒ de tóngxué.”** = *“Who's he?” “He's my classmate.”*

■ 我不喜欢他。**Wǒ bù xǐhuān tā.** = *I don't like him.*

■ 他的朋友都叫他小王。**Tā de péngyou dōu jiào tā Xiǎo Wáng.** = *His friends all call him Xiao Wang.*

tāmen 他们 [suffix: 他 *he, him* + 们 suffix denoting a plural number]

PRONOUN = they, them

■ 他们有困难，我们要帮助他们。**Tāmen yǒu kùnnan, wǒmen yào bāngzhù tāmen.** = *As they're in difficulty, we should help them.*

■ 这是他们的问题，我们没有办法。**Zhè shì tāmen de wèntí, wǒmen méiyǒu bànfǎ.** = *This is their problem. There's nothing we can do.*

tā 它 (宀 5) PRONOUN = it

■ 它是我们的小狗。**Tā shì wǒmen de xiǎo gǒu.** = *It's our puppy.*

tāmen 它们 [suffix: 它 *it* + 们 suffix denoting a plural number] PRONOUN = (non-human) they, them (plural form of 它)

tā 她 (女 6) [女 sign + 也 symb]

PRONOUN = she, her

■ 她是我班上的女同学。**Tā shì wǒ bānshang de nǚ tóngxué.** = *She's a female student in my class.*

tāmen 她们 [suffix: 她 *she, her* + 们 suffix denoting a plural number] PRONOUN = (female) they, them

tái 台 (厶 5) Trad 檯 NOUN = table

Táiwān 台湾 NOUN = Taiwan

tái 抬 (扌 8) [扌 sign + 台 phon **tái**] Trad 擡 VERB = lift, raise
■ 来，咱们俩把桌子抬到外边去。 **Lái, zánmen liǎ bǎ zhuōzi táidào wàibian qù.** = *Come on, let's move the table outside.*

tài 太 (大 4) ADVERB = excessively, too (followed by an adjective)
■ 今天我太累了，不去游泳了。 **Jīntiān wǒ tài lèi le, bú qù yóuyǒng le.** = *Today I'm too tired to go swimming.*

tàitai 太太 NOUN
1 = Mrs (respectful form of address for a married woman, preceded by her husband's family name)
■ 王先生和王太太请我们这个星期日去他们家吃饭。 **Wáng xiānsheng hé Wáng tàitai qǐng wǒmen zhè ge Xīngqīrì qù tāmen jiā chīfàn.** = *Mr and Mrs Wang invited us to dinner at their home this Sunday.*
2 = wife
■ 您太太刚才来电话。 **Nín tàitai gāngcái lái diànhuà.** = *Your wife called just now.*

tàiyang 太阳 [modif: 太 *big, supreme* + 阳 *open, overt, masculine*] NOUN = the sun, sunshine
■ 今天的太阳真好。 **Jīntiān de tàiyang zhēn hǎo.** = *The sunshine's beautiful today.*

tài 态 (心 8) [太 phon **tài** + 心 sign] Trad 態 NOUN = stance

tàidu 态度 [compound: 态 *stance* + 度 *appearance, bearing*] NOUN = attitude, approach
■ 这位服务员的服务态度不好。 **Zhè wèi fúwùyuán de fúwù tàidu bù hǎo.** = *This attendant's work attitude is not good.*

NOTE: Though 态度 **tàidu** is glossed as "attitude" or "approach," it is more commonly used in Chinese than its equivalents in English.

tán 谈 (讠 10) [讠 sign + 炎 phon **yán**] Trad 談 VERB = talk, discuss
■ 我想跟你谈一件事。 **Wǒ xiǎng gēn nǐ tán yí jiàn shì.** = *I'd like to discuss something with you.*

tán yíxià 谈一下 = talk briefly about, give a brief talk about
■ 请你谈一下去中国旅行的情况。 **Qǐng nǐ tán yíxià qù Zhōngguó lǚxíng de qíngkuàng.** = *Please give a brief talk about your trip to China.*

tánhuà 谈话 = have a (serious, formal) talk
■ 校长找他谈话。 **Xiàozhǎng zhǎo tā1 tánhuà.** = *The principal summoned him for a talk.*

tāng 汤 (氵 6) [氵 sign + phon] Trad 湯 NOUN = soup (碗 **wǎn**)

T

■ 妈妈做的汤真好喝。**Māma zuò de tāng zhēn hǎohē!** = *The soup mum prepared is really delicious.*
hē tāng **喝汤** = eat soup

táng 堂 (土 11) NOUN = hall (See 食堂 **shítáng**.)

táng 糖 (米 16) [米 sign + 唐 phon **táng**] NOUN = sugar, candy (块 **kuài**)
■ "你的咖啡里要放糖吗?" "要，请放一块糖。" **"Nǐ de kāfēi li yào fàng táng ma?" "Yào, qǐng fàng yí kuài táng.** = *"Do you want sugar in your coffee?" "Yes, a lump of sugar, please."*
tángguǒ **糖果** = candy, sweets
■ 小孩儿一般都喜欢吃糖果。**Xiǎo háir yìbān dōu xǐhuān chī tángguǒ.** = *Children usually love candy.*

tǎng 躺 (身 14) Trad **躺** VERB = lie
■ 她喜欢躺在床上看书。**Tā xǐhuan tǎng zài chuángshang kànshū.** = *She likes to lie in bed reading.*

tǎo 讨 (讠 5) [讠 sign + 寸 symb] Trad **討** VERB = explore

tǎolùn 讨论 [compound: 讨 *explore* + 论 *discuss*]
1 VERB = discuss
■ 老师们在讨论明年的工作。**Lǎoshīmen zài tǎolùn míngnián de gōngzuò.** = *The teachers are discussing next year's work.*
2 NOUN = discussion (次 cì)
■ 这次讨论对我们很有用。**Zhè cì tǎolùn duì wǒmen hěn yǒuyòng.** = *This discussion is useful to us.*

tè 特 (牛 10) ADVERB = particularly, especially

tèbié 特别 [compound: 特 *special* + 别 *other, unusual*] ADJECTIVE = special, especially
■ 他病得很重，住在特别病房。**Tā bìng de hěn zhòng, zhù zàI tèbié bìngfáng.** = *He's seriously ill and stays in the special ward.*
■ 我特别喜欢吃新西兰的苹果。**Wǒ tèbié xǐhuan chī Xīnxīlán de píngguǒ.** = *I especially like New Zealand apples.*

téng 疼 (疒 10) [疒 sign + 冬 phon **dōng**] VERB = ache, hurt
tóu téng **头疼** = headache, have a headache
■ 我头疼，得躺一会儿。**Wǒ tóu téng, děi tǎng yíhuìr.** = *I have a headache. I have to lie down for a while.*

tī 踢 (足 15) [足 sign + 易 phon] VERB = kick
tīqiú **踢球** = play soccer
■ 一些男孩儿在操场上踢球。**Yìxiē nán háir zài cāochǎng shang tīqiú.** = *Some boys are playing soccer on the sports ground.*
tī zúqiú **踢足球** = play soccer

tí 提 (扌 12) [扌 sign + 是 symb] VERB
1 = carry in the hand (with the arm down)
2 = mention
■ 你见到他的时候，别提这件事。**Nǐ jiàndào tā de shíhou, bié tí zhè jiàn shì.** = *Don't mention this matter when you see him.*
tí wèntí **提问题** = raise a question

T

tígāo 提高 [v+comp: 提 *raise* + 高 *high*] VERB = raise, advance
■ 我要提高自己的中文水平。**Wǒ yào tígāo zìjǐ de Zhōngwén shuǐpíng.** = *I want to increase my proficiency in Chinese.*

tí 题 (是 15) Trad **題** NOUN = question (See 问题 **wèntí**.)

tǐ 体 (亻 7) [亻 sign + 本 symb] Trad **體** ADJECTIVE = physical

tǐyù 体育 [modif: 体 *physical* + 育 *education*] NOUN = physical education, sports
■ 体育和学习，哪个更重要？ **Tǐyù hé xuéxí, nǎ ge gèng zhòngyào?** = *Sports or study, which is more important?*
tǐyù chǎng 体育场 = stadium
tǐyù guǎn 体育馆 = gymnasium

tiān 天 (天 4) NOUN
1 = sky, heaven
■ 秋天，天特别蓝。**Qiūtiān, tiān tèbié lán.** = *In autumn, the sky is especially blue.*
2 = day
■ 我在朋友家住了三天。**Wǒ zài péngyou jiā zhùle sān tiān.** = *I stayed with my friend for three days.*
3 = weather
■ 这位老人下雨天一般不出去。**Zhè wèi lǎorén xià yǔ tiān yìbān bù chūqu.** = *This old man normally does not go out on rainy days.*
tiān shàng 天上 = in the sky
tiān xià 天下 = under heaven (→in the world, on earth)
tiāntiān 天天 = every day
Tiān zhīdào 天知道 = Only God knows!

tiānqì 天气 [compound: 天 *weather* + 气 *weather*] NOUN = weather
■ 天气变化很大。**Tiānqì biànhuà hěn dà.** = *The weather changes dramatically.*

tiáo 条 (木 7) [夂 symb + 木 sign] Trad **條** MEASURE WORD = (for things with a long, narrow shape)
■ 一条河 **yì tiáo hé** = *a river*
■ 两条鱼 **liǎng tiáo yú** = *two fish*

tiáojiàn 条件 [compound: 条 *item, piece* + 件 *item, piece*] NOUN = conditions, environment
shēnghuó tiáojiàn 生活条件 = living conditions
■ 他们那里的生活条件比较差。**Tāmen nàli de shēnghuó tiáojiàn bǐjiào chà.** = *Their living conditions there are rather poor.*
gōngzuò tiáojiàn 工作条件 = working conditions
■ 工人们要求提高工作条件。**Gōngrénmen yāoqiú tígāo gōngzuò tiáojiàn.** = *The workers demand that their working conditions be improved.*

tiào 跳 (足 13) [足 sign + 兆 phon **zhào**] NOUN = jump
■ 他跳得很高，所以篮球打得好。**Tā tiào de hěn gāo, suǒyǐ lánqiú dǎ de hǎo.** = *He can jump high, so he plays basketball well.*
tiào gāo 跳高 = high jump
tiào yuǎn 跳远 = long jump
tiào shuǐ 跳水 = dive

T

tiàowǔ 跳舞 [compound: 跳 *jump* + 舞 *dance*] VERB = dance

■ 我可以请您跳舞吗? **Wǒ kěyǐ qǐng nín tiàowǔ ma?** = *May I have a dance with you?*

tīng 听 (口 7) [口 sign + 斤 symb] Trad 聽 VERB = listen

■ 他每天早上都听广播。**Tā měi tiān zǎoshang dōu tīng guǎngbō.** = *He listens to the radio early every morning.*

tīngjiàn 听见 = hear

■ 我听见有人在花园里叫我。**Wǒ tīngjiàn yǒurén zài huāyuán li jiào wǒ.** = *I heard somebody calling me in the garden.*

tīngshuō 听说 = hear of, people say

■ 听说小明一家搬走了。**Tīngshuō Xiǎo Míng yì jiā bānzǒu le.** = *I've heard that Xiao Ming's family has moved.*

tīngxiě 听写 = dictation, take dictation

tíng 庭 (广 9) [广 sign + 廷 phon **tíng**] NOUN = courtyard (See 家庭 **jiātíng**.)

tíng 停 (亻 11) VERB = stop, park (a vehicle)

tíng xiàlai 停下来 = come to a stop

■ 前面是红灯，车子要停下来。**Qiánmiàn shì hóngdēng, chēzi yào tíng xiàlai.** = *There's a red light in front. The car must stop.*

tíng chē 停车 = park a car

■ 我可以在这儿停车吗? **Wǒ kěyǐ zài zhèr tíng chē ma?** = *May I park my car here?*

tíngchēchǎng 停车场 = parking lot, car park

tǐng 挺 (扌 9) ADVERB = very

■ 她学习挺认真。**Tā xuéxí tǐng rènzhēn.** = *She studies very conscientiously.*

NOTE: 挺 **tǐng** and 很 **tǐng** share the same meaning, but 挺 **tǐng** is colloquial. (See note on 很 **hěn**.)

tōng 通 (辶 10) [辶 sign + 甬 phon **yǒng**]

1 VERB = (of roads, railways) lead to, go to

■ 这条路通到哪里? **Zhè tiáo lù tōngdào nǎli?** = *Where does this road lead?*

2 ADJECTIVE = (of language) grammatical, logical

■ 这句话不通，但是我说不出错在哪里。**Zhè jù huà bù tōng, dànshì wǒ shuōbuchū cuò zài nǎli.** = *This sentence is not quite right, but I can't identify where the mistake is.*

tōngguò 通过 [compound: 通 *go though* + 过 *pass*]

1 VERB = pass through

■ 从我家到机场，要通过城里。**Cóng wǒ jiā dào jīchǎng, yào tōngguò chénglǐ.** = *Going from my home to the airport, one has to pass through the city center.*

2 PREPOSITION = through, as a result of

■ 通过这次访问，我更了解中国了。**Tōngguò zhè cì fǎngwèn, wǒ gèng liǎojiě Zhōngguó le.** = *As a result of this visit, I understand China better.*

tóng 同 (冂 6) ADJECTIVE = same

T

tóngshí 同时 [modif: 同 *same* + 时 *time*] NOUN = at the same time, simultaneously
■ 我和她同时开始学中文。**Wǒ hé tā tóngshí kāishǐ xué Zhōngwén.** = *She and I began to learn Chinese at the same time.*

tóngxué 同学 [modif: 同 *together* + 学 *study*] NOUN = classmate, schoolmate
■ 我的朋友大多是我的同学。**Wǒ de péngyou dà duō shì wǒ de tóngxué.** = *Many of my friends are my schoolmates.*
lǎo tóngxué 老同学 = former schoolmate

> NOTE: (1) In Chinese schools, teachers address students as 同学们 **tóngxuémén**, for example,
> ■ 同学们，我们现在上课了。**Tóngxuémen, wǒmen xiànzài shàngkè le.** = *Class, we're starting class now.*
> (2) 同学 **tóngxué** is also used by a student to address fellow students.

tóngyì 同意 [modif: 同 *same* + 意 *opinion*] VERB = agree, approve (antonym 反对 **fǎnduì**)
■ 我不同意你说的话。**Wǒ bù tóngyì nǐ shuō de huà.** = *I don't agree with what you said.*

tóngzhì 同志 [modif: 同 *same* + 志 *aspiration*] NOUN = comrade

> NOTE: 同志 **tóngzhì** used to be the most common form of address in China before 1980. Now it is seldom used. 同志 **tóngzhì** is almost never used between a Chinese and a foreigner. The common forms of address in China today are 先生 **xiānshen** (to men) and 小姐 **xiǎojiě** (to women, especially young women).

tòng 痛 (疒 12)

tòngkuai 痛快 [compound: 痛 *to one's heart content* + 快 *delight*] ADJECTIVE = overjoyed, very delighted
■ 我在会上说了一直想说的话，心里很痛快。**Wǒ zài huìshang shuōle yìzhí xiǎng shuō de huà, xīn li hěn tòngkuai.** = *At the meeting I said what I'd been wanting to say, and felt extremely pleased.*
■ 上星期日我们玩得真痛快。**Shàng Xīngqīrì wǒmen wán de zhēn tòngkuai.** = *We had a terrific time last Sunday.*

tóu 头 (大 5) Trad 頭
1 NOUN = head
■ 我头疼。**Wǒ tóu téng.** = *My head aches.* (→ *I have a headache.*)
2 MEASURE WORD = (for cattle or sheep)
■ 一头牛 **yì tóu niú** = *a bull/cow*
■ 两头羊 **liǎng tóu yáng** = *two sheep*

tū 突 (穴 9) ADVERB = sudden

tūrán 突然 [suffix: 突 *sudden* + 然 adjectival suffix] ADJECTIVE = sudden, suddenly
■ 他没有给我打电话，也没有给我写信，昨天晚上突然来了。**Tā méiyǒu gěi wǒ dǎ diànhuà, yě méiyǒu gěi wǒ xiě xìn, zuótiān wǎnshang**

T

tūrán lái le. = *He hadn't rung or written to me, but unexpectedly came yesterday evening.*

tuán 团 (口 6) [口 sign + 才 symb] Trad **團** VERB = rally around

tuánjié 团结 [compound: 团 *rally around* + 结 *tie up*] VERB = unite, be in solidarity with
■ 他们家的兄弟姐妹很团结。**Tāmen jiā de xiōngdìjiěmèi hěn tuánjié.** = *The siblings in this family are united.*

tú 图 (口 8) Trad **圖** NOUN = picture

túshūguǎn 图书馆 [modif: 图书 *books* + 馆 *building*] NOUN = library (座 **zuò**)
■ 我们学校的图书馆没有多少中文书。**Wǒmen xuéxiào de túshūguǎn méiyǒu duōshǎo Zhōngwén shū.** = *The library in our school doesn't have many Chinese books.*

tuī 推 (扌 11) [扌 sign + 隹 symb] VERB = push
■ 你要推这个门，不要拉。**Nǐ yào tuī zhège mén, bú yào lā.** = *You should push this door, not pull it.*

tuǐ 腿 (月 13) [月 sign + 退 phon **tuì**] NOUN = leg (条 **tiáo**)
■ 他腿长，跑得快。**Tā tuǐ cháng, pǎo de kuài.** = *He has long legs and runs fast.*

tuì 退 (辶 9) [辶 sign + 艮 symb] VERB = move back, retreat
■ 请你退到黄线后面。**Qǐng nǐ tuìdào huángxiàn hòumian.** = *Please step back behind the yellow line.*

tuō 脱 (月 11) VERB = take off (clothes, shoes, etc.)
tuō yīfu 脱衣服 = take off clothes
■ 这个小孩儿会自己脱衣服吗？**Zhège xiǎoháir huì zìjǐ tuō yīfu ma?** = *Can the child take off his clothes by himself? (→ Can this child undress himself?)*
tuō xié 脱鞋 = take off one's shoes
tuō màozi 脱帽子 = take off one's hat

W

wà 袜 (衤 10) [衤 sign + 末 symb] Trad **襪** NOUN = stocking

wàzi 袜子 [suffix: 袜 *stocking* + 子 *nominal suffix*] NOUN = stocking, sock (只 **zhī**，双 **shuāng**)
■ 我的袜子破了。**Wǒ de wàzi pò le.** = *My socks have holes.*
chuān wàzi 穿袜子 = put on one's socks
tuō wàzi 脱袜子 = take off one's socks

wài 外 (夕 5) NOUN = outside (antonym 里 **lǐ**)
■ 墙外是一条安静的小街。**Qiáng wài shì yì tiáo ānjìng de xiǎo jiē.** = *Beyond the wall is a quiet by-street.*

wàibian 外边 [modif: 外 *outside* + 边 *side*] NOUN = outside (antonym 里边 **lǐbiān**)

T

■ 外边凉快，我们到外边去吧。**Wàibian liángkuai, wǒmen dào wàibian qù ba.** = *It's cool outside. Let's go outside.*

wàiguó 外国 [modif: 外 *outside* + 国 *country*] NOUN = foreign country
■ 你去过外国吗？ **Nǐ qùguo wàiguó ma?** = *Have you been abroad?*
wàigúorén 外国人 = foreigner

wàiwén 外文 [modif: 外 *foreign* + 文 *writing*] NOUN = foreign language (especially the writing of a foreign language) (门 **mén**)
■ 这封信是用外文写的，我看不懂。**Zhè fēng xìn shì yòng wàiwén xiě de, wǒ kàn bu dǒng.** = *This letter is written in a foreign language. I can't read it.*

wàiyǔ 外语 [modif: 外 *foreign* + 语 *language*] NOUN = foreign language (门 **mén**)
■ 懂一门外语很有用。**Dǒng yì mén wàiyǔ hěn yǒuyòng.** = *Knowing a foreign language is useful.*

wān 湾 (氵 12) Trad 灣 NOUN = bay, gulf (See 台湾 **Táiwān**.)

wán 完 (宀 6) VERB = finish, end
■ 电影什么时候完？ **Diànyǐng shénme shíhou wán?** = *When will the movie end?*
chīwán 吃完 = finish eating, eat up
■ 我吃完饭就去开会。**Wǒ chīwán fàn jiù qù kāihuì.** = *I'm going to a meeting as soon as I finish my meal.*
kànwán 看完 = finish reading/watching
■ 我昨天看完电视已经十二点了。**Wǒ zuótiān kànwán diànshì yǐjīng shí'èr diǎn le.** = *It was already twelve o'clock when I finished watching TV last night.*
zuòwán 做完 = finish doing, complete
■ 你什么时候可以做完作业？ **Nǐ shénme shíhou kěyǐ zuòwán zuòyè?** = *When can you finish your homework?*
yòngwán 用完 = use up
■ 我的钱用完了，我要到银行去取钱。**Wǒ de qián yòngwán le. Wǒ yào dào yínháng qù qǔ qián.** = *I've used up my money. I'll go to the bank to get some cash.*

wánchéng 完成 [compound: 完 *finish* + 成 *accomplish*] VERB = accomplish, fulfill
■ 这个计划在明年六月完成。**Zhège jìhuà zài míngnián Liùyuè wánchéng.** = *This plan will be fulfilled in June next year.*

wánquán 完全 [compound: 完 *finished* + 全 *all*] ADJECTIVE = complete
■ 你完全不懂我的意思。**Nǐ wánquán bù dǒng wǒ de yìsi.** = *You completely fail to see my point.*

wán 玩 (王 8) VERB = play

wánr 玩儿 [suffix: 玩 *play* + 儿 *suffix*] VERB = play, have fun
■ 我们一块儿到公园去玩儿吧！**Wǒmen yíkuàir dào gōngyuán qù wánr ba!** = *Let's go to the park to have fun!*

W

NOTE: Although 玩儿 **wánr** is glossed as "to play," its basic meaning is " to have fun" or "to have a good time." It can refer to all kinds of activities and therefore has a very wide application. More examples:
■ 我们常常到小明家去玩儿。**Wǒmen chángcháng dào Xiǎo Míng jiā qù wánr.** = *We often go to Xiao Ming's home to have a good time.* (e.g. singing, dancing, playing cards, playing games, or just chatting)
■ 上星期天我们在海边玩儿得真高兴！ **Shàng Xīngqītiān wǒmen zài hǎi biān wánr de zhēn gāoxìng.** = *We had a wonderful time by the seaside last Sunday.*
■ 我想去香港玩儿。**Wǒ xiǎng qù Xiānggǎng wánr.** = *I'd like to have a holiday in Hong Kong.*

W

wǎn 晚 (日 12) [日 sign + 免 phon **miǎn**] ADJECTIVE = late, not on time
■ 对不起，我来晚了。 **Duìbuqǐ, wǒ lái wǎn le.** = *I'm sorry I'm late.*

wǎnfàn 晚饭 [modif: 晚 *evening* + 饭 *meal*] NOUN = supper (顿 **dùn**)
■ 你们家一般什么时候吃晚饭？ **Nǐmen jiā yìbān shénme shíhou chī wǎnfàn?** = *When do you usually have supper at home?*
zuò wǎnfàn 做晚饭 = prepare supper

wǎnhuì 晚会 [modif: 晚 *evening* + 会 *assembly*] NOUN = evening party, an evening of entertainment
■ 很多重要的人要来参加今天的晚会。**Hěn duō zhòngyào de rén yào lái cānjiā jīntiān de wǎnhuì.** = *Many important people will be attending today's evening party.*

wǎnshang 晚上 NOUN = evening
jīntiān wǎnshang 今天晚上 = this evening
■ 你今天晚上打算做什么？ **Nǐ jīntiān wǎnshang dǎsuàn zuò shénme?** = *What do you plan to do this evening?*
zuótiān wǎnshang 昨天晚上 = yesterday evening

wǎn 碗 (石 13) [石 sign + 宛 phon **wǎn**] NOUN = bowl (只 **zhī**)
■ 中国人吃饭一般用碗，大碗放菜，小碗放米饭。**Zhōngguórén chīfàn yìbān yòng wǎn, dàwǎn fàng cài, xiǎowǎn fàng mǐfàn.** = *Chinese people usually use bowls for meals: big bowls for dishes and small ones for cooked rice.*
fànwǎn 饭碗 = a rice bowl
càiwǎn 菜碗 = a dish bowl
... wǎnfàn … 碗饭 = ... bowl(s) of rice
■ "你一顿吃几碗饭？" "两碗饭。" **"Nǐ yí dùn chī jǐ wǎn fàn?" "Liǎng wǎn fàn."** = *"How many bowls of rice do you have a meal?" "Two."*

wàn 万 (一 3) Trad **萬** NUMERAL = ten thousand
■ 一万两千三百 **yíwàn liǎngquān sānbǎi** = *twelve thousand and three hundred*
■ 二十万 **èrshí wàn** = *two hundred thousand*

Wáng 王 (王 4) NOUN = a common family name

wǎng 往 (彳 8) [彳 sign + 主 symb]
PREPOSITION = towards, in the direction of
■ 你往前走，到红绿灯的地方，往左走，就可以到火车站。**Nǐ wǎng qián zǒu, dào hónglǜ dēng de dìfang, wǎng zuǒ zǒu, jiù kěyǐ dào huǒchēzhàn.** = *Walk straight on, and turn left at the traffic lights. Then you'll reach the railway station.*

wàng 忘 (心 7) [亡 phon **wáng** + 心 sign] VERB = forget
■ 别忘了寄这封信。**Bié wàngle jì zhè fēng xìn.** = *Don't forget to post this letter.*
■ 他叫什么名字？我忘了。**Tā jiào shénme míngzì? Wǒ wàng le.** = *What's his name? I've forgotten.*

wàng 望 (月 11) VERB = look forward to (See 希望 **xīwàng**.)

wēi 危 (刀 6) ADJECTIVE = perilous

wēixiǎn 危险 [compound: 危 *perilous* + 险 *risky*]
1 ADJECTIVE = dangerous, in danger
■ 下雪天开车比较危险。**Xiàxuě tiān kāi chē bǐjiào wēixiǎn.** = *It's rather dangerous to drive on snowy days.*
2 NOUN = danger, risk
■ 我不怕危险。**Wǒ bú pà wēixiǎn.** = *I'm not afraid of danger.*

wéi 围 (口 7) [口 sign + 韦 phon **wěi**]
Trad 圍 VERB = encircle, enclose (See 周围 **zhōuwéi**.)

wěi 伟 (亻 6) [亻 sign + 韦 phon **wěi**)
Trad 偉 ADJECTIVE = big

wěidà 伟大 [compound: 伟 *big* + 大 *big*] ADJECTIVE = great

wèi 为 (丶 4) Trad 為
1 VERB = (do, work) for the benefit of
■ 我为人人，人人为我。**Wǒ wèi rénrén, rénrén wèi wǒ.** = *I work for everybody else and everybody else works for me.* (→ *One for all and all for one.*)
2 PREPOSITION = for, because of
■ 你是为钱工作吗？ **Nǐ shì wèi qián gōngzuò ma?** = *Do you work for money?*

wèile 为了 PREPOSITION = same as 为 **wèi** 2 PREPOSITION

wèishéme 为什么 [v+obj: 为*(do) for* + 什么 *what*] ADVERB = what for, why
■ 你昨天为什么没有来上课？ **Nǐ zuótiān wèishénme méiyǒu lái shàngkè?** = *Why didn't you come to school yesterday?*

wèi 位 (亻 7) [亻 sign + 立 sign]
MEASURE WORD = (a polite measure word, for people)
■ 一位老师 **yí wèi lǎoshī** = *a teacher*
■ 那位先生是谁？ **Nà wèi xiānsheng shì shuí?** = *Who is that gentleman?*

wèi 喂 (口 12) [口 sign + 畏 phon **wèi**) INTERJECTION = hey, hello, hi
■ 喂，你的票呢？ **Wèi, nǐ de piào ne?** = *Hey, where's your ticket?*

■ 喂，这里是大华公司，您找谁？ **Wèi, zhelǐ shì Dàhuá Gōngsī, nín zhǎo shuí?** = *Hello, this is Dahua Company, whom do you seek?* (→ *Who would you like to speak to? May I help you?*)

NOTE: 喂 **wèi** is used in telephone conversation, equivalent to "hello." In other contexts, using 喂 **wèi** is a rude way of getting people's attention. It is more polite to say 对不起 **duìbuqǐ** for example:
■ 对不起，先生，您的票呢？ **Duìbuqǐ, xiānsheng, nín de piào ne?** = *Excuse me, sir, where's your ticket?*

wén 文 (文 4) NOUN = culture

wénhuà 文化 NOUN = culture
■ 语言中有很多文化知识。**Yǔyán zhōng yǒu hěn duō wénhuà zhīshi.** = *A language contains a great deal of cultural knowledge.*
■ 我对中国文化知道得不多。**Wǒ duì Zhōngguó wénhuà zhīdào de bù duō.** = *I don't know much about Chinese culture.*

wénxué 文学 NOUN = literature
■ 我姐姐在大学念英国文学。**Wǒ jiějie zài dàxué niàn Yīngguó wénxué.** = *My elder sister studies English literature in university.*
wénxué jiā 文学家 = (great) writer

wényì 文艺 [compound: 文 *literature* + 艺 *art*] NOUN = literature and art; performing arts
■ 我妈妈喜欢文艺，我爸爸喜欢体育。**Wǒ māma xǐhuan wényì. Wǒ bàba xǐhuan tǐyù.** = *My mother likes literature and art while my father likes sports.*
wényi wǎnhuì 文艺晚会 = an evening of entertainment, soirée

wénzhāng 文章 [compound: 文 *writing* + 章 *essay*] NOUN = essay, article (篇 **piān**)
■ 昨天晚报上有一篇很有意思的文章。**Zuótiān wǎnbào shang yǒu yì piān hěn yǒuyìsi de wénzhāng.** = *There's an interesting article in yesterday's evening paper.*
■ 他文章写得很好。**Tā wénzhāng xiě de hěn hǎo.** = *He writes essays well.*

wén 闻 (门 9) [门 sign + 耳 sign] Trad 聞 NOUN = what is heard (See 新闻 **xīnwén**.)

wèn 问 (门 6) [门 symb + 口 sign] Trad 問 VERB = ask (a question), inquire
■ 我可以问你一个问题吗？ **Wǒ kěyǐ wèn nǐ yí ge wèntí ma?** = *May I ask you a question?*
wèn lù 问路 = ask the way
wèn hǎo 问好 = ask after, give greetings to
■ 请代问您父母亲好。**Qǐng dài wèn nín fùmǔqīn hǎo.** = *Please give my regards to your parents.*

wèntí 问题 [compound: 问 *inquiry* + 题 *question*] NOUN = question (道 **dào** for school examination only)

■ "有什么问题吗?" "有，我有一个问题。" **"Yǒu shénme wèntí ma?" "Yǒu, wǒ yǒu yí ge wèntí."** = *"Do you have any questions?" "Yes, I've got one."*
■ 考试的五个问题，你答对了三道，答错了两道。**Kǎoshì de wǔ ge wèntí, nǐ dá duìle sān dào, dá cuòle liǎng dào.** = *Of the five questions in the examination, you answered three correctly and two incorrectly.*

wǒ 我 (戈 7) PRONOUN = I, me
■ 我是美国人。我在学中文。**Wǒ shì Měiguórén, wǒ zài xué Zhōngwén.** = *I'm an American. I'm learning Chinese.*

wǒmen 我们 [suffox: 我 *I, me* + 们 suffix denoting a plural number] PRONOUN = we, us
■ 我们是学中文的学生。**Wǒmen shì xué Zhōngwén de xuésheng.** = *We're students of Chinese.*

wò 握 (扌 12) [扌 sign + 屋 phon **wū**] VERB = hold

wòshǒu 握手 [v+obj: 握 *hold* + 手 *hand*] VERB = shake hands
■ 他和新认识的朋友握手。**Tā hé xīn rènshi de péngyou wòshǒu.** = *He shook hands with the new friends.*

wū 屋 (尸 9) NOUN = house, room

wūzi 屋子 [suffix: 屋 *house, room* + 子 nominal suffix] NOUN = room (间 **jiān**)
■ 这个房子有几间屋子？ **Zhège fángzi yǒu jǐ jiān wūzi?** = *How many rooms does this house have?*

NOTE: 屋子 **wūzi** in the sense of "room" is only used in North China. To Southern Chinese, 屋子 **wūzi** may mean "house." To avoid ambiguity, it is better to use the word 房间 **fángjiān** for "room."

wǔ 五 (一 4) NUMERAL = five
■ 五五二十五 **Wǔ wǔ èrshíwǔ.** = *Five times five is twenty-five*
wǔxīng hóngqí 五星红旗 = the five-star red flag (the Chinese national flag)

wǔ 午 (十 4) NOUN = noon

wǔfàn 午饭 [modif: 午 *noon* + 饭 *meal*] NOUN = lunch (顿 **dùn**)
■ 我在学校吃午饭。**Wǒ zài xuéxiào chī wǔfàn.** = *I have my lunch in school.*

wǔ 舞 (丿 14) NOUN = dance (See 跳舞 **tiàowǔ**.)

wù 务 (夂 5) [夂 symb + 力 sign] Trad 務 VERB = work (See 服务 **fúwù**.)

wù 物 (牛 8) [牛 sign + 勿 phon **wù**] NOUN = things, objects

wùlǐ 物理 [modif: 物 *things, objects* + 理 *pattern, rule*] NOUN = physics
■ 我弟弟物理、数学都挺好。**Wǒ dìdi wùlǐ, shùxué dōu tǐng hǎo.** = *My younger brother is good at physics and mathematics.*

W

wù 误 (讠 9) Trad 誤 VERB = miss (See 错误 **cuòwù**.)

X

xī 西 (西 6) NOUN = west
■ 河东是一座小城，河西是一大片农场。**Hé dōng shì yí zuò xiǎo chéng, hé xī shì yí dà piàn nóngchǎng.** = *East of the river is a small town, and on the west is a big farm.*

xībiān 西边 [modif: 西 *west* + 边 *side*] NOUN = west, west side
■ 太阳在西边下山。**Tàiyang zài xībiān xiàshān.** = *The sun sets in the west.*

xī 希 (巾 7) VERB = wish

xīwàng 希望 [compound: 希 *wish* + 望 *look forward to*]
1 VERB = hope, wish
■ 我希望你常给我打电话。**Wǒ xīwàng nǐ cháng gěi wǒ dǎ diànhuà.** = *I hope you'll ring me often.*
■ 希望你旅行愉快! **Xīwàng nǐ lǖ3xíng yúkuài.** = *I wish you a happy journey.* (→ *Bon voyage!*)
2 NOUN = hope, wish
■ 孩子是父母的希望。**Háizi shì fù-mǔ de xīwàng.** = *Children are their parents' hope.*

xī 息 (心 10) VERB = pause (See 消息 **xiāoxi**, 休息 **xiūxi**.)

xí 习 (冫 3) Trad 習 VERB = practise

xíguàn 习惯 [compound: 习 *be familiar with* + 惯 *be accustomed to*]
1 NOUN = habit
■ 他有一个坏习惯，我希望他改掉。**Tā yǒu yí ge huài xíguàn, wǒ xīwàng tā gǎidiào.** = *He has a bad habit. I hope he'll get rid of it.*
2 VERB = be accustomed to, be used to
■ 很多中国人不习惯站着吃饭。**Hěn duō Zhōngguórén bù xíguàn zhànzhe chī fàn.** = *Many Chinese are not used to eating their meals while standing up.*

xǐ 洗 (氵 9) [氵 sign + 先 phon **xiān**] VERB = wash
■ 吃饭前要洗手。**Chī fàn qián yào xǐ shǒu.** = *Hands should be washed before having a meal.*

xǐshǒujiān 洗手间 = toilet, restroom, washroom
■ 请问，洗手间在哪里? **Qǐngwèn, xǐshǒujiān zài nǎlǐ?** = *Excuse me, where's the washroom?*

NOTE: 洗手间 **xǐshǒujiān** literally means "room for washing hands" and is a common euphemism for "toilet." The formal word for "toilet" is 厕所 **cèsuǒ**, e.g. 男厕所 **nán cèsuǒ** = Men's room, Gents', 女厕所 **nǚ cèsuǒ** = Ladies' room, Ladies'.

xǐzǎo 洗澡 [compound: 洗 *wash* + 澡 *bathe, take a bath*] VERB = take a bath, take a shower
■ 有人每天早上洗澡，有人每天晚上洗澡。**Yǒurén měi tiān zǎoshang xǐzǎo, yǒurén měi tiān wǎnshang xǐzǎo.** = *Some people take a bath*

early every morning, and others in the evening.

xǐzǎojiān 洗澡间 = bathroom, shower room

xǐ 喜 (士 12) VERB = be fond of

xǐhuān 喜欢 [compound: 喜 *be fond of* + 欢 *pleasure*] VERB = like, be fond of

■ 你喜欢不喜欢中国音乐？ **Nǐ xǐhuan bu xǐhuan Zhōngguó yīnyuè?** = *Do you like Chinese music?*

xì 戏 (戈 6) Trad 戲 VERB = have fun (See 游戏 **yóuxì**.)

xì 系 (糸 7) NOUN = department (of a university)

■ 这座大学有十二个系，最大的是电脑系。**Zhè zuò dàxué yǒu shí'èr ge xì, zuì dà de shì diànnǎo xì.** = *This university has twelve departments; the biggest is the Computing Science Department.*

xì 细 (纟 8) Trad 細 ADJECTIVE = thin, slender (of objects shaped like a strip)

■ 中国面条又细又长，是我最喜欢吃的东西。**Zhōngguó miàntiáo yòu xì yòu cháng, shì wǒ zuì xǐhuan chī de dōngxi.** = *Chinese noodles are thin and long; they are my favorite food.*

xià 下 (一 3)

1 NOUN = below, underneath (antonym 上 **shàng**)

■ 树下很凉快。**Shù xià hěn liángkuai.** = *It's cool under the tree.*

2 VERB = go (come) down (antonym 上 **shàng**)

xiàlai 下来 = come down

■ 晚饭做好了，快下来吃吧！ **Wǎnfàn zuòhǎo le, kuài xiàlai chī ba!** = *Supper is ready. Come down and eat!*

xiàqu 下去 = go down

■ 时间不早了，我们（从山上）下去吧。**Shíjiān bù zǎo le, wǒmen (cóng shānshang) xiàqu ba.** = *It's quite late. Let's go down [the hill].*

xiàkè 下课 = finish class

■ 你们每天几点钟下课？ **Nǐmen měi tiān jǐ diǎnzhōng xiàkè?** = *When does school finish every day?*

xiàbān 下班 = get off work

■ 我下班以后要去买菜。**Wǒ xiàbān yǐhòu yào qù mǎi cài.** = *I'll go and do grocery shopping after work.*

xiàchē 下车 = get off a vehicle

■ 到了，下车吧！ **Dàole, xiàchē ba!** = *We've arrived. Let's get off the car (the bus, etc.).*

3 MEASURE WORD = (used with certain verbs to indicate the number of times the action is done)

■ 我试了几下，都不行。**Wǒ shìle jǐ xia, dōu bù xíng.** = *I tried several times, but it didn't work.*

... yīxià …一下 = (used after a verb to indicate the action is done briefly or tentatively)

■ 我看一下电视就去洗澡。**Wǒ kàn yíxià diànshì, jiù qù xǐzǎo.** = *I'll watch TV for a short while, then go and take a bath.*

xiàbian 下边 [modif: 下 *below, underneath* + 边 *side*] NOUN = below, under (antonym 上边 **shàngbiān**)

X

■ 椅子下边有几本书，是谁的？ **Yǐzi xiàbian yǒu jǐ běn shū, shì shéi de?** = *There are some books under the chair. Whose are they?*

xiàwǔ 下午 [modif: 下 *lower half* + 午 *noon*] NOUN = afternoon (antonym 上午 **shàngwǔ**)

■ 上午多云，下午天晴了。**Shàngwǔ duō yún, xiàwǔ tiān qíng le.** = *It was cloudy in the morning, but it cleared up in the afternoon.*

xià 夏 (一 10) NOUN = summer

xiàtiān 夏天 NOUN = summer

■ 北京的夏天热吗？ **Běijīng de xiàtiān rè ma?** = *Is summer in Beijing hot?*

■ 我们夏天常常到海边去游泳。**Wǒmen xiàtiān chángcháng dào hǎibiān qù yóuyǒng.** = *We often go swimming by the seaside in summer.*

xiān 先 (儿 6) ADVERB = first (in time sequence) (antonym 后 **hòu**)

xiān...zài... 先…再… = first ... and then ...

■ 他每天早上先跑步，再吃早饭。**Tā měitiān zǎoshang xiān pǎobù, zài chī zǎofàn.** = *Every morning he first jogs and then has breakfast.*

xiānsheng 先生 [modif: 先 *first, before* + 生 *born*] NOUN

1 = Mr, sir

■ 王先生，这位是张先生。**Wáng xiānsheng, zhè wèi shì Zhāng xiānsheng.** = *Mr Wang, this is Mr Zhang.*

■ 先生，有事吗？ **Xiānsheng, yǒu shì ma?** = *Is there anything I can do for you, sir?*

2 = husband

■ 您先生在哪儿工作？ **Nín xiānsheng zài nǎr gōngzuò?** = *Where does your husband work?*

xiǎn 险 (阝 9) Trad 險 ADJECTIVE = risky (See 危险 **wēixiǎn**.)

xiàn 现 (王 8) Trad 現 NOUN = present, now

xiàndài 现代 [modif: 现 *present* + 代 *generation*] NOUN = modern times, the contemporary age

■ 我祖父不喜欢现代音乐。**Wǒ zǔfù bù xǐhuan xiàndài yīnyuè.** = *My grandfather does not like modern music.*

xiànzài 现在 [compound: 现 *present* + 在 *being*] NOUN = the present time, now

■ 我现在没有时间，晚上再打电话给他。**Wǒ xiànzài méiyǒu shíjiān, wǎnshang zài dǎ diànhuà gei tā.** = *I don't have time now, I'll ring him this evening.*

xiāng 相 (木 9) ADVERB = each other, mutually

xiāngxìn 相信 [modif: 相 *each other* + 信 *trust*] VERB = believe, believe in

■ 我不相信他会做这种事。**Wǒ bù xiāngxìn tā huì zuò zhè zhǒng shì.** = *I don't believe that he would do such a thing.*

X

xiāng 香 (禾 9) [禾 sign + 日 symb] ADJECTIVE = fragrant, sweet-smelling
■ 这花真香！ **Zhè huā zhēn xiāng!** = *How fragrant this flower is!*

Xiānggǎng 香港 [modif: 香 *fragrant* + 港 *harbor*] NOUN = Hong Kong
■ 香港是买东西的好地方。 **Xiānggǎng shì mǎi dōngxi de hǎo dìfang.** = *Hong Kong is a good place for shopping.*

xiāngjiāo 香蕉 [modif: 香 *fragrant* + 蕉 *banana*] NOUN = banana
■ 这些香蕉还没有熟，过两天再吃吧。 **Zhē xiē xiāngjiāo hái méiyǒu shú, guò liǎng tiān zài chī ba.** = *These bananas aren't ripe yet. Let's wait a few days before eating them.*

xiǎng 响 (口 9) [口 sign + 向 phon **xiàng**) Trad 響 ADJECTIVE = loud, noisy
■ 你们说话声音别这么响，教室里在考试。 **Nǐmen shuōhuà shēngyīn bié zhème xiǎng, jiàoshì li zài kǎoshì.** = *Don't you talk so loudly. An examination is going on in the classroom.*

xiǎng 想 (心 13) [相 phon **xiāng** + 心 sign] VERB = think
■ 这个问题我要想想。 **Zhège wèntí wǒ yào xiǎngxiang.** = *I need to think over this problem.*

xiǎng yíxià 想一下 = think for a while, give it some thought
■ 明天晚上跟不跟他一块儿去看电影？让我想一下。 **Míngtiān wǎnshang gēn bu gēn tā yíkuàir qù kàn diànyǐng, ràng wǒ xiǎng yíxià.** = *Shall I go to the movie with him tomorrow evening? Let me think about it.*

xiǎng bànfa 想办法 = think of a way (to do something)
■ 没关系，我来想办法。 **Méi guānxi, wǒ lái xiǎng bànfǎ.** = *It's OK. I'll think of a way.*

xiàng 向 (丿 6)
1 PREPOSITION = in the direction of, towards
■ 中国的长江，黄河都向东流。 **Zhōngguó de Chángjiāng, Huánghé dōu xiàng dōng liú.** = *China's Yangtze and Yellow River flow to the east.*
2 VERB = face
■ 这个房间有两个窗子，一个向南，另一个向东。 **Zhège fángjiān yǒu liǎng ge chuāngzi, yí ge xiàng nán, lìng yí ge xiàng dōng.** = *There are two windows in this room. One faces south and the other faces east.*

xiàng 相 (木 9) NOUN = appearance (See 照相 **zhàoxiàng**.)

xiàng 像 (亻 13) [亻 sign + 象 phon **xiàng**]
1 VERB = bear resemblance to, be like
■ 她很像妈妈。 **Tā hěn xiàng māma.** = *She takes after her mother.*
2 NOUN = likeness of (a human being), portrait
■ 墙上挂着祖父的像。 **Qiángshang guàzhe zǔfù de xiàng.** = *On the wall hangs grandfather's portrait.*

xiāo 消 (氵 10) VERB = vanish

xiāoxi 消息 NOUN = news (条 **tiáo**)
■ 今天报上有什么消息？ **Jīntiān bàoshang yǒu shénme xiāoxi?** = *What's the news in today's paper?*
■ 我先告诉你一个好消息，再告诉你一个坏消息。**Wǒ xiān gàosu nǐ yí ge hǎo xiāoxi, zài gàosu nǐ yí ge huài xiāoxi.** = *I'll first tell you a piece of good news, and then tell you a piece of bad news.*

xiǎo 小 (小 3) ADJECTIVE
1 = small, little (antonym 大 **dà**)
■ 这双鞋太小了。有没有大一点儿的？ **Zhè shuāng xié tài xiǎo le, yǒu méiyǒu dà yìdiǎnr de?** = *This pair of shoes is too small. Do you have a bigger size?*
2 = young (antonym 老 **lǎo**)
■ 我姓李，您就叫我小李吧。**Wǒ xìng Lǐ, nín jiù jiào wǒ Xiǎo Lǐ ba.** = *My family name is Li. You can call me Xiao Li.*

NOTE: "小 **xiǎo** + family name," like 小李 **Xiǎo Lǐ**, is a casual, friendly form of address to a person younger than oneself. (See note on 老 **lǎo** for forms of address like 老李 **Lǎo Lǐ**.)

xiǎoháir 小孩儿 [suffix: 小孩 *young child* + 儿 diminutive nominal suffix] NOUN = same as 孩子 **háizi**.

xiǎojiě 小姐 [compound: 小 *young* + 姐 *elder sister*] NOUN = young lady; Miss
■ 有一位小姐要见你。**Yǒu yí wèi xiǎojiě yào jiàn nǐ.** = *There's a young lady who wants to see you.*
■ 王先生、王太太和他们的女儿王小姐都在美国旅行。**Wáng xiānsheng, Wáng tàitai hé tāmen de nǚ'er Wáng xiǎojiě dōu zài Měiguó lǚxíng.** = *Mr and Mrs Wang, with their daughter Miss Wang, are all travelling in the United States.*

NOTE: 小姐 **xiǎojiě** is a common form of address to a young (or not so young) woman. If her family name is not known, just use 小姐 **xiǎojiě.** 小姐 **xiǎojiě** is also the form of address for a waiter or attendant, e.g.
■ 小姐，请给我一杯水。**Xiǎojiě, qǐng gěi wǒ yì bēi shuǐ.** = *Excuse me, please give me a glass of water.*

xiǎoshí 小时 [modif: 小 *small* + 时 *time*] NOUN = hour
■ 我等你等了一个半小时了。**Wǒ děng nǐ děng le yí ge bàn xiǎoshí le.** = *I've been waiting for you for an hour and a half.*
bàn xiǎoshí 半小时 = half an hour

xiǎoxué 小学 [modif: 小 *small* + 学 *school*] NOUN = primary school (座 **zuò**)
■ 这里附近有没有有名的小学？ **Zhèli fùjìn yǒu méiyǒu yǒumíng de xiǎoxué?** = *Are there any famous primary schools nearby?*

xiào 笑 (竹 10) VERB = laugh, smile (antonym 哭 **kū**)
■ 他笑着和我握手。**Tā xiàozhe hé wǒ wòshǒu.** = *He shook my hand, smiling.*

X

dà xiào 大笑 = laugh
xiàohua 笑话 = joke
■ 他很会讲笑话。**Tā hěn huì jiǎng xiàohua.** = *He's good at telling jokes.*

xiào 校 (木 10) NOUN = school (See 学校 **xuéxiào**.)

xiē 些 (止 8) MEASURE WORD = some, a few, a little
■ 午饭我吃了些面包。**Wǔfàn wǒ chīle xiē miànbāo.** = *I had some bread for lunch.*
hǎoxiē 好些 = quite a few, a lot of
■ 昨天晚上他和老朋友谈了很久，喝了好些酒。**Zuótiān wǎnshang tā hé lǎo péngyou tánle hěn jiǔ, hēle hǎoxiē jiǔ.** = *Yesterday evening he chatted with his old friends for a long time and drank a lot of wine.*

xié 鞋 (革 15) NOUN = shoe (只 **zhī**, 双 **shuāng**)
■ 他总是穿一双黑鞋。**Tā zǒngshì chuān yì shuāng hēi xié.** = *He always wears a pair of black shoes.*
yùndòng xié 运动鞋 = sports shoes
liáng xié 凉鞋 = sandals
xié dài 鞋带 = shoelace, shoestring

xiě 写 (冖 5) Trad 寫 VERB = write
■ 这个汉字怎么写？ **Zhège Hànzì zěnme xiě?** = *How do you write this Chinese character?*
■ 他在写一篇文章。**Tā zài xiě yì piān wēnzhāng.** = *He is writing an essay.*

xiè 谢 (讠 12) Trad 謝 VERB = thank

xièxie 谢谢 VERB = thank
■ "谢谢你。" "不客气。" **"Xièxie nǐ." "Bú kèqi."** = *"Thank you." "You're welcome."*
■ 你给我这么大帮助，我不知道怎么谢谢你才好。**Nǐ gěi wǒ zhème dà bāngzhù, wǒ bù zhīdào zěnme xièxie nǐ cái hǎo.** = *You've given me so much help. I don't know how to thank you enough.*

NOTE: There are many ways of replying 谢谢你 **xièxie nǐ**, e.g.:
■ 不客气！ **Bú kèqi.** = *You don't have to be so polite.*
■ 不用谢。**Bú yòng xiè.** = *You don't have to thank me.*
■ 没关系。**Méi guānxi.** = *It doesn't matter.* (→*No problem.*)

xīn 心 (心 4) NOUN = the heart
■ 这个人心真好！**Zhège rén xīn zhēn hǎo!** = *This person is really kindhearted.*
yòngxīn 用心 = apply oneself to
■ 你学习不太用心。**Nǐ xuéxí bú tài yòngxīn.** = *You don't really apply yourself to your study.*
fàngxīn 放心 = feel relieved, be assured, not worried
■ 你一个人去爬山，我不放心。**Nǐ yí ge rén qù páshān, wǒ bú fàngxīn.** = *I'd be worried if you go mountain-climbing all by yourself.*

xīn 辛 (辛 7) ADJECTIVE = spicy hot

xīnkǔ 辛苦 [compound: 辛 *spicy hot* + 苦 *bitter*]
1 ADJECTIVE = hard and toilsome (job); harsh (life)

X

■ 这个工作很辛苦。**Zhège gōngzuò hěn xīnkǔ.** = *This is a tough job.*
■ 你们辛苦了！ **Nǐmen xīnkǔ le!** = *You've been working hard!*
2 VERB = (used to request somebody's service)
■ 辛苦你把这些书搬到楼上去。**Xīnkǔ nǐ bǎ zhè xiē shū bān dào lóushàng qu.** = *Would you please move these books upstairs?*

NOTE: 你(们)辛苦了！ **Nǐ(men) xīnkǔ le!** is used by a superior to express appreciation of hard work done by subordinate(s). When somebody has done you a service, you can say 辛苦你了！ **Xīnkǔ nǐ le!**

xīn 新 (斤 13) ADJECTIVE = new (antonym 旧 **jiù**)
■ 你觉得我这件新衣服怎么样？ **Nǐ juéde wǒ zhè jiàn xīn yīfu zěnmeyàng?** = *What do you think of my new dress?*

Xīnjiāpō 新加坡 NOUN = Singapore
■ 大多数新加坡人会说华语。**Dàduōshù Xīnjiāpōrén huì shuō Huáyǔ.** = *Most Singaporeans can speak Chinese.*

NOTE: In Singapore and other Southeast Asian countries, Mandarin Chinese is known as 华语 **Huáyǔ**. 华 **huá** means China; ethnic Chinese in Southeast Asian countries and elsewhere are called 华人 **Huárén.**

xīnnián 新年 [modif: 新 *new* + 年 *year*] NOUN = New Year
■ 新年好! **Xīnnián hǎo!** = *Happy New Year!*
■ 祝您新年快乐! **Zhù nín xīnnián kuàilè!** = *I wish you a happy New Year!*

xīnwén 新闻 [modif: 新 *new* + 闻 *what is heard*] NOUN = news (of current affairs) (条 **tiáo**)
■ 你是怎么样得到新闻的 – 读报纸、听广播、还是看电视？ **Nǐ shì zěnmeyàng dédào xīnwén de—dú bàozhǐ, tīng guǎngbō, háishì kàn diànshì?** = *How do you get news—by reading newspapers, listening to the radio or watching television?*

Xīnxīlán 新西兰 NOUN = New Zealand
■ 每年很多外国人去新西兰旅游。**Měi nián hěn duō wàiguórén qù Xīnxīlán lǚyóu.** = *Every year, many foreigners go to New Zealand for sightseeing.*

xìn 信 (亻 9) [亻 sign + 言 sign] NOUN = letter (封 **fēng**)
■ 现在人们很少写信。**Xiànzài rénmen hěn shǎo xiě xìn.** = *Nowadays, people seldom write letters.*
jì xìn 寄信 = post a letter
shōudào xìn 收到信 = receive a letter
xìnfēng 信封 = envelope

xīng 星 (日 9)

xīngqī 星期 NOUN = week
■ 一年有五十二个星期。**Yì nián yǒu wǔshí'èr ge xīngqī.** = *There are fifty-two weeks in a year.*
Xīngqīyī 星期一 = Monday
Xīngqī'èr 星期二 = Tuesday
Xīngqīsān 星期三 = Wednesday

Xīngqīsì 星期四 = Thursday
Xīngqīwǔ 星期五 = Friday
Xīngqīliù 星期六 = Saturday
Xīngqīrì 星期日 = Sunday
Xīngqītiān 星期天 = Sunday
shàng xīngqī 上星期 = last week
xià xīngqī 下星期 = next week

xíng 行 (彳 6) [彳 sign + 亍 symb]
1 VERB = all right, OK, (that) will do
■ "我可以用一下你的词典吗?" "行。" **"Wǒ kěyǐ yòng yíxià nǐ de cídiǎn ma?" "Xíng."** = *"May I use your dictionary?" "OK."*
■ 学中文不学汉字不行。**Xué Zhōngwén bù xué Hànzì bù xíng.** = *It won't do to learn Chinese without learning Chinese characters.*
2 ADJECTIVE = competent, capable
■ 你又赢了，真行！ **Nǐ yòu yíng le, zhēn xíng!** = *You've won (the game) again. You're really great!*

xìng 兴 (八 6) Trad 興 ADJECTIVE = excited (See 高兴 **gāoxìng**.)

xìng 幸 (土 8) NOUN = good fortune

xìngfú 幸福 [compound: 幸 *good fortune* + 福 *happiness*] ADJECTIVE = happy, fortunate
■ 多么幸福的家庭！ **Duōme xìngfú de jiātíng!** = *What a happy family!*

NOTE: 幸福 **xìngfú** is used in a sublime sense, denoting a profound and almost perfect "happiness." So it has a much more limited use than its English equivalents *happy* or *fortunate*. The usual Chinese word for "happy," as in: "I'm happy to hear the news" is 高兴 **gāoxìng**:
■ 听到这个消息，我很高兴。**Tīngdào zhège xiāoxi, wǒ hěn gāoxìng.** = *I'm happy to hear the news.*

xìng 姓 (女 8) [女 sign + 生 symb]
NOUN = family name, surname
■ 中国人最常用的三个姓是李、张、王。**Zhōngguórén zuì cháng yòng de sān ge xìng shì Lǐ, Zhāng, Wáng.** = *The three most common family names of the Chinese are Li, Zhang and Wang.*
guìxìng 贵姓 = (polite usage, often in a question) your family name
■ "您贵姓?" "我姓王。" **"Nín guìxìng?" "Wǒ xìng Wáng."** = *"What's your family name?" "Wang."*
xìngmíng 姓名 = family name and given name, full name

NOTE: The character 姓 **xìng** has the signific graph of 女 **nǚ**, meaning "female," an indication that the Chinese once had a matriarchal society.

xiū 休 (亻 5) [亻 sign + 木 sign] NOUN = leisure

xiūxi 休息 [compound: 休 *leisure* + 息 *pause*] VERB = rest, take a rest
■ 我们工作了两个小时了，休息一会儿吧。**Wǒmen gōngzuòle liǎng ge xiǎoshí le, xiūxi yíhuìr ba.** = *We've been working for over two hours. Let's take a break.*

xiū 修 (亻 9) VERB = repair

xiūlǐ 修理 VERB = repair, fix
■ 自行车坏了，你会修理吗？ **Zìxíngchē huài le, nǐ huì xiūlǐ ma?** = *The bike has broken down. Can you fix it?*

xū 须 (纟 9) Trad 須 MODAL VERB = need, have to (See 必须 **bìxū**.)

xū 需 (雨 14) VERB = need

xūyào 需要 [compound: 需 *need* + 要 *want*]
1 VERB = need, be in need of
■ 我需要一本好词典。**Wǒ xūyào yì běn hǎo cídiǎn.** = *I need a good dictionary.*
2 NOUN = need, requirement
■ "你有什么需要，可以跟我说。" "谢谢，没有什么需要。" **"Nǐ yǒu shénme xūyào, kěyǐ gēn wǒ shuō." "Xièxie, méiyǒu shénme xūyào."** = *"If there's anything you need, let me know." "Thank you, but there's nothing I need."*

xǔ 许 (讠 6) Trad 許 ADVERB = approximately, perhaps

xǔduō 许多 [compound: 许 *approximate* + 多 *many, much*]
ADJECTIVE = many, much
■ 妈妈买回来许多好吃的东西。**Māma mǎi huílai xǔduō hǎochī de dōngxi.** = *Mum bought lots of delicious food.*

xù 续 (纟 11) Trad 續 VERB = keep on (See 继续 **jìxù**.)

xué 学 (子 8) [symb + 子 sign]
Trad 學 VERB = learn, study
■ "你哥哥在大学学什么？" "学电脑。" **"Nǐ gēge zài dàxué xué shénme?" "Xué diànnǎo."** = *"What does your elder brother study in university?" "Computer science."*

xuésheng 学生 [modif: 学 *study* + 生 *scholar*] NOUN = student, pupil (个 **gè**)
■ "这个班有多少学生？" "二十二个。" **"Zhège bān yǒu duōshǎo xuésheng?" "Èrshí'èr ge."** = *"How many students are there in this class?" "Twenty-two."*

xuéxí 学习 [compound: 学 *learn* + 习 *practise*]
1 VERB = study, learn
■ 年轻的时候，应该多学习些知识。**Niánqīng de shíhou, yīnggāi duō xuéxí xiē zhīshi.** = *One should learn lots of knowledge when young.* (→ *When young, one should acquire much knowledge.*)
xiàng...xuéxi 向…学习 = learn from ..., emulate
■ 你工作很认真，我要向你学习。**Nǐ gōngzuò hěn rènzhēn, wǒ yào xiàng nǐ xuéxí.** = *You work conscientiously. I must emulate you.*

xuéxiào 学校 [modif: 学 *study* + 校 *school*] NOUN = school (座 **zuò**)
■ 王老师每天八点前就到学校来了。**Wáng lǎoshī měi tiān bā diǎn qián jiù dào xuéxiào lái le.** = *Every day, Teacher Wang is in school before eight o'clock.*

X

xuéyuàn 学院 [compound: 学 *study* + 院 *place* (for certain activities)] NOUN = college, institute (of higher education) (座 **zuò**)
■ 在中国有些大学叫"学院"，例如，"教育学院"。**Zài Zhōngguó yǒuxiē dàxué jiào "xuéyuàn," lìrú, "jiàoyù xuéyuàn."** = *In China some universities are called "college," "college of education" for example.*

xuě 雪 (雨 11) [雨 sign + ⺕ symb] NOUN = snow
xià xuě 下雪 = to snow
■ "香港冬天下雪吗？""不下。" **"Xiānggǎng dōngtiān xià xuě ma?" "Bú xià."** = *"In Hong Kong, does it snow in winter?" "No."*

Y

yā 呀 (口 7) [口 sign + 牙 phon **yá**]
1 INTERJECTION = oh, ah (expressing surprise)
■ 呀，你还会说上海话！ **Yā, nǐ hái huì shuō Shànghǎi huà!** = *Oh, you can even speak the Shanghai dialect!*
2 PARTICLE = (the same as 啊 **ā**; used after a, e, i, o, ü)
■ 你还会说上海话呀! **Nǐ hái huì shuō Shànghǎi huà ya!** = *Oh, you can even speak the Shanghai dialect!*
■ 这个苹果真大呀！ **Zhège píngguǒ zhēn dà ya!** = *How big this apple is!*

yán 言 (言 7) NOUN = speech (See 语言 **yǔyán**.)

yán 研 (石 11) [石 sign + 开 symb]

yánjiū 研究 [compound: 研 *research* + 究 *investigate*]
1 VERB = research, study
■ 科学家正在研究一种新药。**Kēxuéjiā zhèngzài yánjiū yì zhǒng xīn yào.** = *Scientists are researching a new medicine.*
2 NOUN = research work, study
■ 这个问题需要好好研究。**Zhège wèntí xūyào hǎohǎo yánjiū.** = *This problem needs a great deal of study.*
yánjiūshēng 研究生 = graduate student
yánjiūshēng yuàn 研究生院 = graduate school (of a university)
yánjiūyuán 研究员 = research fellow
yánjiūsuǒ 研究所 = research institute

yán 颜 (页 15) Trad 顏 NOUN = complexion

yánsè 颜色 [compound: 颜 *complexion* + 色 *color*] NOUN = color
■ "你最喜欢什么颜色？""蓝颜色。" **"Nǐ zuì xǐhuan shénme yánsè?" "Lán yánsè."** = *"What's your favorite color?" "Blue."*

yǎn 眼 (目 11) [目 sign + 艮 symb] NOUN = eye

yǎnjing 眼睛 [compound: 眼 *eye* + 睛 *eyeball*] NOUN = eye
■ 打电脑时间太长，我的眼睛累了。**Dǎ diànnǎo shíjiān tài cháng, wǒ de yǎnjing lèi le.** = *I've been working on the computer for too long; my eyes are tired.*

zuǒyǎn 左眼 = the left eye
yòuyǎn 右眼 = the right eye
yǎnkē yīshēng 眼科医生 = ophthalmologist

yǎn 演 (氵 14) VERB = put on (a play)

yǎnchū 演出
1 VERB = put on a theatrical performance, perform
■ 这次音乐会有两位有名的歌唱家演出。**Zhè cì yīnyuèhuì yǒu liǎng wèi yǒumíng de gēchàngjiā yǎnchū.** = *Two well-known singers will perform at the concert.*
2 NOUN = theatrical performance
■ 他们的演出精彩极了! **Tāmen de yǎnchū jīngcǎi jí le!** = *How wonderful their performance was!*

yàn 宴 (宀 10) NOUN = feast

yànhuì 宴会 [modif: 宴 *feast* + 会 *meet*] NOUN = banquet, feast, dinner party
■ 他们回国以前，举行了告别宴会。**Tāmen huíguó yǐqián, jǔxíngle gàobié yànhuì.** = *Before returning to their country, they gave a farewell banquet.*
huānyíng yànhuì 欢迎宴会 = welcome banquet
jiéhūn yànhuì 结婚宴会 = wedding banquet
cānjiā yànhuì 参加宴会 = attend a banquet

yàn 验 (马 10) Trad 驗 NOUN = test (See 经验 **jīngyàn**.)

yáng 羊 (羊 6) NOUN = sheep, goat, lamb
■ 春天是生小羊的时候。**Chūntiān shì shēng xiǎoyáng de shíhou.** = *Spring is the lambing season.*
xiǎoyáng 小羊 = lamb
shānyáng 山羊 = goat
yángròu 羊肉 = mutton
yángmáo 羊毛 = wool
yángpí 羊皮 = sheepskin

yáng 扬 (扌 6) Trad 揚 VERB = raise, make known (See 表扬 **biǎoyáng**.)

yáng 阳 (阝 6) [阝 symb + 日 sign] Trad 陽 NOUN = what is open, overt, masculine (See 太阳 **tàiyang**.)

yàng 样 (木 10) [木 symb + 羊 phon **yáng**] Trad 樣 NOUN = appearance

yàngzi 样子 NOUN = appearance, manner
■ 几年不见，你还是以前的样子。**Jǐ nián bú jiàn, nǐ hái shì yǐqián de yàngzi.** = *It's years since I saw you last and you still look the way you did.*

yāoqiú 要求 [compound: 要 *ask* + 求 *request*]
1 VERB = demand, require, ask
■ 老师要求我们每天都读课文。**Lǎoshī yāoqiú wǒmen měi tiān dōu dú kèwén.** = *The teacher requires us to read the texts every day.*
2 NOUN = demand, requirement
■ 我想提两个要求，可以吗？ **Wǒ xiǎng tí liǎng ge yāoqiú, kěyǐ ma?** = *I'd like to set two requirements, is that all right?*

yào 药 (艹 9) [艹 sign + 约 symb]
Trad 藥 NOUN = medicine, drug
■ 这种药你每天吃两次，每次吃一片。**Zhè zhǒng yào nǐ měi tiān chī liǎng cì, měi cì chī yí piàn.** = *You should take this medicine twice a day, one pill each time.*
chī yào 吃药 = take medicine
zhōngyào 中药 = traditional Chinese medicine
xīyào 西药 = western medicine
cǎoyào 草药 = herbal medicine
yàoshuǐ 药水 = liquid medicine
yàofāng 药房 = pharmacist's, pharmacy
yàopiàn 药片 = pill, tablet

yào 要 (西 9)
1 VERB = want, would like to, ask (somebody to do something)
■ 我要一间安静的房间。**Wǒ yào yì jiān ānjìng de fángjiān.** = *I want a quiet room.*
■ 我哥哥要我问你好。**Wǒ gēge yào wǒ wèn nǐ hǎo.** = *My brother asked me to send you his regards.*
2 MODAL VERB = should, must
■ 你想学好中文，就要多听、多讲。**Nǐ xiǎng xué hǎo Zhōngwén, jiù yào duō tīng, duō jiǎng.** = *If you want to learn Chinese well, you should listen more and speak more.*

yàoshì 要是 CONJUNCTION = if
■ 要是你明天不能来，请给我打个电话。**Yàoshì nǐ míngtiān bù néng lái, qǐng gěi wǒ dǎ ge diànhuà.** = *If you're unable to come tomorrow, please give me a call.*

yě 也 (乙 3) ADJECTIVE
1 = also, too
■ 我喜欢打球，也喜欢游泳。**Wǒ xǐhuan dǎ qiú, yě xǐhuan yóuyǒng.** = *I like ballgames, and I also like swimming.*
■ 你想去北京学习，我也想去北京学习。**Nǐ xiǎng qù Běijīng xuéxí, wǒ yě xiǎng qù Běijīng xuéxí.** = *You want to study in Beijing, so do I.*
2 = nor, neither
■ 你没有看过这个电影，我也没有看过这个电影。**Nǐ méiyǒu kànguo zhè ge diànyǐng, wǒ yě méiyǒu kànguo zhège diànyǐng.** = *You haven't seen this movie, nor have I.*

yěxǔ 也许 ADVERB = perhaps, maybe
■ 天上有云，也许会下雨。**Tiān shang yǒu yún, yěxǔ huì xià yǔ.** = *It's cloudy. Perhaps it'll rain.*

yè 业 (业 5) Trad 業 NOUN = industry
(See 工业 **gōngyè**, 农业 **nóngyè**, 作业 **zuòyè**.)

yè 页 (页 6) Trad 頁 NOUN = page
■ 请把书翻到二十页。**Qǐng bǎ shū fāndào èrshí yè.** = *Please turn to page twenty of your book.*

yè 夜 (夕 8) NOUN = night, evening
■ 她昨天夜里十一点钟才回家。**Tā zuótiān yèli shíyī diǎnzhōng cái huíjiā.** = *Last night she returned home as late as eleven o'clock.*
yèli 夜里 = at night
yèbān 夜班 = night shift
yèchē 夜车 = night train
yèxiào 夜校 = evening school

yī 一 (一 1) NUMERAL = one
■ 一百十一 **yībǎi shīyī** = *one hundred and eleven*

> NOTE: 一 undergoes tone changes (tone sandhi). When standing alone, 一 is pronounced with the first tone, i.e. **yī**. When followed by a sound in the fourth tone, 一 changes to the second tone, e.g. 一定 **yídìng**. 一 is pronounced in the fourth tone in all other circumstances, e.g. 一般 **yìbān**. Pay attention to the various tones of 一 here and in following words.

yī 衣 (衣 6) NOUN = clothing

yīfu 衣服 [compound: 衣 *clothing* + 服 *clothing*] NOUN = clothes, a piece of clothing (件 **jiàn**)
■ 她每年花很多钱买衣服。**Tā měi nián huā hěn duō qián mǎi yīfu.** = *She spends a lot of money buying clothes every year.*

> NOTE: 衣服 **yīfu** may denote "clothes" or "a piece of clothing." 一件衣服 **yíjiàn yīfu** may be a jacket, a coat, a dress or a sweater, but not a pair of trousers, which is 一条裤子 **yìtiáo kùzi**.

yī 医 (匚 7) Trad 醫 VERB = heal, cure

yīshēng 医生 [modif: 医 *medicine* + 生 *scholar*] NOUN = medical doctor (位 **wèi**)
■ 你要听医生的话。**Nǐ yào tīng yīshēng de huà.** = *You should follow the doctor's advice.*
■ 我们的家庭医生是张医生。**Wǒmen de jiātíng yīshēng shì Zhāng yīshēng.** = *Our family doctor is Dr Zhang.*

yīyuàn 医院 [modif: 医 *medicine* + 院 *place* (for certain activities)] NOUN = hospital (座 **zuò**)
■ 马上送医院！ **Mǎshàng sòng yīyuàn!** = *Take him to the hospital right now!*
sòng ... qù yīyuàn 送…去医院 = take ... to the hospital
zhù yīyuàn 住医院 = be hospitalized
■ 他病得很重，得住医院。**Tā bìng de hěn zhòng, děi zhù yīyuàn.** = *He is seriously ill and has to be hospitalized.*

> NOTE: In colloquial Chinese 住院 **zhù yuàn** is often used instead of 住医院 **zhù yīyuàn**.

yídìng 一定 ADJECTIVE = fixed, specified
■ 他吃饭没有一定的时间。**Tā chīfàn méiyǒu yídìng de shíjiān.** = *He has no fixed mealtimes.*

yígòng 一共 ADVERB = in all, totally, all together
■ 你们学校一共有多少学生？ **Nǐmen xuéxiào yígòng yǒu duōshǎo xuésheng?** = *How many students are there altogether in your school?* (→ *What is the total number of students in your school?*)

yīhuìr 一会儿
1 ADVERB = in a very short time, in a moment

Y

■ 不用麻烦倒茶，我一会儿就走。 **Bú yòng máfan dào chá, wǒ yīhuìr jiù zǒu.** = *Please don't bother making tea. I'll be leaving in a moment.*

2 NOUN = a very short time, a moment
■ 昨天我只看了一会儿电视。 **Zuótiān wǒ zhǐ kànle yīhuìr diànshì.** = *Yesterday I watched TV for a very short time only.*

yīkuàir 一块儿 ADVERB = together
■ 咱们一块儿去吃饭吧。 **Zánmen yīkuàir qù chīfàn ba.** = *Let's go and have a meal together.*

yíqiè 一切
1 ADJECTIVE = all, each and every without exception
■ 一切工作都做完，才能放假。 **Yíqiè gōngzuò dōu zuòwán, cái néng fàng jià.** = *You can have a holiday only after all the work is done.*
2 PRONOUN = all, everything
■ 我了解她的一切。 **Wǒ liáojiě tā de yíqiè.** = *I know everything about her.*

yíxiàr 一下儿 ADVERB = (used after a verb to indicate the action is done briefly or casually)
■ 请您等一下儿，王先生马上就来。 **Qǐng nǐ děng yíxiàr, Wáng xiānsheng mǎshàng jiù lái.** = *Please wait for a while. Mr Wang will be here in a moment.*

NOTE: It is very common in spoken Chinese to use 一下儿 **yíxiàr** after a verb, especially as an informal request. Some native Chinese speakers use 一下 **yíxià** instead of 一下儿 **yíxiàr**. More examples:
■ 请您来一下。 **Qǐng nín lái yíxiàr.** = *Please come over for a while.*
■ 我们在这里停一下吧。 **Wǒmen zài zhèlǐ tíng yíxià ba.** = *Let's stop here for a while.*
■ 让我想一下儿再回答。 **Ràng wǒ xiǎng yíxiàr zài huídá.** = *Let me think a while before I answer.*

yíyàng 一样 ADJECTIVE = same, identical
■ "一下"和"一下儿"是一样的。 **"Yíxià" he "yíxiàr" shì yíyàng de.** = *"Yixia" and "Yixiar" are the same.*

yí 宜 (宀 8) ADJECTIVE = suitable (See 便宜 **piányi**.)

yǐ 已 (已 3) PREPOSITION = by means of, according to

yǐjīng 已经 ADVERB = already
■ 我已经学了三年中文了。 **Wǒ yǐjīng xuéle sān nián Zhōngwén le.** = *I've already studied Chinese for three years.*

yǐ 以 (人 4) PREPOSITION = by means of, according to

yǐhòu 以后 NOUN = after, later
■ 做完作业以后，要检查一下。 **Zuòwán zuòyè yǐhòu, yào jiǎnchá yíxià.** = *After you've done the assignment, you should check it (for mistakes).*
■ 这个问题我们以后再谈。 **Zhège wèntí wǒmen yǐhòu zài tán.** = *We'll discuss this problem later.*

Y

yǐqián 以前 NOUN = before, some time ago

■ 回答问题以前，先要想一下。**Huídá wèntí yǐqián, xiān yào xiǎng yíxià.** = *Before answering a question, you should think first.*

bùjiǔ yǐqián 不久以前 = not long ago

■ 他不久以前给我发来一个电子邮件。**Tā bùjiǔ yǐqián gěi wǒ fālái yí ge diànzǐ yóujiàn.** = *He sent me an e-mail not long ago.*

yǐwéi 以为 VERB = think (usually mistakenly)

■ 我一直以为他是日本人，现在才知道他是中国人。**Wǒ yìzhí yǐwéi tā shì Rìběnrén, xiànzài cái zhīdào tā shì Zhōngguórén.** = *I always thought he was Japanese; only now I know he is Chinese.*

yǐ 椅 (木 12) [木 sign + 奇 phon **qí**] NOUN = chair

yǐzi 椅子 [suffix: 椅 *chair* + 子 nominal suffix] NOUN = chair (把 **bǎ**)

■ 房间里有一张桌子和四把椅子。**Fángjiān lǐ yǒu yì zhāng zhuōzi hé sì bǎ yǐzi.** = *In the room are a table and four chairs.*

yìbān 一般 ADJECTIVE = average, commonplace

■ 他的学习成绩一般。**Tā de xuéxí chéngjì yìbān.** = *His school grades are just average.*

yìbiān...yìbān... 一边…一边… CONJUNCTION = at the same time

■ 不少大学生一边学习一边工作。**Bù shǎo dàxuéshēng yìbiān xuéxí yìbiān gōngzuò.** = *Quite a few university students study and work at the same time.*

NOTE: 一边…一边… **yìbiān...yìbān...** links two verbs to indicate the two actions denoted by the verbs take place simultaneously. Another example:

■ 他常常一边做作业，一边听音乐。**Tā chángcháng yìbiān zuò zuòyè, yìbān tīng yīnyuè.** = *He often does his assignments while listening to music.*

yìdiǎnr 一点儿 NOUN = a tiny amount, a bit

■ 那个菜不好吃，我只吃了一点儿。**Nàge cài bù hǎo chī, wǒ zhǐ chīle yìdiǎnr.** = *That dish isn't tasty. I ate only a tiny bit of it.*

yìqǐ 一起 ADVERB = same as 一块儿 **yíkuàir**

yìxiē 一些 MEASURE WORD = a small amount of, a bit of

■ 请你在我的茶里放一些糖。**Qǐng nǐ zài wǒ de chá lǐ fàng yìxiē táng.** = *Please put a little sugar in my tea.*

yìzhí 一直 ADVERB = always, all the time

■ 我一直住在这个城市。**Wǒ yìzhí zhù zài zhège chéngshì.** = *I've always been living in the city.*

yì 义 (丿 3) Trad 義 NOUN = meaning (See 意义 **yìyì**.)

Y

yì 亿 (亻 3) Trad 億 NUMERAL = one hundred million
■ 中国有十三亿人口。**Zhōngguó yǒu shísān yì rénkǒu.** = *China has a population of 1.3 billion.*

yì 艺 (艹 4) Trad 藝 NOUN = art

yìshù 艺术 [modif: 艺 *art* + 术 *craft, skill*] NOUN = art
■ 我祖父不懂现代艺术。**Wǒ zǔfù bù dǒng xiàndài yìshù.** = *My grandfather does not understand modern art.*
yìshùjiā 艺术家 = artist

yì 译 (讠 7) Trad 譯 VERB = translate, interpret (See 翻译 **fānyì**.)

yì 易 (日 8) ADJECTIVE = easy (See 容易 **róngyì**.

yì 谊 (讠 10) Trad 誼 NOUN = friendship (See 友谊 **yǒuyì**.)

yì 意 (心 13) [音 symb + 心 sign] NOUN = idea, meaning

yìjiàn 意见 [compound: 意 *idea* + 见 *viewpoint*] NOUN = opinion, view (条 **tiáo**)
■ 对这个问题你有什么意见？ **Duì zhège wèntí nǐ yǒu shénme yìjiàn?** = *What is your opinion on this issue?*

yìsi 意思 [compound: 意 *meaning* + 思 *thought*] NOUN = meaning
■ 这个字是什么意思？ **Zhège zì shì shénme yìsi?** = *What's the meaning of this character?*
■ 这句话的意思不清楚。**Zhè jù huà de yìsi bù qīngchu.** = *The meaning of this sentence is not clear.*

yìyì 意义 [compound: 意 *meaning* + 义 *meaning*] NOUN = significance
■ 这件事有很大的历史意义。**Zhè jiàn shì yǒu hěn dà de lìshǐ yìyì.** = *This event has great historical significance.*

yīn 阴 (阝 6) [阝 symb + 月 sign] ADJECTIVE = cloudy, overcast
■ 昨天上午天晴，下午阴天，晚上下雨。**Zuótiān shàngwǔ tiānqíng, xiàwǔ yīntiān, wǎnshang xià yǔ.** = *Yesterday it was fine in the morning, cloudy in the afternoon and it rained in the evening.*

yīn 因 (口 6) CONJUNCTION = because

yīnwèi 因为 CONJUNCTION = because
■ 因为没有时间，所以我很少去看朋友。**Yīnwèn méiyǒu shíjiān, suǒyǐ wǒ hěn shǎo qù kàn péngyou.** = *I seldom go and visit friends because I don't have the time.*

> NOTE: 因为 **yīnwèn** is usually followed by 所以 **suǒyi**: 因为…, 所以… **yīnwèn ..., suǒyi ....**

yīn 音 (音 9) NOUN = sound

yīnyuè 音乐 [compound: 音 *sound* + 乐 *music*] NOUN = music
■ 星期天我常常跟朋友一块儿听音乐。**Xīngqītiān wǒ chángcháng gēn péngyou yīkuàir tīng yīnyuè.** = *I often listen to music with my friends on Sundays.*

Y

yīnyuè huì 音乐会 = concert
yīnyuè jiā 音乐家 = musician

NOTE: 乐 is pronounced **yuè** in 音乐 **yīnyuè**, but **lè** in 快乐 **kuàilè**.

yín 银 (钅 11) [钅 sign + 艮 symb] Trad 銀 NOUN = silver

yínháng 银行 [modif: 银 *silver, money* + 行 *firm*] NOUN = bank (家 **jiā**)
■ 他打算到银行去借钱。**Tā dǎsuàn dào yínháng qù jiè qián.** = *He plans to get a loan from the bank.*

NOTE: 行 is pronounced **háng** in 银行 **yínháng**, but **xíng** in 不行 **bù xíng** (see 行 **xíng**).

yīng 应 (广 7) Trad 應 MODAL VERB = should, ought to

yīnggāi 应该 MODAL VERB = should, ought to
■ 你的朋友有困难，你应该帮助他。**Nǐ de péngyou yǒu kùnnan, nǐ yīnggāi bāngzhu tā.** = *When your friend is in difficulty, you should help him.*

yīng 英 (艹 8) ADJECTIVE = heroic

Yīngguó 英国 NOUN = England, Britain, the UK
■ 英国一年中夏天最好。**Yīngguó yìnián zhōng xiàtiān zuì hǎo.** = *In England, summer is the best season of the year.*

Yīngwén 英文 [modif: 英 *English* + 文 *writing*] NOUN = the English language (especially the writing)

Yīngyǔ 英语 [modif: 英 *English* + 语 *language*] NOUN = the English language
■ 你用英语说吧，大家都听得懂。**Nǐ yòng Yīngyǔ shuō ba, dàjiā dōu tīng de dǒng.** = *You can say it in English. Everybody here understands it.*

yíng 迎 (辶 7) [辶 sign + symb] VERB = meet (See 欢迎 **huānyíng**.)

yíng 赢 (亠 17) VERB = win (a game), beat (a rival)
■ 昨天的球赛谁赢了？ **Zuótiān de qiúsài shéi yíng le?** = *Who won the ball game yesterday?*

yǐng 影 (彡 15) NOUN = shadow

yǐngxiǎng 影响 [compound: 影 *shadow* + 响 *sound*]
1 VERB = influence, affect
■ 经济发展慢，影响了生活水平的提高。**Jīngjì fāzhǎn màn, yǐngxiǎngle shēnghuó shuǐpíng de tígāo.** = *Slow economic development affects the improvement of living standards.*
2 NOUN = influence
■ 中学生受谁的影响大一父母，还是朋友？ **Zhōngxuéshēng shòu shéi de yǐngxiǎng dà—fùmǔ, háishì péngyou?** = *Who has more influence on high school students—parents or friends?*

yǒng 永 (丶 5) ADVERB = forever

yǒngyuǎn 永远 [compound: 永 *forever* + 远 *remote*] ADVERB = forever
■ 我们永远是好朋友。**Wǒmen yǒngyuǎn shì hǎo péngyou.** = *We'll be good friends forever.*

yǒng 泳 (氵8) [氵sign + 永 phon **yǒng**] VERB = swim (See 游泳 **yóuyǒng.**)

yòng 用 (用 5) VERB = use, (do something) with
■ 我可以用一下你的自行车吗？**Wǒ kěyǐ yòng yíxià nǐ de zìxíngchē ma?** = *May I use your bicycle?*
■ 我会用电脑写汉字。**Wǒ huì yòng diànnǎo xiě Hànzì.** = *I can use a computer to write Chinese characters.*
yǒuyòng 有用 = useful
■ 这本词典非常有用。**Zhè běn cídiǎn fēicháng yǒuyòng.** = *This dictionary is very useful.*
méiyǒuyòng 没有用 = useless
■ 这本书太旧了，没有用了。**Zhè běn shū tài jiù le, méiyǒu yòng le.** = *This book is too outdated, it's of no use.*

yóu 尤 (一 4) ADVERB = especially

yóuqí 尤其 ADVERB = especially
■ 新西兰的天气很舒服，尤其是夏天。**Xīnxīlán de tiānqì hěn shūfu, yóuqí shì xiàtiān.** = *The weather in New Zealand is very pleasant, especially in summer.*

yóu 邮 (阝7) [阝symb + 由 phon **yóu**] Trad **郵** NOUN = post

yóujú 邮局 [modif: 邮 *post* + 局 *office*] NOUN = post office
■ 请问，附近有没有邮局？**Qǐngwèn, fùjìn yǒuméiyǒu yóujú?** = *Excuse me, is there a post office nearby?*

yóupiào 邮票 [modif: 邮 *post* + 票 *ticket*] NOUN = postal stamp (张 **zhāng**)
■ 这封信寄到台湾，要多少邮票？**Zhè fēng xìn jìdào Táiwān, yào duoshao youpiao?** = *How much is the postage for this letter to Taiwan?*
■ 我买十块钱邮票。**Wǒ mǎi shí kuài qián yóupiào.** = *I want to buy ten yuan worth of stamps.*

yóu 油 (氵8) [氵sign + 由 phon **yóu**] NOUN = oil (See 黄油 **huángyóu.**)

yóu 游 (氵12) [氵sign + phon] VERB = swim

yóuyǒng 游泳 [compound: 游 *swim* + 泳 *swim*] VERB = swim
■ 他游泳游得很好。**Tā yóuyǒng yóu de hěn hǎo.** = *He swims very well.*

yóuxì 游戏 [compound: 游 *play* + 戏 *have fun*] NOUN = game
■ 我们来做游戏！ **Wǒmen lái zuò yóuxì!** = *Let's play a game.*
diànnǎo yóuxì 电脑游戏 = computer game

yǒu 友 (又 4) NOUN = friend

yǒuhǎo 友好 [compound: 友 *friendly* + 好 *amiable*] ADJECTIVE = friendly

■ 她对所有的人都很友好。**Tā duì suóyǒu de rén dōu hěn yǒuhǎo.** = *She is friendly to everyone.*
■ 你这么做不大友好。**Nǐ zhème zuò bú dà yǒuhǎo.** = *It's not friendly of you to do so.* (→ *It's not very nice of you to do this.*)

yǒuyì 友谊 [compound: 友 *friendly* + 谊 *congeniality*] NOUN = friendship
■ 我希望我们能发展我们之间的友谊。**Wǒ xīwàng wǒmen néng fāzhǎn wǒmen zhījiān de yǒuyì.** = *I hope we will be able to develop the friendship between us.*

yǒu 有 (月 6) VERB
1 = possess, have
■ 他们有一座房子、一辆汽车，在银行里还有一些钱。**Tāmen yǒu yí zuò fángzi, yí liàng qìchē, zài yínháng li háiyǒu yìxiē qián.** = *They have a house, a car and some money in the bank.*
2 = exist, there is/are
■ 世界上有多少国家？ **Shìjiè shang yǒu duōshǎo guójiā?** = *How many countries are there in the world?*
měiyǒu 没有 = do not possess, do not have, have no…; do not exist, there is no…
■ 我没有汽车。**Wǒ méiyǒu qìchē.** = *I don't have a car.*
■ 教室里没有人。**Jiàoshì li méiyǒu rén.** = *There is nobody in the classroom.*

yǒude 有的 PRONOUN = some
■ 有的人喜欢体育，有的人喜欢艺术，也有的人什么也不喜欢。**Yǒude rén xǐhuan tǐyù, yǒude rén xǐhuan yìshù, yě yǒude rén shénme yě bù xǐhuan.** = *Some people are fond of sports, others are fond of art, and still others are not fond of anything.*

yǒumíng 有名 [v+obj: 有 *have* + 名 *fame*] ADJECTIVE = famous, well-known
■ 这座大学很有名。**Zhè zuò dàxué hěn yǒumíng.** = *This is a famous university.*

yǒushíhou 有时候 ADVERB = sometimes
■ 爸爸有时候忙，有时候不那么忙。**Bàba yǒushíhou máng, yǒushíhou bú nàme máng.** = *Sometimes father is busy, sometimes he isn't so busy.*

yǒuxiē 有些 PRONOUN = (same as 有的 **yǒude**)

yǒu yìsi 有意思 [v+obj: 有 *have* + 意思 *meaning*] ADJECTIVE = meaningful, interesting
■ 这本书很有意思，每个人都应该看看。**Zhè běn shū hěn yǒu yìsi, měi ge rén dōu yīnggāi kànkan.** = *This book is very meaningful. Everybody should read it.*
méiyǒu yìsi 没有意思 = uninteresting, meaningless
■ 那个电影没有意思。**Nàge diànyǐng méiyǒu yìsi.** = *That movie isn't interesting.*

yòu 右 (口 5) NOUN = the right side (antonym 左 **zuǒ**)
■ 你右边的那座房子就是图书馆。**Nǐ yòubian de nà zuò fángzi jiù shì**

Y

túshūguǎn. = *The building on your right is the library.*

yòu 又 (又 2) ADVERB = again
■ 电脑昨天刚修好，今天又坏了。**Diànnǎo zuótiān gāng xiūhǎo, jīntiān yòu huài le.** = *The computer was fixed yesterday, but it broke down again today.*

NOTE: See 冉 **zài**.

yú 鱼 (鱼 8) Trad 魚 NOUN = fish (条 **tiáo**)
■ 河里有鱼吗？ **Hé li yǒu yú ma?** = *Is there any fish in the river?*

yú 愉 (忄 12) [忄 sign + 俞 phon **yú**] NOUN = pleasure

yúkuài 愉快 [compound: 愉 *pleasure* + 快 *delight*] ADJECTIVE = pleasant, joyful; pleased, happy
■ 祝你假期愉快！ **Zhù nǐ jiàqī yúkuài!** = *I wish you a happy holiday.* (→ *Happy holidays!*)
■ 听到这句话，我很不愉快。**Tīngdào zhè jù huà, wǒ hěn bù yúkuài.** = *Hearing this, I was very displeased.*

yǔ 雨 (雨 8) NOUN = rain
■ 这里夏天多雨。**Zhèli xiàtiān duō yǔ.** = *It often rains here in summer.*
■ 我看马上要下雨了。**Wǒ kàn mǎshàng yào xià yǔ le.** = *It seems to me that it's going to rain soon.*
xià yǔ 下雨 = to rain
yǔyī 雨衣 = raincoat
yǔtiān 雨天 = rainy day

yǔ 语 (讠 9) [讠 sign + 吾 symb] Trad 語 NOUN = language

yǔfǎ 语法 [modif: 语 *language* + 法 *law, rule*] NOUN = grammar
■ 我不大懂汉语语法，我想学一点儿。**Wǒ bú dà dǒng Hànyǔ yǔfǎ, wǒ xiǎng xué yìdiǎnr.** = *I don't quite understand Chinese grammar; I'd like to learn a little.*

yǔyán 语言 [compound: 语 *language* + 言 *speech*] NOUN = language
■ 要了解一个民族，就要学它的语言。**Yào liǎojiě yí ge mínzú, jiù yào xué tā de yǔyán.** = *If you want to understand an ethnic group, you should study its language.*

yù 育 (月 8) VERB = educate, nurture (See 教育 **jiàoyù**, 体育 **tǐyù**.)

yù 遇 (辶 12) VERB = encounter

yùdào 遇到 VERB = encounter, come across
■ 我在中国旅行的时候，遇到不少好心人。**Wǒ zài Zhōngguó lǚxíng de shíhou, yùdào bù shǎo hǎoxīn rén.** = *When I traveled in China, I came across many kindhearted people.*

yù 预 (页 10) Trad 預 ADJECTIVE = preparatory, in advance

yùxí 预习 [modif: 预 *preparatory* + 习 *study*] VERB = prepare lessons before class, preview
■ 明天上语法课，我要先预习一下。

Míngtiān shàng yǔfǎ kè, wǒ yào xiān yùxí yíxià. = *Tomorrow there'll be a grammar lesson, and I want to prepare for it.*

yuán 元 (二 4) MEASURE WORD = (the basic unit of Chinese currency: 1 元 **yuán** = 10 角 **jiǎo**/毛 **máo** = 100 分 **fēn**) *yuan,* dollar
■ 五十元 **wǔshí yuán** = *fifty yuan; fifty dollars*
Měiyuán 美元 = US dollar
Rìyuán 日元 = Japanese yen

> NOTE: 元 **yuán** is the formal word for the basic unit of Chinese currency. In spoken Chinese 块 **kuài** is more common. For instance, the sum of fifty *yuan* is usually written as 五十元 **wǔshí yuán**, but spoken of as 五十块 **wǔshí kuài**.

yuán 员 (口 7) Trad 員 See 服务员 **fúwùyuán**, 官员 **guānyuán**.

yuán 园 (囗 7) [囗 sign + 元 phon **yuán**] Trad 園 ADJECTIVE = garden (See 公园 **gōngyuán**, 动物园 **dòngwùyuán**.)

yuán 原 (厂 10) ADJECTIVE = original, former

yuánlái 原来 ADJECTIVE = original, former
■ 她原来的计划是去英国工作一段时间。**Tā yuánlái de jìhuà shì qù Yīngguó gōngzuò yí duàn shíjiān.** = *Her original plan was to go to England and work there for a period of time.*

yuánliàng 原谅 VERB = pardon, excuse, forgive
■ 我今天上午没有能到飞机场去接您，请多原谅。**Wǒ jīntiān shàngwǔ méiyǒu néng dào fēijīchǎng qù jiē nín, qǐng duō yuánliàng.** = *Please forgive me for not having been able to meet you at the airport this morning.*
■ "你这样做，我不能原谅。" **Nǐ zhèyàng zuò, wǒ bù néng yuánliàng.** = *I can't forgive you for such behavior.*

yuán 圆 (囗 10) [囗 sign + 员 phon **yuán**) Trad 圓 ADJECTIVE = round, circular
■ 地球是圆的。**Dìqiú shì yuán de.** = *The Earth is round.*

yuǎn 远 (辶 7) [辶 sign + 元 phon **yuán**] Trad 遠 ADJECTIVE = far, distant, remote
■ "这里离火车站有多远?" "大概两公里。" **"Zhèli lí huǒchēzhàn yǒuduōyuǎn?" "Dàgài liǎng gōnglǐ."** = *"How far is it from here to the railway station?" "About two kilometers."*

yuàn 院 (阝 9) NOUN = place (for certain activities) (See 学院 **xuéyuàn**, 医院 **yīyuàn**.)

yuàn 愿 (心 14) [原 phon **yuán** + 心 sign] VERB = wish, hope

yuànyì 愿意 [compound: 愿 *wish* + 意 *desire*]
1 MODAL VERB = be willing
■ 我愿意帮助你。**Wǒ yuànyì bāngzhù nǐ.** = *I'm willing to help you.*

■ 你愿意去就去，你不愿意去就不去。**Nǐ yuànyì qù jiù qù, nǐ bú yuànyì qù jiù bú qù.** = *If you're willing to go, then go; if you're not willing to go, then don't go.*

2 VERB = wish, want

■ 父母都愿意自己的孩子幸福。**Fùmǔ dōu yuànyì zìjǐ de háizi xìngfú.** = *All parents want their children to be happy.*

yuè 月 (月 4) NOUN

1 = month

■ 我在那里住了八个月。**Wǒ zài nàlǐ zhùle bā ge yuè.** = *I stayed there for eight months.*

2 = the moon

Yīyuè 一月 = January

Èryuè 二月 = February

Shí'èryuè 十二月 = December

yuèliang 月亮 = the moon

■ 今天晚上的月亮真好！ **Jīntiān wǎnshang de yuèliang zhēn hǎo!** = *What a fine moon it is, tonight!*

yùnqíu 月球 = the moon (as a scientific term)

yuè 乐 (丿 5) Trad **樂** NOUN = music (See 音乐 **yīnyuè**.)

yún 云 (云 4) Trad **雲** NOUN = cloud

■ 蓝天白云，好看极了！ **Lán tiān bái yún, hǎokàn jíle.** = *White clouds in the blue sky, how beautiful!*

duōyún 多云 = cloudy

■ 今天多云。**Jīntiān duōyún.** = *It's cloudy today.*

yùn 运 (辶 7) [辶 sign + 云 phon **yún**] Trad **運** VERB = move (something)

yùndòng 运动 [compound: 运 *move* + 动 *move*]

1 VERB = do physical exercises

■ 你每天运动吗？ **Nǐ měi tiān yùndòng ma?** = *Do you exercise every day?*

2 NOUN = physical exercises

■ "你做什么运动？""我有时候打球，有时候跑步。" **"Nǐ zuò shénme yùndòng?" "Wǒ yǒushíhou dǎ qiú, yǒushíhou pǎobù."** = *"What physical exercises do you do?" "Sometimes I play ball games and sometimes I jog."*

Z

zá 杂 (木 6) Trad **雜** ADJECTIVE = miscellaneous (See 复杂 **fùzá**.)

zài 再 (一 6) ADVERB = again

■ 我没听清楚，请您再说一遍。**Wǒ méi tīng qīngchu, qǐng nín zài shuō yībiàn.** = *I did not hear it clearly. Please say it again.*

■ 你的电脑我修好了，要是再坏，我就没有办法了。**Nǐ de diànnǎo wǒ xiūhǎo le, yàoshì zài huài, wǒ jiù méiyǒu bànfǎ le.** = *I've fixed your computer. If it breaks down again, there'll be nothing I can do.*

NOTE: 再 **zài** and 又 **yòu** are both glossed as "again," but they have different usage: 又 **yòu** is used in the context of a past situation while 再 **zài** is used for a future situation. For example:

■ 她昨天又迟到了。**Tā zuótiān yòu chídào le.** = *She was late (for work, school, etc.) again yesterday.*
■ 明天你不要再迟到了。**Míngtiān nǐ bú yào zài chídào le.** = *Please do not be late again tomorrow.*

zàijiàn 再见 [modif: 再 *again* + 见 *see*] VERB = see you again, goodbye
■ "我回家了，再见！""再见，明天见！" **"Wǒ huíjiā le, zàijiàn!" "Zàijiàn, míngtiān jiàn!"** = *"I'm going home. Goodbye!" "Bye! See you tomorrow!"*

zài 在 (土 6)
1 PREPOSITION = in, on, at
■ 我在两年以前开始学中文。**Wǒ zài liǎng nián yǐqián kāishǐ xué Zhōngwén.** = *I began learning Chinese two years ago.*
■ 在新加坡很多人会说中文。**Zài Xīnjiāpō hěn duō rén huì shuō Zhōngwén.** = *In Singapore many people speak Chinese.*
zài ... shang 在 … 上 = on, above
■ 在桌子上有两本书。**Zài zhuōzi shang yǒu liǎng běn shū.** = *There are two books on the desk.*
zài ... xia 在 … 下 = under, below, beneath
■ 在床下有一双鞋。**Zài chuáng xia yǒu yì shuāng xié.** = *There's a pair of shoes under the bed.*
zài ... li 在 … 里 = in, within
■ 他在房间里休息。**Tā zài fángjiān li xiūxi.** = *He's resting in the room.*
zài ... zhījiān 在 … 之间 = between
■ 我要在这两棵树之间种一些花。**Wǒ yào zài zhè liǎng kē shù zhījiān zhòng yìxiē huā.** = *I'm going to plant some flowers between the two trees.*
2 VERB = be in
■ "你爸爸在家吗？""他不在家。" **"Nǐ bàba zài jiā ma?" "Tā bú zài jiā."** = *"Is your father home?" "No, he isn't."*
■ "小明在哪里？""他在操场。" **"Xiǎo Míng zài nǎli?" "Tā zài cāochǎng."** = *"Where's Xiao Ming?" "He's on the sports ground."*
3 ADVERB = (used before a verb to indicate the action is in progress)
■ "你在做什么？""我在找东西。" **"Nǐ zài zuò shénme?" "Wǒ zài zhǎo dōngxi."** = *"What are you doing?" "I'm looking for something."*

zán 咱 (口 9) PRONOUN = same as 咱们 **zánmen**

zánmen 咱们 [suffix: 咱 *we, us* + 们 suffix denoting a plural number] PRONOUN = we, us (including the person or persons spoken to)
■ 你在学中文，我也在学中文，咱们都在学中文。**Nǐ zài xué Zhōngwén, wǒ yě zài xué Zhōngwén, zánmen dōu zài xué Zhōngwén.** = *You're learning Chinese. I'm learning Chinese. We're both learning Chinese.*
■ 咱们去吃饭吧！ **Zánmen qù chīfàn ba!** = *Let's go and have our meal.*

NOTE: 咱们 **zánmen** is only used in colloquial Chinese, and has a northern dialect flavor. You can always just use 我们 **wǒmen**, even to include the person(s) spoken to, for example:

■ 你在学中文，我也在学中文，我们都在学中文。**Nǐ zài xué Zhōngwén, wǒ yě zài xué Zhōngwén, wǒmen dōu zài xué Zhōngwén.** = *You're learning Chinese. I'm learning Chinese. We're both learning Chinese.*
■ 我们去吃饭吧！**Wǒmen qù chīfàn ba!** = *Let's go and have our meal.*

zāng 脏 (月 10) Trad 髒 ADJECTIVE = dirty (antonym 干净 **gānjìng**)
■ 这些衣服脏了，要洗一下。**Zhèxiē yīfu zāng le, yào xǐ yíxia.** = *These clothes are dirty; they need washing.*

zǎo 澡 (氵 16) [氵 sign + phon] VERB = bathe (See 洗澡 **xǐzǎo**.)

zǎo 早 (日 6) [日 sign + 十 symb] ADJECTIVE = early
■ 现在才三点钟，还早呢！**Xiànzài cái sān diǎnzhōng, hái zǎo ne!** = *It's only three o'clock. It's still early.*
■ 李先生每天很早上班，很晚下班。**Lǐ xiānsheng měi tiān hěn zǎo shàngbān, hěn wǎn xiàbān.** = *Every day Mr Li goes to work early and comes off work late.*

zǎochén 早晨 [modif: 早 *early* + 晨 *early morning*] NOUN = early morning (approximately 6–9 a.m.)
■ 他早晨六点半起床。**Tā zǎochén liù diǎn bàn qǐchuáng.** = *He gets up at half past six.*

NOTE: See note on 上午 **shàngwǔ**.

zǎofàn 早饭 [modif: 早 *early* + 饭 *meal*] NOUN = breakfast (顿 **dùn**)
■ 我今天起得太晚了，没有时间吃早饭。**Wǒ jīntiān qǐ de tài wǎn le, méiyǒu shíjiān chī zǎofàn.** = *I got up too late today and didn't have time for breakfast.*

zǎoshang 早上 NOUN = same as 早晨 **zǎochén**

zé 责 (王 8) Trad 責 NOUN = responsibility (See 负责 **fùzé**.)

zěn 怎 (心 9) PRONOUN = how

zěnme 怎么 PRONOUN
1 = in what manner, how
■ 这个汉字怎么念？**Zhège hànzì zěnme niàn?** = *How do you pronounce this Chinese character?*
2 = how come, why
■ 你今天怎么这么高兴？**Nǐ jīntiān zěnme zhème gāoxìng?** = *Why are you so happy today?*

zěnmeyàng 怎么样 PRONOUN = how; how about that, how's that
■ 你今天觉得怎么样？**Nǐ jīntiān juéde zěnmeyàng?** = *How are you feeling today?*
■ 我们每个人讲一个故事，怎么样？**Wǒmen měi ge rén jiǎng yí ge gùshi, zěnmeyàng?** = *We each tell a story, how about that?*

zěnyàng 怎样 PRONOUN = how
■ 你今天觉得怎样？**Nǐ jīntiān juéde zěnyàng?** = *How are you feeling today?*

NOTE: As the example shows, 怎样 **zěnyàng** often has the same meaning as 怎么样 **zěnmeyàng**, but 怎样 **zěnyàng** is only used in written Chinese.

zēng 增 (土 15) VERB = increase

zēngjiā 增加 [compound: 增 *increase* + 加 *add*] VERB = increase
■ 在过去十年中这个学校的学生增加了一倍。**Zài guòqù shí nián zhōng zhège xuéxiào de xuésheng zēngjiāle yí bèi.** = *In the past ten years the student number in this school has increased by 100 percent.*

zhǎn 展 (尸 10) Trad 展 VERB = display

zhǎnlǎn 展览 [modif: 展 *display* + 览 *view*]
1 VERB = put on display, exhibit
■ 这个画儿画得真好，可以去展览。**Zhège huàr huà de zhēn hǎo, kěyǐ qù zhǎnlǎn.** = *This picture is done so well, it can be put on display.*
2 NOUN = exhibition, show
■ 我上个星期参观了一个很有意思的展览。**Wǒ shàng ge xīngqī cānguānle yí ge hěn yǒu yìsi de zhǎnlǎn.** = *Last week I visited a very interesting exhibition.*

zhǎnlǎnhuì 展览会 = same as 展览 **zhǎnlǎn** 2 NOUN

zhàn 占 (卜 5) VERB = occupy
■ 你一个人不能占两个座位。**Nǐ yí ge rén bù néng zhàn liǎng ge zuòwèi.** = *You're only one person and can't take two seats.*

zhàn 站 (立 10) [立 sign + 占 phone **zhàn**]
1 VERB = stand
■ 房间里有些人站着，有些人坐着。**Fángjiān li yǒuxiē rén zhànzhe, yǒuxiē rén zuòzhe.** = *In the room some are standing, and some are seated.*
zhàn qǐlai 站起来 = stand up
■ 老师走进教室，学生们都站起来。**Lǎoshī zǒujìn jiàoshì, xuéshengmen dōu zhàn qǐlai.** = *When the teacher entered the room, all the students stood up.*
2 NOUN = station, stop
■ 我要一辆出租汽车去火车站。**Wǒ yào yí liàng chūzū qìchē qù huǒchē zhàn.** = *I want a taxi to go to the railway station.*
huǒchē zhàn 火车站 = railway station
qìchē zhàn 汽车站 = coach/bus station; bus stop
chūzū qìchē zhàn 出租汽车站 = taxi stand
zhànzhǎng 站长 = railway/coach station master

zhāng 张 (弓 7) Trad 張
1 MEASURE WORD = (for paper, beds, tables, desks)
■ 一张纸 **yì zhāng zhǐ** = *a piece of paper*
■ 两张床 **liǎng zhāng chuáng** = *two beds*
■ 三张桌子 **sān zhāng zhuōzi** = *three tables/desks*
2 NOUN = a common family name
■ 张先生 **Zhāng xiānsheng** = *Mr Zhang*

Z

zhāng 章 (立 11) NOUN = essay (See 文章 **wénzhāng**.)

zhǎng 长 (丿 4) VERB = grow
■ 孩子长高了。**Háizi zhǎnggāo le.** = *The child has grown taller.*

zhǎng 掌 (手 12) [尚 phon + 手 sign] VERB = be in charge

zhǎngwò 掌握 [compound: 掌 *be in change* + 握 *take ... in one's hands*] VERB = have a good command of, know well
■ 要掌握一门外语是不容易的。**Yào zhǎngwò yì mén wàiyǔ shì bù róngyì de.** = *It is not easy to gain a good command of a foreign language.*

zhàng 丈 (一 3) NOUN = senior

zhàngfu 丈夫 NOUN = husband (antonym 妻子 **qīzi**)
■ 你认识她的丈夫吗？ **Nǐ rènshi tā de zhàngfu ma?** = *Do you know her husband?*

zháo 着 (羊 11) VERB = catch

zháojí 着急 ADJECTIVE = anxious, worried
■ 已经快十二点了，女儿还没回家，妈妈很着急。**Yǐjīng kuài shíèr diǎn le, nǚ'er hái méi huíjiā, māma hěn zháojí.** = *It was almost twelve o'clock and her daughter was still not home. The mother was very worried.*
■ 别着急。**Bié zháojí.** = *Don't worry.*

zhǎo 找 (扌 7) [扌 sign + 戈 symb] VERB = look for, search for
■ "你在找什么？" "我在找我的手表。" **"Nǐ zài zhǎo shénme?" "Wǒ zài zhǎo wǒ de shǒubiǎo."** = *"What are you looking for?" "I'm looking for my watch."*

zhǎodào 找到 = find
■ 我姐姐在香港找到了一个好工作。**Wǒ jiějie zài Xiānggǎng zhǎodàole yí ge hǎo gōngzuò.** = *My elder sister has found a good job in Hong Kong.*

zhǎo bu dào 找不到 = cannot find
■ 我找不到那本书。**Wǒ zhǎo bu dào nà ben shū.** = *I can't find the book.*

zhào 照 (灬 13) [昭 phon **zhāo** + 灬 sign] VERB = look after, shine on

zhàogù 照顾 [compound: 照 *look after* + 顾 *attend to*] VERB = look after, care for
■ 她每个星期六下午到老人院去照顾老人。**Tā měi ge Xīngqīliù xiàwǔ dào lǎorényuàn qù zhàogù lǎorén.** = *Every Saturday afternoon she goes to a senior citizens' home to look after the senior citizens there.*
■ 我在中国的时候，我的中国朋友对我照顾得很好。**Wǒ zài Zhōngguó de shíhou, wǒ de Zhōngguó péngyou duì wǒ zhàogù de hěn hǎo.** = *When I was in China, my Chinese friends took good care of me.*

zhàoxiàng 照相 [v+obj: 照 *illuminate* + 相 *photograph*] VERB = take a picture
■ 请你给我们照个相。**Qǐng nǐ gěi wǒmen zhào ge xiàng.** = *Please take a picture of us.*

zhàoxiàngjī 照相机 = camera
■ 明天出去玩，别忘了带照相机！ **Míngtiān chūqu wán, bié wàngle dài zhàoxiàngjī.** = *Tomorrow we're going on an outing; don't forget to bring the camera.*

zhě 者 (日 8) NOUN = person, thing
(See 或者 **huòzhě**.)

zhè 这 (辶 7) Trad 這 PRONOUN = this
■ 这是什么？ **Zhè shì shénme?** = *What's this?*

zhège 这个 [modif: 这 *this* + 个 *one*] PRONOUN = this one, this
■ 这个太大，给我小一点儿的。 **Zhège tài dà, gěi wǒ xiǎo yìdiǎnr de.** = *This one is too big. Give me a smaller one.*

zhèli 这里 PRONOUN = this place, here
■ 你在这里住了几年了？ **Nǐ zài zhèli zhùle jǐnián le?** = *How long have you been living here?*
■ 我刚来的时候，不习惯这里的天气。 **Wǒ gāng lái de shíhou, bù xíguàn zhèli de tiānqì.** = *When I first came, I wasn't used to the weather here.*

NOTE: In spoken Chinese 这里 **zhèli** can be replaced by 这儿 **zhèr**.

Z

zhème 这么 PRONOUN = like this, in this manner, so
■ 这件衣服这么贵，我没想到。 **Zhè jiàn yīfu zhème guì, wǒ méi xiǎngdào.** = *I did not expect this dress to be so expensive.*

zhèxiē 这些 PRONOUN = these
■ 这些书你都看过吗？ **Zhè xiē shū nǐ dōu kànguo ma?** = *Have you read all these books?*

zhèyàng 这样 PRONOUN = same as 这么 **zhème**

zhe 着 (目 11) PARTICLE = (used after a verb to indicate the action or state is going on)
■ 门开着，灯亮着，可是房间里没有人。 **Mén kāizhe, dēng liàngzhe, kěshì fāngjiān lǐ méiyǒu rén.** = *The door was open and the light was on but there was no one in the room.*

zhēn 真 (十 10) ADVERB = real, really, true, truly, indeed
■ 中国真大呀！ **Zhōngguó zhēn dà ya!** = *China is really big!*
■ 我真不愿意去参加那个晚会。 **Wǒ zhēn bú yuànyì qù cānjiā nàge wǎnhuì.** = *I really don't want to attend that evening party.*

zhēnzhèng 真正 [compound: 真 *real* + 正 *proper*] ADJECTIVE = genuine, real
■ 真正的友谊是天长地久的。 **Zhēnzhèng de yǒuyì shì tiān-cháng-dì-jǐu de.** = *Genuine friendship is everlasting.*

zhěng 整 (束 16) [敕 symb + 正 phon **zhèng**] ADJECTIVE = neat

zhěngqí 整齐 [compound: 整 *neat* + 齐 *orderly*] ADJECTIVE = in good order, neat and tidy (antonym 乱 **luàn**)

zhěng-zhěng-qí-qi 整整齐齐 = an emphatic form of 整齐 **zhěngqí**
■ 十几双鞋排得整整齐齐。**Shí jǐ shuāng xié pái de zhěng-zhěng-qí-qí.** = *Over a dozen pairs of shoes were arranged in a very orderly way.*

zhèng 正 (一 5) ADJECTIVE = proper

zhèngquè 正确 [compound: 正 *proper* + 确 *true*] ADJECTIVE = correct, accurate (antonym 错误 **cuòwù**)
■ 你的回答不正确。**Nǐde huídá bú zhèngquè.** = *Your answer isn't correct.*

zhèngzài 正在 ADVERB = used before a verb to indicate the action is in progress
■ 他正在看电视。**Tā zhèngzài kàn diànshì.** = *He's watching TV.*

zhèngzài ... ne 正在…呢 = same as 正在 **zhèngzài** but with a casual, friendly tone
■ 他正在看电视呢。**Tā zhèngzài kàn diànshì ne.** = *He's watching TV.*

zhèng 政 (攵 9) [正 phon **zhèng** + 攵 symb] NOUN = governance

zhèngfǔ 政府 [modif: 政 *governance* + 府 *building*] NOUN = government

zhèngzhì 政治 [compound: 政 *governance* + 治 *administering*] NOUN = politics
■ 我对这个国家的政治情况了解不多。**Wǒ duì zhège guójiā de zhèngzhì qíngkuàng liǎojiě bù duō.** = *I don't know much about the political situation in this country.*

zhī 之 (丶 3)

zhījiān 之间 PREPOSITION = between
■ 我希望我们能发展我们之间的友谊。**Wǒ xīwàng wǒmen néng fāzhǎn wǒmen zhījiān de yǒuyì.** = *I hope we will be able to develop the friendship between us.*

zhī 支 (支 4) MEASURE WORD = (used with nouns denoting sticklike things)
■ 一支笔 **yì zhī bǐ** = *a pen*

zhī 只 (口 5) Trad 隻 MEASURE WORD = (with certain nouns denoting animals, utensils, or objects)
■ 一只手 **yì zhī shǒu** = *a hand*
■ 两只狗 **liǎng zhī gǒu** = *two dogs*

zhī 知 (矢 8) VERB = know

zhīdào 知道 VERB = know, be aware (of)
■ 我不知道这件事。**Wǒ bù zhīdào zhè jiàn shì.** = *I wasn't aware of this matter.*

zhīshi 知识 [compound: 知 *know* + 识 *understanding*] NOUN = knowledge
■ 旅行使人学到知识。**Lǚxíng shǐ rén xuédào zhīshi.** = *Traveling enables one to gain knowledge.*

zhīshi jīngjì 知识经济 NOUN = knowledge economy

Z

zhī 织 (纟 8) [纟 sign + 只 phon **zhǐ**] Trad 織 VERB = weave (See 组织 **zǔzhī**.)

zhí 直 (十 8) ADJECTIVE = straight (See 一直 **yìzhí**.)

zhǐ 只 (口 5) Trad 祇 ADVERB = only
■ 我只有一个弟弟，没有哥哥，也没有姐妹。**Wǒ zhǐ yǒu yí ge dìdi, méiyǒu gēge, yě méiyǒu jiěmèi.** = *I've only got a younger brother. I don't have an elder brother or sisters.*

zhǐhǎo 只好 ADVERB = have no choice but, have to
■ 他自行车坏了，只好走路去上学。**Tā zìxíngchē huàile, zhǐhǎo zǒulù qù shàngxué.** = *His bicycle broke down, so he has to walk to school.*

zhǐ 纸 (纟 7) [纟 sign + 氏 phon **shì**] Trad 紙 NOUN = paper (张 **zhāng**)
■ 请给我几张纸。**Qǐng gěi wǒ jǐ zhāng zhǐ.** = Please give me some paper.

zhǐ 指 (扌 9) [扌 sign + 旨 phon **zhǐ**] VERB = point at, point to
■ 你不知道那东西叫什么，就用手指。**Nǐ bù zhīdào nà dōngxi jiào shénme, jiù yòng shǒu zhǐ.** = *If you don't know what it's called, just point at it with your finger.*

zhì 志 (士 7) [士 symb + 心 sign] NOUN = aspiration (See 同志 **tóngzhì**.)

zhì 治 (氵 8) VERB = administer (See 政治 **zhèngzhì**.)

zhōng 中 (丨 4)
1 NOUN = center, middle
■ 东南西北中 **Dōng, nán, xī, běi, zhōng** = *the east, the south, the west, the north and the center*
2 ADJECTIVE = middle, medium

Zhōngguó 中国 [modif: 中 *middle, central* + 国 *kingdom*] NOUN = China
■ 中国历史长，人口多。**Zhōngguó lìshǐ cháng, rénkǒu duō.** = *China has a long history and a large population.*

zhōngjiān 中间 noun = center, middle, among
■ 花园的中间有一棵很大的树。**Huāyuán de zhōngjiān yǒu yì kē hěn dà de shù.** = *In the middle of the garden there is a very big tree.*
■ 我的朋友中间，他体育最好。**Wǒ de péngyou zhōngjiān, tā tǐyù zuì hǎo.** = *Among my friends he is the best sportsman.*

Zhōngwén 中文 [modif: 中 *China* + 文 *writing*] NOUN = the Chinese language (especially Chinese writing)
■ 世界上有十几亿人用中文。**Shìjiè shang yǒu shíjǐ yì rén yòng Zhōngwén.** = *Over a billion people in the world use Chinese.*

NOTE: See the note on 汉语 **Hànyǔ**.

zhōngwǔ 中午 [modif: 中 *middle* + 午 *noon*] NOUN = noon
■ 我们中午休息一个小时。**Wǒmen zhōngwǔ xiūxi yí ge xiǎoshí.** = *We have a one-hour break at noon.*

Z

zhōngxué 中学 [modif: 中 *middle* + 学 *school*] NOUN = secondary school, high school, middle school
■ 这座城市有十多个中学。**Zhè zuò chénshì yǒu shí duō ge zhōngxué.** = *This city has over ten secondary schools.*

zhōng 钟 (钅9) [钅 sign + 中 phon **zhōng**] Trad **鐘** NOUN = clock (座 **zuò**)
■ 这座钟慢了三分钟。**Zhè zuò zhōng mànle sān fēnzhōng.** = *This clock is three minutes slow.*

zhōngtóu 钟头 NOUN = same as 小时 **xiǎoshí**, but used only in spoken Chinese

zhǒng 种 (禾9) [禾 sign + 中 phon **zhōng**] Trad **種**
1 NOUN = seed, race
Báizhǒngrén 白种人 = Caucasians
Hēizhǒngrén 黑种人 = Black people
Huángzhǒngrén 黄种人 = the Yellow race
■ 世界上黄种人最多。**Shìjiè shang Huángzhǒngrén zuì duō.** = *In the world, the Yellow race is most numerous.*
2 MEASURE WORD = kind, sort
■ 你最喜欢吃哪种水果？ **Nǐ zuì xǐhuan chī nǎ zhǒng shuǐguǒ?** = *Which kinds of fruit do you like the best?*

zhòng 重 (丿9) ADJECTIVE = heavy (antonym 轻 **qīng**)
■ 这个机器太重了，我们两个人搬不动。**Zhè ge jīqì tài zhòng le, wǒmen liǎng ge rén bān bu dòng.** = *This machine is too heavy for us two to move.*

zhòngyào 重要 [compound: 重 *heavy* + 要 (in this context) *important*] ADJECTIVE = important
■ 这件事非常重要，你别忘了！**Zhè jiàn shì fēicháng zhòngyào, nǐ bié wàng le.** = *This matter is very important. Don't you forget it.*
■ 我有一个重要的消息告诉你。**Wǒ yǒu yī ge zhòngyào de xiāoxi gàosu nǐ.** = *I've important news to tell you.*

zhōu 周 (冂8) NOUN = week
■ "你们学校寒假放几周？" "三周。" **"Nǐmen xuéxiào hánjià fàng jǐ zhōu?" "Sān zhōu."** = *"How many weeks of winter holiday does your school have?" "Three weeks."*

NOTE: 周 **zhōu** and 星期 **xīngqī** both mean "week," but 周 **zhōu** is usually used in writing only. In spoken Chinese, normally 星期 **xīngqī** is used.

zhōuwéi 周围 [compound: 周 *circuit* + 围 *encircle*] NOUN = surrounding area, all around
■ 新西兰周围都是大海。**Xīngxīlán zhōuwéi dōu shì dàhǎi.** = *All around New Zealand are oceans and seas.*

zhū 猪 (犭11) [犭 sign + 者 symb] NOUN = pig (只 **zhī**)
■ 这只猪真大呀！ **Zhèzhī zhū zhēn dà ya!** = *How big this pig is!*

zhūròu 猪肉 = pork

■ 中国人一般吃猪肉，不大吃牛肉、羊肉。**Zhōngguórén yìbān chī zhūròu, búdà chī niúròu, yángròu.** = *The Chinese usually eat pork; they don't eat much beef or mutton.*

zhǔ 主 (丶 5) NOUN = master, owner, lord

zhǔyì 主意 [compound: 主 *advocate* + 意 *idea*] NOUN = definite view, idea

■ 这件事我没有什么主意，你看呢？ **Zhè jiàn shì wǒ méiyǒu shénme zhǔyì, nǐ kàn ne?** = *I don't have any definite views on this matter. What do you think?*

zhǔyào 主要 [compound: 主 *major* + 要 (in this context) *important*] ADJECTIVE = major, chief, main

■ 这不是主要的问题，可以以后再讨论。**Zhè bú shì zhǔyào de wèntí, kěyǐ yǐhòu zài tǎolùn.** = *This is not a major issue. We can discuss it later.*

zhù 住 (亻 7) [亻 sign + 主 phon **zhǔ**] VERB = live, reside

■ "你住在哪里？" "我住在学校附近。" **"Nǐ zhù zài nǎli?" "Wǒ zhù zài xuéxiào fùjìn."** = *"Where do you live?" "I live near the school."*

zhù 助 (力 7) [且 symb + 力 sign] VERB = help (See 帮助 **bāngzhù**.)

zhù 注 (氵 8) VERB = pay attention to

zhùyì 注意 VERB = pay attention to, take notice of

■ 说话的时候，要注意语法。**Shuōhuà de shíhou, yào zhùyì yǔfǎ.** = *One should pay attention to grammar when speaking.*

■ 请大家注意！明天张老师要开一个重要的会，所以不上课。**Qǐng dàjiā zhùyì! Míngtiān Zhāng lǎoshī yào kāi yī ge zhòngyào de huì, suǒyǐ bú shàngkè.** = *Attention, please! Tomorrow Teacher Zhang will be attending an important meeting, so there will be no class.*

zhù 祝 (礻 9) [礻 sign + 兄 symb] VERB = express good wishes, wish

■ 祝你生日快乐！ **Zhù nǐ shēngrì kuàilè!** = *I wish you a happy birthday!*

zhuāng 装 (衣 12) Trad 裝 VERB = pretend

■ 她不想跟他说话，所以装没看见。**Tā bù xiǎng gēn tā shuōhuà, suǒyǐ zhuāng méi kànjiàn.** = *She did not want to talk to him, so she pretended not to see him.*

zhǔn 准 (冫 10) ADJECTIVE = accurate

zhǔnbèi 准备

1 VERB = prepare

zhǔnbèi hǎo 准备好 = be well prepared

■ 明天考试，你们准备好了吗？ **Míngtiān kǎoshì, nǐmen zhǔnbèi hǎo le ma?** = *There'll be an examination tomorrow. Are you well prepared?*

2 NOUN = preparation

■ 老师上课以前要做很多准备。**Lǎoshī shàngkè yǐqián yào zuò hěnduō zhǔnbèi.** = *Teachers need to do a lot of preparation before class.*

Z

zhuō 桌 (木 10) [symb + 木 sign] VERB = table

zhuōzi 桌子 [suffix: 桌 *table* + 子 nominal suffix] NOUN = table, desk (张 **zhāng**)
■ 桌子上有几本书和一个杯子。**Zhuōzi shang yǒu jǐ běn shū he yì ge bēizi.** *There are some books and a cup on the table.*

zì 自 (自 6) PRONOUN = self

zìjǐ 自己 PRONOUN = self, one's own
■ 自己的工作自己做。**Zìjǐ de gōngzuò zìjǐ zuò.** = *Each must do their own work.*
wǒ zìjǐ 我自己 = myself
wǒmen zìjǐ 我们自己 = ourselves
nǐ zìjǐ 你自己 = yourself
tāmen zìjǐ 他们自己 = themselves

zìxíngchē 自行车 [modif: 自 *self* + 行 *walking* + 车 *vehicle*] NOUN = bicycle (辆 **liàng**)
■ 我会骑自行车，但是不会修自行车。**Wǒ huì qí zìxíngchē, dànshì búhuì xiū zìxíngchē.** = *I can ride a bicycle, but I can't fix it.*

zì 字 (宀 6) NOUN = Chinese character
■ 中国字很有意思。**Zhōngguó zì hěn yǒu yìsi.** = *Chinese characters are very interesting.*
■ 这个字是什么意思？ 怎么念？**Zhège zì shì shénme yìsi? Zěnme niàn?** = *What is the meaning of this Chinese character? How is it pronounced?*
Hànzì 汉字 = Chinese character

zi 子 (子 3) PARTICLE = (a nominal suffix) (See 杯子 **bēizi**, 本子 **běnzi**, 电子 **diànzǐ**, 儿子 **érzi**, 房子 **fángzi**, 饺子 **jiǎozi**, 妻子 **qīzi**, 日子 **rìzi**, 橘子 **júzi**, 句子 **jùzi**, 裤子 **kùzi**, 筷子 **kuàizi**, 帽子 **màozi**, 袜子 **wàzi**, 屋子 **wūzi**, 样子 **yàngzi**, 椅子 **yǐzi**, 桌子 **zhuōzi**.)

zǒng 总 (心 9) Trad 總 ADVERB = same as 总是 **zǒngshì**

zǒngshì 总是 ADVERB = always
■ 他总是觉得自己正确。**Tā zǒngshì juéde zìjǐ zhèngquè.** = *He always thinks himself correct.*
■ 她晚上总是在家。**Tā wǎnshang zǒngshi zài jiā.** = *She is always at home in the evenings.*

zǒu 走 (走 7) VERB = walk; leave
■ 我家离学校很近，我每天走到学校。**Wǒjiā li xuéxiào hěn jìn, wǒ měi tiān zuǒudào xuéxiào.** = *My home is close to the school. I walk to school every day.*
■ 时间不早了，我们得走了。**Shíjiān bù zǎo le, wǒmen děi zǒu le.** = *It's quite late. We've got to go.*

zū 租 (禾 10) VERB = rent, hire (See 出租 **chūzū**.)

zú 足 (足 7) NOUN = foot

zúqiú 足球 [modif: 足 *foot* + 球 *ball*] NOUN = soccer
tī zúqiú 踢足球 = play soccer
■ 我爸爸年轻的时候，常常踢足球，现在还喜欢看足球比赛。**Wǒ bàba niánqīng de shíhou, chángcháng tī**

zúqiú, xiànzài hái xǐhuan kàn zúqiú bǐsài. = *When my father was young he often played soccer; now he still enjoys watching soccer games.*

zú 族 (方 11) NOUN = clan, nationality (See 民族 **mínzú**.)

zǔ 组 (纟 8) [纟 sign + 且 phon] Trad 組 NOUN = group

zǔzhī 组织
1 VERB = organize
■ 学校正在组织到北京去旅行。**Xuéxiào zhèngzài zǔzhī dào Běijīng qù lǚxíng.** = *The school is organizing a trip to Beijing.*
2 NOUN = organization
■ 我父亲不参加任何组织。**Wǒ fùqin bù cānjiā rènhé zǔzhī.** = *My father hasn't joined any organization.*

zǔ 祖 (礻 9) [礻 sign + 且 phon] NOUN = ancestor

zǔfù 祖父 [modif: 祖 *ancestor* + 父 *father*] NOUN = grandfather
■ 我祖父七十多岁了，还每天锻炼身体。**Wǒ zǔfù qīshí duō suì le, hái měi tiān duànliàn shēntǐ.** = *My grandfather is over seventy and still exercises every day.*

zǔguó 祖国 [modif: 祖 *ancestor* + 国 *country*] NOUN = motherland
■ 我爱祖国。**Wǒ ài zǔguó.** = *I love my motherland.*

zǔmǔ 祖母 (母 5) [modif: 祖 *ancestor* + 母 *mother*] NOUN = grandmother
■ 我祖母一个人住，我们常去看她。**Wǒ zǔmǔ yígerén zhù, wǒmen cháng qù kàn tā.** = *My grandmother lives by herself. We often go to see her.*

zuǐ 嘴 (口 16) [口 sign + symb] NOUN = the mouth

zuì 最 (曰 12) ADVERB = (used before an adjective to indicate the superlative degree), most …
■ 中国是世界上人口最多的国家。**Zhōngguó shì shìjiè shang rénkǒu zuì duō de guójiā.** = *China is the most populous country in the world.*

zuìchū 最初 NOUN = the initial stage, initially
■ 我最初不习惯那里的生活。**Wǒ zuìchū bù xíguàn nàli de shēnghúo.** = *Initially I was not used to the life there.*

zuìhòu 最后 NOUN = the final stage, finally
■ 笑得最后，才笑得最好。**Xiào de zuìhòu, cái xiào de zuìhǎo.** = *He who laughs last laughs best.*

zuìjìn 最近 NOUN = recent time, recently
■ 我最近特别忙。**Wǒ zuìjìn tèbié máng.** = *I'm particularly busy these days.*

zuó 昨 (日 9) [日 sign + 乍 phon] NOUN = yesterday

zuótiān 昨天 [modif: 昨 *past* + 天 *day*] NOUN = yesterday

■ 你昨天晚上去哪里了? **Nǐ zuótiān wǎngshang qù nǎlǐ le?** = *Where were you yesterday evening?*

zuǒ 左 (工 5) NOUN = the left side
■ 我弟弟用左手吃饭、写字。**Wǒ dìdi yòng zuǒshǒu chīfàn, xiězì.** = *My younger brother eats and writes using the left hand.*

zuò 作 (亻 7) VERB = same as 做 **zuò**

NOTE: 做 **zuò** and 作 **zuò** have the same pronunciation and often the same meaning, but 做 **zuò** is much more commonly used in everyday Chinese while 作 **zuò** occurs only in certain set expressions.

zuòyè 作业 NOUN = school assignment, homework
■ 中国的中小学生每天要做很多作业。**Zhōngguó de zhōng-xiǎo xuésheng měi tiān yào zuò hěn duō zuòyè.** = *Schoolchildren in China have lots of homework to do every day.*

zuò 坐 (土 7) VERB = sit
■ 请坐! **Qǐng zuò!** = *Sit down, please!*
■ 她正坐在窗边看书。**Tā zhèng zuò zài chuāngbiān kànshū.** = *She's sitting by the window, reading.*

zuò 座 (广 10) [广 sign + 坐 phon **zuò**] MEASURE WORD = (for large and solid objects, such as a large building)
■ 一座大楼 **yí zuò dàlóu** = *a big building*
■ 一座山 **yí zuò shān** = *a mountain*
■ 一座工厂 **yí zuó gōngchǎng** = *a factory*
■ 一座大学 **yí zuò dàxuě** = *a university*
■ 一座桥 **yí zuò qiáo** = *a bridge*
■ 一座城市 **yí zuò chéngshì** = *a city*

zuò 做 (亻 11) VERB
1 = do
■ 这件事我不会做。**Zhè jiàn shì wǒ búhuì zuò.** = *I don't know how to do this.*
■ "你会做这个作业吗?" "会，我已经做好了。" **"Nǐ huì zuò zhège zuòyè ma?" "Huì, wǒ yǐjīng zuòhǎo le."** = *"Can you do this assignment?" "Yes, I can. I've already done it."*
2 = make
■ 这张桌子是我爸爸做的。**Zhè zhāng zhuōzi shì wǒ bàba zuòde.** = *This table was made by my father.*

zuògōng 做工 = do manual work, work
■ 今年夏天你要去哪里做工? **Jīnnián xiàtiān nǐ yào qù nǎli zuògōng?** = *Where are you going to work this summer?*

zuòfàn 做饭 = cook
■ "你们家里谁做饭?" "我，我做饭做得最好。" **"Nǐmen jiālǐ shéi zuòfàn?" "Wǒ, wǒ zuòfàn zuò de zuì hǎo."** = *"Who does cooking in your family?" "I do. I'm the best cook."*

List of Radicals

1 stroke

丶	1
一	2
乙	3
丨	4
丿	5

2 strokes

亠	6
冫	7
讠	8
二	9
十	10
厂	11
匚	12
匕	13
卜	14
刂	15
冖	16
冂	17
勹	18
刀	19
力	20
八	21
亻	22
人	23
儿	24
几	25
又	26
凵	27
厶	28
廴	29
阝	30

3 strokes

氵	31
忄	32
小	33
宀	34
丬	35
广	36
门	37
辶	38
工	39
干	40
土	41
士	42
上	43
艹	44
廾	45
大	46
寸	47
扌	48
口	49
囗	50
巾	51
山	52
彳	53
彡	54
夕	55
夂	56
犭	57
饣	58
彐	59
尸	60
已	61
己	62
巳	63
弓	64
女	65
子	66
纟	67
马	68
个	69

4 strokes

灬	70
文	71
方	72
心	73
户	74
王	75
木	76
犬	77
歹	78
瓦	79
车	80
比	81
曰	82
日	83
贝	84
见	85
父	86
攵	87
牛	88
手	89
毛	90
气	91
片	92
斤	93
爪	94
月	95
欠	96
天	97
风	98
殳	99
火	100
礻	101
戈	102
水	103
止	104

5 strokes

石	105
业	106
目	107
田	108
钅	109
矢	110
禾	111
白	112
用	113
母	114
鸟	115
疒	116
立	117
穴	118
衤	119
示	120
主	121
母	122
去	123
疋	124

6 strokes

老	125
耳	126
西	127
页	128
虫	129
舌	130
竹	131
自	132
舟	133
衣	134
亦	135
羊	136
米	137
羽	138

7 strokes

走	139
里	140
足	141
身	142
角	143
言	144
辛	145
系	146
東	147
非	148
酉	149

8 strokes

隹	15
青	151
鱼	152
雨	153

9 strokes

革	154
是	155
食	156
音	157

11 strokes

麻	158

12 strokes

黑	159

Radical Index

All characters are listed here under their radical plus the number of additional strokes needed to write them. For more information on looking up a character by its radical, see Section 2.1 of the Guide (page xi).

126 耳

取 qǔ
联 lián

127 西

西 xī
要 yào, yāo
票 piào

128 页

页 yè
顿 dùn
顾 gù
预 yù
领 lǐng
颜 yán

129 虫

蛋 dàn

130 舌

乱 luàn

131 竹

笔 bǐ
笑 xiào
第 dì
等 děng
简 jiǎn
筷 kuài
算 suàn
篇 piān
篮 lán

132 自

自 zì

133 舟

般 bān
船 chuán

134 衣

衣 yī
表 biǎo
装 zhuāng

135 亦

变 biàn

136 羊

羊 yáng
美 měi
差 chà
着 zháo, zhe

137 米

米 mǐ
精 jīng
糖 táng

138 羽

翻 fān

139 走

走 zǒu
起 qǐ

140 里

里 lǐ

141 足

足 zú
践 jiàn
跑 pǎo
跟 gēn
路 lù
跳 tiào
踢 tī

142 身

身 shēn
躺 tǎng

143 角

角 jiǎo
解 jiě

144 言

言 yán

145 辛

辛 xīn

146 系

系 xì

147 束

束 shù
整 zhěng

148 非

非 fēi

149 酉

酸 suān

150 隹

集 jí

151 青

青 qīng

152 鱼

鱼 yú

153 雨

雨 yǔ
雪 xuě
零 líng
需 xū

154 革

鞋 xié

155 是

题 tí

156 食

食 shí

157 音

音 yīn

158 麻

麻 má

159 黑

黑 hēi

Stroke Index

This index lists all characters in the dictionary according to the number of strokes used to write them. Characters with the same number of strokes are grouped together according to the first stroke used. These groups are listed in the order 一, 丨, 丿, 丶, ㇗ and ㇆ or 乙.

6 strokes

退 tuì
险 xiǎn
院 yuàn

10 strokes

一

班 bān
础 chǔ
都 dōu
顿 dùn
哥 gē
根 gēn
顾 gù
换 huàn
教 jiāo, jiào
破 pò
起 qǐ
桥 qiáo
热 rè
夏 xià
校 xiào
样 yàng
原 yuán
真 zhēn

丨

啊 ā
紧 jǐn
哭 kū
圆 yuán
桌 zhuō

丿

爱 ài
般 bān
倍 bèi
笔 bǐ
倒 dǎo
饿 è
候 hòu
健 jiàn
脚 jiǎo
借 jiè
留 liú
拿 ná
脑 nǎo
铅 qiān
钱 qián
特 tè
息 xī
笑 xiào
脏 zāng
租 zū

丶

被 bèi
病 bìng
部 bù
差 chà
调 diào
读 dú
烦 fán
高 gāo
海 hǎi
家 jiā
酒 jiǔ
课 kè
离 lí
凉 liáng
谅 liàng
流 liú
旅 lǚ
旁 páng
瓶 píng
请 qǐng
容 róng
谁 shuí, shéi
谈 tán
疼 téng
袜 wà
消 xiāo
宴 yàn
谊 yì
站 zhàn
准 zhǔn
座 zuò

乚

继 jì
能 néng
娘 niáng

𠃌 乙

难 nán
通 tōng
验 yàn
预 yù
展 zhǎn

11 strokes

一

菜 cài
掉 diào
辅 fǔ
黄 huáng
基 jī
检 jiǎn
接 jiē
理 lǐ
历 lì
辆 liàng
排 pái
票 piào
球 qiú
推 tuī
雪 xuě
研 yán

丨

常 cháng
唱 chàng
晨 chén
啦 la
累 lèi
啤 pí
堂 táng
眼 yǎn

丿

彩 cǎi
船 chuán
得 dé, de, děi
第 dì
够 gòu
馆 guǎn
忽 hū
假 jià
利 lì
脸 liǎn
领 lǐng
猫 māo
您 nín
停 tíng
脱 tuō
银 yín
猪 zhū
做 zuò

丶

港 gǎng
惯 guàn
寄 jì
康 kāng
麻 má
清 qīng
情 qíng
商 shāng
深 shēn
宿 sù
望 wàng
章 zhāng
着 zháo, zhe
族 zú

乚

婚 hūn
绩 jì
绿 lǜ
续 xù

𠃌 乙

蛋 dàn

12 strokes

13 strokes

14 strokes

15 strokes

16 strokes

17–18 strokes

English-Chinese Word Finder List

A

able to **néng, nénggòu** 能，能够 89
above **shàng, shàngbiān, zài...shang** 上，上边，在…上 103, 104, 148
abundant **fēngfù** 丰富 37
accept **shōu** 收 109
accomplish **wánchéng** 完成 121
accurate **zhěngquè** 正确 153
ache (v.) **téng** 疼 116
achieve **qǔdé** 取得 99
achievement **chéngjì** 成绩 15
activity **huódòng** 活动 55
add **jiā** 加 59
advance (v.) **tígāo** 提高 117
affair **shìqing** 事情 109
affect **guānxì, yǐngxiǎng** 关系，影响 45, 142
(be) afraid **pà** 怕 92
after **jīngguò** 经过 66
after (n.) **yǐhòu** 以后 139
afternoon **xiàwǔ** 下午 128
afterwards **ránhòu** 然后 100
again **yòu, zài** 又，再 145, 147
age **niánjì** 年纪 89
agree **tóngyì** 同意 119
agriculture **nóngyè** 农业 91
ah **ā, yā** 啊，呀 1, 135
air (n.) **kōngqì** 空气 72
airplane **fēijī** 飞机 36
airport **fēijīchǎng, jīchǎng** 飞机场，机场 36, 56
alcoholic beverage **jiǔ** 酒 67
all (adj.) **quánbù, suǒyǒu, yíqiè** 全部，所有，一切 99, 114, 139
all (adv.) **doū** 都 30
all (of people) **dàjiā, quántǐ** 大家，全体 21, 99
all (pron.) **yíqiè** 一切 139
all around **zhōuwéi** 周围 155
all kinds of **gè zhǒng** 各种 42
all right **hǎo, xíng** 好，行 49, 133
all the time **yìzhí** 一直 140
all together **yígòng** 一共 138
allow **ràng** 让 100
already **yǐjīng** 已经 139
also **yě** 也 137
alter **gǎi** 改 39
although **suīrán** 虽然 113
always **yìzhí, zǒngshì** 一直，总是 140, 157
America **Měiguó** 美国 84
among **zhōngjiān** 中间 154
and **gēn, hé** 跟，和 42, 51
animal **dòngwù** 动物 29
answer (telephone) **tīngdiànhuà** 听电话 27
anxious **jí, zháojí** 急，着急 57, 151
any **rènhé** 任何 101
anyone **rènhé rén** 任何人 101
anything **rènhé shì** 任何事 101
appear **chūxiàn** 出现 17
appearance **yàngzi** 样子 136
applaud **pāishǒu** 拍手 92
apple **píngguǒ** 苹果 95
apply **shíjiàn, shǐyòng** 实践，使用 108

appreciate **gǎnxiè** 感谢 40
approach **tàidu** 态度 115
appropriate **héshì** 合适 50
approve **tóngyì** 同意 119
arrange **ānpái, bǎi** 安排, 摆 2, 3
arrive **dào** 到 23
art **yìshù** 艺术 141
article **wénzhāng** 文章 124
artist **huàjiā, yìshùjiā** 画家, 艺术家 59, 141
as a result of **tōngguò** 通过 118
ask **qǐng, wèn, yāoqiú** 请, 问, 要求 98, 124, 136
aspect **fāngmiàn** 方面 35
assemble **jíhé** 集合 57
assembly **huì** 会 55
assign **pài** 派 93
assignment (school) **zuòyè** 作业 159
assist **bāngzhù** 帮助 5
association **huì** 会 55
(be) assured **fàngxīn** 放心 131
at **zài** 在 148
at once **lìkè, mǎshàng** 立刻, 马上 77, 82
at the same time **tóngshí** 同时 119
attend **cānjiā** 参加 13
attend school **dú** 读 30
attendant **fúwùyuán** 服务员 37
attitude **tàidu** 态度 115
audio tape **cídài** 磁带 19
Australia **Àodàlìyà** 澳大利亚 2
automobile **qìchē** 汽车 96
autumn **qiūtiān** 秋天 99
avenue **mǎlù** 马路 82
average **yìbān** 一般 140
(be) aware of **zhīdào** 知道 153

B

back (n.) **hòu, hòubiān** 后, 后边 52
bad **huài** 坏 53
ball, ball game **qiú** 球 99
banana **xiāngjiāo** 香蕉 129
bank **yínháng** 银行 142
banquet **yànhuì** 宴会 136
base **jīchǔ** 基础 56
basic **jīběn** 基本 56
basketball **lánqiú** 篮球 74
(take a) bath **xǐzǎo** 洗澡 126
bathroom **xǐzǎojiān** 洗澡间 127
be **shì** 是 109
bear in mind **jì** 记 58
beat (a rival) **yíng** 赢 142
beautiful **hǎokàn** 好看 50
because **yīnwèi** 因为 141
become **chéng** 成 15
bed **chuáng** 床 18
beef **niúròu** 牛肉 91
beer **píjiǔ** 啤酒 94
before (n.) **yǐqián** 以前 140
begin, beginning **kāishǐ** 开始 69
Beijing **Běijīng** 北京 6
believe **xiāngxìn** 相信 128
below **xià, xiàbiān** 下, 下边 127
below, beneath **zài...xia** 在…下 148
benefit (n.) **hǎochu** 好处 49
benefit from **lìyòng** 利用 77
besides **chúle** 除了 17
between **zhījiān** 之间 153
bicycle **zìxíngchē** 自行车 157
bird **niǎo** 鸟 90
birthday **shēngrì** 生日 106
(a) bit of **yìdiǎnr, yìxiē** 一点儿, 一些 140
bitter **kǔ** 苦 73
black **hēi** 黑 51
blackboard **hēibǎn** 黑板 51
blow **chuī** 吹 18
blow (wind) **guā** 刮 44
blue **lán** 蓝 74
board a ship **shàng chuán** 上船 103

boast **chuīniú** 吹牛 18
boat **chuān** 船 18
body (human) **shēntǐ** 身体 105
boiled water **kāishuǐ** 开水 111
book (n.) **shū** 书 110
border **biān** 边 7
borrow **jiè** 借 65
both (adv.) **dōu** 都 30
bother (v.) **máfan** 麻烦 82
bottle (n.) **píng, píngzi** 瓶, 瓶子 95
bowl (n.) **wǎn** 碗 122
boy **nán háizi** 男孩子 88
brag **chuīniú** 吹牛 18
brain **nǎo** 脑 88
bread **miànbāo** 面包 85
break (v.) **pò** 破 95
breakfast **zǎofàn** 早饭 149
bridge **qiáo** 桥 97
brief (v.) **jièshào** 介绍 64
bright **liàng** 亮 79
bring **dài** 带 22
Britain **Yīngguó** 英国 142
broadcast, broadcasting **guǎngbō** 广播 46
brother (elder) **gēge** 哥哥 41
brother (younger) **dìdi** 弟弟 25
brush (for art) **huàbǐ** 画笔 7
buffalo **niú, shuǐniú** 牛, 水牛 91
build **jiànshè** 建设 61
building (n.) **guǎn, lóu** 馆, 楼 45, 80
bull **gōngniú** 公牛 91
bump into **pèng** 碰 93
burn the midnight oil **kāi yèchē** 开夜车 69
bus (public) **gōnggòng qìche** 公共汽车 43
bus stop **qìchē zhàn** 汽车站 150
business **shāngyè** 商业 103
business (small) **mǎimai** 买卖 82
businessman **shāngrén** 商人 103
busy **máng** 忙 83
but **dànshì** 但是 22
butter **huángyóu** 黄油 54
buy **mǎi** 买 82
by (agent) **bèi** 被 6

C

cadre **gànbù** 干部 40
calculate **suàn** 算 113
calf **niú , xiǎoniú** 牛, 小牛 90, 91
call **jiào** 叫 62
call (telephone) **gěi…dǎdiànhuà** 给…打电话 27
call out **hǎn** 喊 48
camera **zhàoxiàngjī** 照相机 152
can **huì, néng** 会, 能 54, 89
Canada **Jiānádà** 加拿大 59
candy **táng, tángguǒ** 糖, 糖果 116
cap **màozi** 帽子 83
capable **xíng** 行 133
capital city **shǒudū** 首都 110
car **chē, qìchē** 车, 汽车 15, 96
car park **tíngchēchǎng** 停车场 118
care for **guānxīn, zhàogù** 关心, 照顾 45, 151
carry in hand **ná** 拿 87
carry in hand (arm down) **tí** 提 116
cat **māo** 猫 83
catch a cold **gǎnmào** 感冒 40
cattle **niú** 牛 90
celebrate a birthday **guò shēngrì** 过生日 106
celebrate a festival **guò jié** 过节 63
cent **fēn** 分 36
center (n.) **zhōng, zhōngjiān** 中, 中间 154
chair **yǐzi** 椅子 140
chance **jīhuì** 机会 56

change (n.) **gǎi** 改 39
change (n., v.) **biàn, biànchéng, biànhuà** 变, 变成, 变化 8
change (v.) **gǎi , gǎibiàn** 改, 改变 39
chaotic **luàn** 乱 81
cheap **piányi** 便宜 94
check (v.) **chá, jiǎnchá** 查, 检查 14, 60
chick **xiǎojī** 小鸡 57
chicken **jī** 鸡 56
chicken meat **jīròu** 鸡肉 102
chief **zhǔyào** 主要 156
child **háizi, xiǎoháir** 孩子, 小孩儿 48, 130
China **Zhōngguó** 中国 154
Chinese (language) **Hànyǔ** 汉语 49
Chinese character **zì, hànzì** 字, 汉字 157
Chinese language **Zhōngwén** 中文 154
Chinese New Year **chūnjié** 春节 18
chopsticks **kuàizi** 筷子 73
Christmas **shèngdànjié** 圣诞节 73
circular **yuán** 圆 146
circumstance **qíngkuàng** 情况 98
city **chéng, chéng shì, shì** 城, 城市, 市 16, 16, 108
clap **pāi, pāishǒu** 拍, 拍手 92
class **bān, kè** 班, 课 3, 72
classmate **tóngxué** 同学 119
classroom **jiàoshì** 教室 62
clean **gānjìng** 干净 39
clear (speech, image) **qīngchu** 清楚 98
clear (weather) **qíng** 晴 98
climb **pá** 爬 92
clock (n.) **zhōng** 钟 155
close (v.) **guān** 关 45
close to (adj.) **jìn, lí...jìn** 近, 离…近 66, 76
cloth (cotton/linen) **bù** 布 11
clothes **yīfu** 衣服 138
cloud(s) **yún** 云 147
cloudy **yīn, duōyún** 阴, 多云 141, 147
coach (v.) **fǔdǎo** 辅导 37
Coca-cola **kěkǒukělè** 可口可乐 71
coffee **kāfēi** 咖啡 68
cold (adj.) **hán, lěng** 寒, 冷 48, 76
college **xuéyuàn** 学院 135
color (n.) **yánsè** 颜色 135
come **lái** 来 74
come across **yùdào** 遇到 145
come down **xiàlai** 下来 127
come in **jìnlai** 进来 65
come out **chūlái** 出来 16
come over **guòlai** 过来 47
come up **shànglai** 上来 103
comfortable **shūfu** 舒服 110
commence **kāishǐ** 开始 69
commend **biǎoyáng** 表扬 9
commerce **shāngyè** 商业 103
commonplace **yībān** 一般 140
compare **bǐ** 比 7
compete **bǐsài** 比赛 7
competent **xíng** 行 133
complete (adj.) **quán, wánquán** 全, 完全 99, 121
complex (adj.) **fùzá** 复杂 38
complicated **fùzá** 复杂 38
comprehend **dǒng** 懂 29
computer **diànnǎo** 电脑 27
comrade **tóngzhì** 同志 119
concerned **guānxīn** 关心 45
concert **yīnyuè huì** 音乐会 142
condition (n.) **tiáojiàn** 条件 117
conduct (v.) **jìnxíng** 进行 65
connection **guānxì, liánxì** 关系, 联系 45, 78
conscientious **rènzhēn** 认真 101
consider **rènwéi** 认为 101
construct, construction activity **jiànshè** 建设 61

contact (v.) **liánxì** 联系 78
contemplate **dăsuàn** 打算 20
content **nèiróng** 内容 89
contest **bĭsài** 比赛 7
continue **jìxù** 继续 59
convenient **fāngbiàn** 方便 35
converse, conversation **huìhuà** 会话 55
cook **zuòfàn** 做饭 159
cooked (adj.) **shú** 熟 110
cooked rice **fàn** 饭 34
cool **liáng, liángkuai** 凉，凉快 78
correct (adj.) **duì, zhèngquè** 对，正确 31, 153
correct (v.) **găi** 改 39
cough **késou** 咳嗽 71
count (v.) **shŭ** 数 111
country **guó, guójiā** 国，国家 46
course book **kèběn** 课本 72
cow **niú, năiniú** 牛，奶牛 90, 91
crawl **pá** 爬 92
criticize, criticism **pīpíng** 批评 93
cross (v.)v **guò** 过 47
crowd, crowded **jĭ** 挤 58
cry **kū** 哭 73
cry out **jiào** 叫 62
cultural level **wénhuà shuĭpíng** 文化水平 112
culture **wénhuà** 文化 124
cup **bēi** 杯 5

D

daddy **bāba** 爸爸 2
damage (v.), damaged **pò** 破 95
dance **tiàowŭ** 跳舞 118
danger, dangerous **wēixiăn** 危险 123
dare **găn** 敢 40
dark **hēi** 黑 51
date (n.) **hào, rì, rìzi** 号，日，日子 50, 101, 102
daughter **nǚ'ér** 女儿 92
day **rì, rìzi** 日，日子 101, 102
daytime **báitiān** 白天 3
decide, decision **juédìng** 决定 68
deep **shēn** 深 105
definite view **zhŭyì** 主意 156
delegate (n.) **dàibiăo** 代表 21
delicious **hăochī** 好吃 49
delighted **gāoxìng** 高兴 41
deliver **sòng** 送 113
demand **yāoqiú** 要求 136
depart **lí, líkāi** 离，离开 76
department (of university) **xì** 系 127
desk **zhuōzi** 桌子 157
determine **juédìng** 决定 68
develop (economy) **fāzhăn** 发展 33
dialogue **huìhuà** 会话 55
dictation **tīngxiě** 听写 118
dictionary **cídiăn** 词典 19
did not **méiyŏu** 没有 84
die **sĭ, qùshì** 死，去世 113
different **bùtóng** 不同 11
difficult **kùnnán, nán** 困难，难 73, 88
difficult to understand **shēn** 深 105
difficulty **kùnnán** 困难 73
(a) dime **jiăo** 角 62
dining hall **shítáng** 食堂 107
dinner party **yànhuì** 宴会 136
direction **fāngxiàng** 方向 35
dirty **zāng** 脏 149
discard **diūdiào** 丢掉 28
discover **fāxiàn** 发现 33
discuss **tán, tăolùn** 谈，讨论 115, 116
discussion **tăolùn** 讨论 116
disease **bìng** 病 10
dish (cooked) **cài** 菜 12
disorderly **luàn** 乱 81
dispatch (v.) **pài** 派 93
display (v.) **biăoxiàn** 表现 9

distant **yuǎn** 远 146
dive (into water) **tiào shuǐ** 跳水 117
divide **fēn** 分 36
do **gàn, zuò** 干, 做 40, 159
do (profession) **gǎo** 搞 41
do business **zuò mǎimài** 做买卖 83
doctor **dàifu, yīshēng** 大夫, 医生 21
dog **gǒu** 狗 44
dollar **kuài** 块 73
don't **bié, búyào** 别, 不要 9, 10
door **mén** 门 84
doorway **ménkǒu** 门口 84
dormitory **sùshè** 宿舍 113
downstairs **lóuxià** 楼下 80
draw **huà** 画 53
drawing (n.) **huàr** 画儿 53
dressed in **chuānzhe** 穿着 17
drill (v.) **liànxí** 练习 78
drink **hē** 喝 50
drip (v.) **diǎn** 点 26
drive a car **kāi chē** 开车 15
drop (n.) **diǎn** 点 25
drop (v.) **diào** 掉 28
drug **yào** 药 137
dry (adj.) **gān** 干 39

E

e-mail **diànzi yóujiàn** 电子邮件 28
each **gè, měi** 各, 每 42, 84
each other **hùxiāng** 互相 52
early **zǎo** 早 149
earnest **rènzhēn** 认真 101
east **dōng, dōngbiān** 东，东边 28
easy **qiǎn, róngyì** 浅, 容易 97, 102
eat **chī** 吃 16
economy **jīngjì** 经济 66
educate, education **jiàoyù** 教育 62
educator **jiàoyùjiā** 教育家 59
egg (chicken) **jīdàn** 鸡蛋 57
eight **bā** 八 2
elderly **lǎo** 老 75
electric light **diàndēng** 电灯 27
electricity **diàn** 电 26
electron **diànzi** 电子 28
electronics **diàn** 电 26
embrace **bào** 抱 5
emerge **chūxiàn** 出现 17
emerge from **chū** 出 16
emulate **xiàng...xuéxi** 向…学习 134
encounter **yùdào** 遇到 145
end (v.) **jiéshù, wán** 结束, 完 64, 121
end work **xiàbān** 下班 127
England **Yīngguó** 英国 142
English (language) **Yīngwén, Yīngyǔ** 英文, 英语 142
enough **gòu** 够 44
enter **jìn** 进 65
enthusiastic **rèqíng** 热情 100
envelope **xìnfēng** 信封 132
environment (n.) **tiáojiàn** 条件 117
error **cuòwù** 错误 20
especially **tèbié, yóuqí** 特别, 尤其 116, 143
essay (n.) **wénzhāng** 文章 124
ethnic group **mínzú** 民族 86
even **lián...dōu...** 连…都… 78
even if **jiù** 就 67
even more **gèng** 更 42
evening **wǎnshang, yè** 晚上, 夜 122, 137
evening party **wǎnhuì** 晚会 122
every **gè, měi** 各, 每 42, 84
everybody **dàjiā, quántǐ** 大家, 全体 21, 99
everything **rènhé shì, yíqiè** 任何事, 一切 101, 139
examination **kǎoshì** 考试 70
examine **jiǎnchá** 检查 60
(be) examined **kǎoshì** 考试 70

(for) example **lìrú** 例如 77
except **chúle** 除了 17
excessively **tài** 太 115
exchange **huàn** 换 54
excuse (v.) **yuánliàng** 原谅 146
Excuse me, … **Qǐngwèn, ...** 请问, ... 98
exercise **liànxí** 练习 78
exercise (physical, v.) **huódòng, yùndòng** 活动, 运动 55, 147
exhausted **lèi** 累 76
exhibit (v.), exhibition **zhǎnlǎn** 展览 150
exist **yǒu** 有 144
expensive **guì** 贵 46
experience (n.) **jīngyàn** 经验 66
experienced **yǒu jīngyàn de** 有经验的 66
explain, explanation **shuōmíng** 说明 112
express (v.) **biǎoshì** 表示 8
extensive **guǎng** 广 46
extremely **jíle** 极了 57
eye (n.) **yǎnjing** 眼睛 135

F

face **liǎn** 脸 78
face (v.) **cháo, xiàng** 朝, 向 15, 129
facsimile, fax **chuánzhēn** 传真 17
faction **pài** 派 93
factory **gōngchǎng** 工厂 43
fall **dǎo** 倒
fall (season) **qiūtiān** 秋天 99
fall asleep **shuìzháo** 睡着 112
familiar with **shú** 熟 110
family **jiā, jiātíng** 家, 家庭 59
family name **xìng** 姓 133
(your) family name **guìxìng** 贵姓 46
famous **yǒumíng** 有名 144
far **yuǎn** 远 146
far away from **lí...yuǎn** 离…远 76
farm **nóngchǎng** 农场 91
farmer **nóngmín** 农民 91
farming area **nóngcūn** 农村 91
fast (adj.) **kuài** 快 73
fat (adj.) **pàng** 胖 93
father **fùqin** 父亲 38
fax **chuánzhēn** 传真 17
fear (v.) **pà** 怕 92
feast (n.) **yànhuì** 宴会 136
feel **gǎndào, juéde** 感到, 觉得 40, 68
female (human) **nǚ** 女 92
festival **jié** 节 63
festival day **jiérì** 节日 64
few **shǎo** 少 104
field **chǎng** 场 14
film **diànyǐng** 电影 27
finally **jiéguǒ, zuìhòu** 结果,最后 64, 158
find (v.) **zhǎodào** 找到 151
find out **fāxiàn** 发现 33
fine (weather) **qíng** 晴 98
finish (v.) **wán, zuòwán** 完, 做完 121
finish class **xiàkè** 下课 127
fire **huǒ** 火 55
first (adv.) **xiān** 先 128
(the) first **dì-yī** 第一 25
fish **yú** 鱼 145
five **wǔ** 五 125
fix (v.) **xiūlǐ** 修理 134
fixed **yídìng** 一定 138
flesh **ròu** 肉 102
floor (level) **céng, lóu** 层, 楼 13, 80
flow **liú** 流 80
flower **huā** 花 52
fly **fēi** 飞 36
follow **gēn** 跟 42
following (prep.) **cóng** 从 19
(be) fond of **xǐhuān** 喜欢 27
foot **jiǎo** 脚 62
football **zúqiú** 足球 157
for **gěi, wèi** 给, 为 42, 123

grandfather **zǔfù** 祖父 158
grandmother **zǔmǔ** 祖母 158
grass **cǎo** 草 13
(be) grateful **gǎnxiè** 感谢 40
great **wěidà** 伟大 123
green **lǜ, qīng** 绿, 青 81, 97
ground **chǎng** 场 14
grow **zhǎng** 长 151
gymnasium **tǐyù guǎn** 体育馆 117

H

ha ha **hāhā** 哈哈 47
habit **xíguàn** 习惯 126
hair **máo** 毛 83
half **bàn** 半 4
hand (n.) **shǒu** 手 109
hand over **jiāo** 交 62
handle **bàn** 办 4
hang up **guà** 挂 44
happen **fāshēng** 发生 33
happy **gāoxìng, xìngfú, yúkuài** 高兴, 幸福, 愉快 41, 133, 145
hard (life) **kǔ** 苦 73
hard, toilsome (job) **xīnkǔ** 辛苦 131
harsh (life) **xīnkǔ** 辛苦 131
hat **màozi** 帽子 83
have **yǒu** 有 144
have to **děi** 得 24
have to **zhǐhǎo** 只好 154
he **tā** 他 114
head (n.) **tóu** 头 119
headache **tóu téng** 头疼 116
health **jiànkāng, shēntǐ** 健康, 身体 61, 105
healthy **jiànkāng** 健康 61
hear **tīngjiàn** 听见 118
(the) heart **xīn** 心 131
heavy **zhòng** 重 155
hello **wèi** 喂 123
help **bāngzhù** 帮助 5
hen **jī, mǔjī** 鸡, 母鸡 56
here **zhèlǐ** 这里 152
hey **wèi** 喂 123
hi **wèi** 喂 123
high **gāo** 高 41
high jump **tiàogāo** 跳高 117
high school **zhōngxué** 中学 155
high up **shàngbiān** 上边 104
hill **shān** 山 103
hire **chūzū** 出租 17
history **lìshǐ** 历史 77
hit **dǎ** 打 20
hold ná 拿 87
holiday **jiàqī** 假期 60
(be on) holiday **fàngjià** 放假 36
home **jiā** 家 59
homework **gōngkè, zuòyè** 功课, 作业 42, 159
Hong Kong **Xiānggǎng** 香港 129
hope **xīwàng** 希望 126
horse **mǎ** 马 82
hospital **yīyuàn** 医院 138
hostel **sùshè** 宿舍 113
hot **rè** 热 100
hotel **fàndiàn** 饭店 34
hour **xiǎoshí** 小时 130
house **fángzi** 房子 35
household **jiā** 家 59
how **zěnme, zěnyàng** 怎么, 怎样 149
how about that **zěnmeyàng** 怎么样 149
how many **jǐ** 几 57
how many/much **duōshǎo** 多少 32
how...! **hǎo** 好 49
how... !/? **duō, duōme** 多, 多么 32
hug **bào** 抱 5
human being **rén** 人 100
human body **shēntǐ** 身体 105
hundred **bǎi** 百 3

hungry **è** 饿 32
hurt (v.) **téng** 疼 116
husband **xiānsheng, zhàngfu** 先生，丈夫 128, 151

I

I, me **wǒ** 我 125
idea **zhǔyì** 主意 156
identical **yíyàng** 一样 139
if **rúguǒ** 如果 102
if (conj.) **yàoshi** 要是 137
(be) ill, illness **bìng** 病 9
immediately **lìkè, mǎshàng** 立刻，马上 77, 82
impatient person **jíxìngzi** 急性子 57
impetuous person **jíxìngzi** 急性子 57
important **zhòngyào** 重要 155
impossible, impossibly **méiyǒu kěnéng** 没有可能 71
in **lǐbiān, zài, zài...lǐ** 里边，在，在...里 77, 148, 148
in a moment **yíhuìr** 一会儿 138
in all **yígòng** 一共 138
in that case **nàme** 那么 87
in the end **jiéguǒ** 结果 64
increase **zēngjiā** 增加 150
indeed (adj.) **quèshí** 确实 100
indeed (adv.) **zhēn** 真 152
indicate **biǎoshì** 表示 8
inexpensive **piányi** 便宜 94
influence **yǐngxiǎng** 影响 142
inform **gàosu** 告诉 41
initially **zuìchū** 最初 158
inquire **wèn** 问 124
inside **lǐ, lǐbiān, nèi** 里，里边，内 77, 77, 89
inspect **jiǎnchá** 检查 60
institute (academic) **xuéyuàn** 学院 135
interesting **yǒu yìsi** 有意思 144
interesting (to read/watch) **hǎokàn** 好看 50
international students **liúxuéshēng** 留学生 80
interpret, interpreter **fānyì** 翻译 34
interview **fǎngwèn** 访问 35
introduce **jièshào** 介绍 64
invite **qǐng** 请 98
it **tā** 它 114

J

Japan **Rìběn** 日本 101
Japanese (language) **Rìwén, Rìyǔ** 日文，日语 101
job **gōngzuò, huór** 工作，活儿 43, 55
jog (v.) **pǎobù** 跑步 93
join **cānjiā** 参加 13
joke **xiàohua** 笑话 131
jump **tiào** 跳 117
just (adv.) **cái, gāng** 才，刚 12, 40
just now **gāngcái** 刚才 40

K

kick (v.) **tī** 踢 116
kilogram **gōngjīn** 公斤 43
kilometer **gōnglǐ** 公里 43
kindhearted **hǎoxīn** 好心 49
knife **dāo** 刀 22
know **liǎojiě, rènshi, zhīdào** 了解，认识，知道 79, 101, 153
know well **shú, zhǎngwò** 熟，掌握 110, 151
knowledge **zhīshi** 知识 153

L

labor (manual, v.) **láodòng** 劳动 74
lack **chà** 差 14

M

mail (v.) **jì** 寄 59
main **zhǔyào** 主要 156
main street **dàjiē** 大街 63
major **zhǔyào** 主要 156
make **zuò** 做 159
make friends with **gēn/hé...jiāo péngyou** 跟 / 和…交朋友 93
make great efforts **nǔlì** 努力 91
make use of **lìyòng** 利用 77
male (human) **nán** 男 88
man, men **nánrén** 男人 88
manage **bàn** 办 4
manner **yàngzi** 样子 136
manual (n.) **shuōmíng** 说明 112
manufacture **shēngchǎn** 生产 105
manufacturing industry **gōngyè** 工业 43
many **duō, hǎoduo, xǔduō** 多, 好多, 许多 31, 49, 134
market **shì, shìchǎng** 市, 市场 108
marry **jiēhūn** 结婚 64
master worker **shīfu** 师傅 107
materialize **shíxiàn** 实现 108
mathematics **shùxué** 数学 111
matter (n.) **shìqing** 事情 109
may **kěnéng, kěyǐ** 可能, 可以 71
maybe **yěxǔ** 也许 137
me, I **wǒ** 我 125
(a) meal **fàn** 饭 34
meaning **yìsi** 意思 141
meaningful **yǒu yìsi** 有意思 144
meaningless **méiyǒu yìsi** 没有意思 144
meat **ròu** 肉 102
medicine **yào** 药 137
medium (adj.) **zhōng** 中 154
meet **jiànmiàn** 见面 60
meet and greet **jiē** 接 63
meet unexpectedly **pèngdào** 碰到 93
meeting **huì** 会 55
memorize new words **jì shēngcí** 记生词 105
mental illness **jīngshénbìng** 精神病 67
mention (v.) **tí** 提 116
method **bànfǎ, fāngfǎ** 办法, 方法 4, 35
Mid-Autumn Festival **zhōngqīujié** 中秋节 163
middle (adj.) **zhōng** 中 154
middle (n.) **zhōng, zhōngjiān** 中, 中间 154
middle school **zhōngxué** 中学 155
milk (from cow) **niúnǎi** 牛奶 91
minute (n.) **fēn, fēnzhōng** 分, 分钟 36
miserable (life) **kǔ** 苦 73
Miss **xiǎojiě** 小姐 130
(be) missing **shǎo** 少 104
mistake **cuòwù** 错误 20
modern times **xiàndài** 现代 128
modest **kèqi** 客气 72
mom, mommy **māma** 妈妈 81
(a) moment **yīhuìr** 一会儿 138
Monday **Xīngqīyī** 星期一 132
money **qián** 钱 97
month **yuè** 月 147
(the) moon **yuè, yuèliàng** 月, 月亮 147
more **duō, gèng** 多, 更 31, 42
more or less **dàgài** 大概 21
moreover **érqie** 而且 32
morning (after 9 a.m.) **shàngwǔ…** 上午 104
morning (early) **zǎochén, zǎoshang** 早晨, 早上 149
mother **mǔqin** 母亲 86
motherland **zǔgu** 祖国 158
mountain **shān** 山 103
mouth (n.) **kǒu, zuǐ** 口, 嘴 72, 158
move (something) **bān** 搬 4
move (v.) **dòng** 动 29

one **yī** 一 138
one another **hùxiāng** 互相 52
one hundred million **yì** 亿 141
one's own **zìjǐ** 自己 157
only (adv.) **zhǐ** 只 154
open **kāi** 开 69
open (for business) **kāimén** 开门 69
ophthalmologist **yǎnkē yīshēng** 眼科医生 136
opinion **yìjiàn** 意见 141
opportunity **jīhuì** 机会 56
oppose **fǎnduì** 反对 34
or **huòzhě** 或者 56
orderly (adj.) **zhěngqí** 整齐 152
organize, organization **zǔzhī** 组织 158
orientation **fāngxiàng** 方向 35
original **yuánlái** 原来 146
other **biéde** 别的 9
others **biérén** 别人 9
otherwise **huòzhě** 或者 56
ought to **gāi, yīnggāi** 该, 应该 39, 142
ourselves **wǒmen zìjǐ** 我们自己 157
out of order **huài** 坏 53
outside **wài, wàibiān** 外, 外边 120
over (numeral) **duō** 多 32
overcast **yīn** 阴 141
overjoyed **tòngkuai** 痛快 119
overweight **pàng** 胖 93
ox **niú, huángniú** 牛, 黄牛 90, 91

P

(the) past **cóngqián** 从前 19
(sometime in the) past **guòqù** 过去 47
paddy rice **mǐ** 米 85
page (n.) **yè** 页 137
paint **huà** 画 53
paintbrush (for art) **huàbǐ** 画笔 7
painter (art) **huàjiā** 画家 59
painting **huàr** 画儿 53
pajamas **shuìyī** 睡衣 112
papa **bāba** 爸爸 2
paper **zhǐ** 纸 154
pardon (v.) **yuánliàng** 原谅 146
park (n.) **gōngyuán** 公园 43
park (v.) **tíng** 停 118
parking lot **tíngchēchǎng** 停车场 118
part **bùfen** 部分 11
participate **cānjiā** 参加 13
pass (something) on **chuán** 传 17
pass (v.) **guò** 过 47
pass by **jīngguò** 经过 66
pass through **tōngguò** 通过 118
pat (v.) **pāi** 拍 92
patient (n.) **bìngrén** 病人 10
pay attention to **zhùyì** 注意 156
peace **ān** 安 1
peaceful **ānjìng** 安静 1
peasant **nóngmín** 农民 91
Peking (Beijing) **Běijīng** 北京 6
pen **bǐ** 笔 7
(fountain) pen **gāngbǐ** 钢笔 40
pencil **bǐ, qiānbǐ** 笔, 铅笔 7, 96
pencil sharpener **qiānbǐdāo** 铅笔刀 22
penknife **shuǐguǒ dāo** 水果刀 111
people **rénmen** 人们 100
people (of a state) **rénmín** 人民 100
perceive **jiàn** 见 60
perform, performance **biǎoyǎn, yǎnchū** 表演, 演出 9, 136
performing arts **wényì** 文艺 124
perhaps **yěxǔ** 也许 137
(a) period of time **yí duàn shíjiān, shíjiān** 一段时间, 时间 31, 107
persist **jiānchí** 坚持 60
person **rén** 人 100
pharmacy **yàofáng** 药房 137
physical education **tǐyù** 体育 117
physical exercise **yùndòng** 运动 147

physics **wùlǐ** 物理 125
pick up (from ground) **shí** 拾 108
picture **huàr** 画儿 53
pig **zhū** 猪 155
pill **yàopiàn** 药片 137
place (n.) **dìfāng** 地方 25
place (v.) **bǎi** 摆 3
plain boiled water **báikāishuǐ** 白开水 3
plan (n.) **jìhuà** 计划 58
plan (v.) **dǎsuàn, jìhuà** 打算, 计划 20, 58
play (certain games) **dǎ** 打 20
play (v.) **wánr** 玩儿 121
play a joke **kāi wánxiào** 开玩笑 69
play soccer **tīqiú, tī zúqiú** 踢球, 踢足球 116
playground **cāochǎng** 操场 13
pleasant **yúkuài** 愉快 145
plus **jiā** 加 59
point **fēn** 分 36
point at/to **zhǐ** 指 154
point in time **shíhou** 时候 107
polite **kèqi** 客气 72
politics **zhèngzhì** 政治 153
pop (soft drink) **qìshuǐ** 汽水 96
population **rénkǒu** 人口 100
pork **zhūròu** 猪肉 156
portion **bùfen** 部分 11
portrait **xiàng** 像 129
possess **yǒu** 有 144
possibility **kěnéng** 可能 71
possible, possibly **kěnéng, yǒu kěnéng** 可能, 有可能 71
post (v.) **jì** 寄 59
post a letter **jì xìn** 寄信 132
post office **yóujú** 邮局 143
postal stamp **yóupiào** 邮票 143
power (electric) **diàn** 电 26
practice **shíjiàn** 实践 108
praise (v.) **biǎoyáng** 表扬 9
prepare lessons **yùxí** 预习 145
prepare, preparation **zhǔnbèi** 准备 156
(at) present **mùqián** 目前 86
present (gift, n.) **lǐwù** 礼物 76
pretend **zhuāng** 装 156
pretty **hǎokàn, měi, piàoliang** 好看, 美, 漂亮 50, 84, 94
preview **yùxí** 预习 145
price **jiàqián** 价钱 59
primary school **xiǎoxué** 小学 130
principle **dàolǐ** 道理 23
probably **huì** 会 54
produce **shēngchǎn** 生产 105
proficiency (in language) **shuǐpíng** 水平 112
profound **shēn** 深 105
program **jiémù** 节目 63
prove **shuōmíng** 说明 112
province **shěng** 省 106
public **gōnggòng** 公共 43
puff (v.) **chuī** 吹 18
pull **lā** 拉 74
pupil **xuésheng** 学生 134
push (v.) **tuī** 推 120
put **bǎi, fàng** 摆, 放 3, 35
put in order **shōushi** 收拾 109
put on **chuān, dài** 穿, 戴 17, 22

Q

question (n.) **wèntí** 问题 124
quick **kuài** 快 173
quiet **ānjìng** 安静 1

R

race (n.) **zhǒng** 种 155
rain **yǔ** 雨 145
raincoat **yǔyī** 雨衣 145

raise (v.) **jǔ, tái, tígāo** 举, 抬, 提高 68, 115, 117
raise a question **tí wèntí** 提问题 116
read **dú, kàn, niàn, kànshū** 读, 看, 念, 看书 30, 70, 90, 110
read aloud **niàn** 念 90
real (adj.) **zhēnzhèng** 真正 152
real, really (adv.) **zhēn** 真 152
reason **dàolǐ** 道理 23
reasonable **yǒudàolǐ** 有道理 23
recall **jìdé** 记得 58
receive **jiē, shōu, shōudào** 接, 收, 收到 63, 109, 109
recently **zuìjìn** 最近 158
record (v.) **jì** 记 58
record, recording (sounds) **lùyīn** 录音 80
red **hóng** 红 51
relation **guānxì** 关系 45
remain **liú** 留 80
remember **jì, jìdé** 记, 记得 58
rent (v.) **chūzū** 出租 17
repair (v.) **xiūlǐ** 修理 134
replace **huàn** 换 54
represent, representative **dàibiǎo** 代表 21
request (v.) **qǐng** 请 98
require **yāoqiú** 要求 136
requirement **xūyào, yāoqiú** 需要, 要求 134, 136
research **yánjiū** 研究 135
research (scientific) **kēxué yánjiū** 科学研究 71
resemble **xiàng** 像 129
reside **zhù** 住 156
resourceful **yǒu bànfǎ** 有办法 4
(be) responsible **fùzé** 负责 38
rest (v.) **xiūxi** 休息 133
restaurant **fàndiàn, fànguǎn** 饭店, 饭馆 34, 45
restroom **xǐshǒujiān** 洗手间 126
retreat **tuì** 退 120
return (something) **huán** 还 53
return (somewhere) **huí** 回 54
review **fùxí** 复习 38
rice (cooked) **mǐfàn** 米饭 85
rice (uncooked) **mǐ** 米 85
rich **fēngfù** 丰富 37
ride (horse, bicycle) **qí** 骑 96
right hand **yòushǒu** 右手 109
(the) right side **yòu** 右 144
ring (telephone someone) **gěi... dǎdiànhuà** 给...打电话 27
ripe **shú** 熟 110
rise (v.) **qǐ, qǐlai** 起, 起来 96
risk **wēixiǎn** 危险 123
river **hé, jiāng** 河, 江 51, 61
road **lù** 路 81
room (house) **fángjiān, wūzi** 房间, 屋子 35, 125
room (space) **dìfāng** 地方 25
rooster **jī, gōngjī** 鸡, 公鸡 56, 57
root **gēn** 根 42
round **yuán** 圆 146
row (n.) **pái** 排 92
run (v.) **pǎo** 跑 93
run a fever **fāshāo** 发烧 33
rural area **nóngcūn** 农村 91

S

same **yíyàng** 一样 139
sandals **liáng xié** 凉鞋 131
satisfied, satisfactory **mǎnyì** 满意 83
Saturday **Xīngqīliù** 星期六 133
say **shuō** 说 112
school **xuéxiào** 学校 134

school (of thought) **pài** 派 93
schoolmate **tóngxué** 同学 119
science **kēxué** 科学 71
scientific research **kēxué yánjiū** 科学研究 71
scientist **kēxuéjiā** 科学家 71
scold **pīpíng** 批评 93
sea **hǎi** 海 48
search for **zhǎo** 找 151
seaside **hǎi biān** 海边 48
second **dì-èr, èr** 第二，二 25, 33
secondary school **zhōngxué** 中学 155
secondhand **jiù** 旧 67
section **duàn** 段 31
see **jiàn, kànjiàn** 见，看见 60, 70
see a doctor **kànbìng** 看病 70
seed **zhǒng** 种 155
seem to be **hǎoxiàng shì** 好像是 50
seldom **bùcháng, shǎo** 不常，少 14, 104
self **zìjǐ** 自己 157
sell **mài** 卖 82
sell out **màidiào** 卖掉 28
send (by mail) **jì** 寄 59
send out **fā** 发 33
sentence (n.) **jùzi** 句子 68
serious **rènzhēn** 认真 101
serve **fúwù** 服务 37
serve as **dāng** 当 22
set off (on a journey) **chūfā** 出发 16
settle (an issue) **jiějué** 解决 64
seven **qī** 七 95
several **jǐ** 几 57
shake hands **wòshǒu** 握手 125
shallow **qiǎn** 浅 97
Shanghai **Shànghǎi** 上海 104
she **tā** 她 114
sheep **yáng** 羊 136
sheepskin **yángpí** 羊皮 136
shift (n.) **bān** 班 3
ship **chuán** 船 18
shoe **xié** 鞋 131
shoelace, shoestring **xié dài** 鞋带 131
shop (n.) **shāngdiàn** 商店 103
shopping mall **shāngchǎng** 商场 103
short (height) **ǎi** 矮 1
short (length, time) **duǎn** 短 30
(be) short of **shǎo** 少 104
(a) short time ago **cái** 才 12
should **gāi, yào, yīnggāi** 该，要，应该 39, 137, 142
shout **hǎn** 喊 48
shout **jiào** 叫 62
show (n.) **biǎoyǎn, zhǎnlǎn** 表演，展览 9, 150
show (v.) **biǎoshì, biǎoxiàn, biǎoyǎn, shuōmíng** 表示，表现，表演，说明 8, 9, 9, 112
(take a) shower **xǐzǎo** 洗澡 126
sickness **bìng** 病 10
side **biān, fāngmiàn, pángbiān** 边，方面，旁边 7, 35, 93
sightseeing **lǚyóu** 旅游 81
(be) similar to **hǎoxiàng** 好像 50
significance **yìyì** 意义 141
simple **jiǎndān** 简单 60
simultaneously **tóngshí** 同时 119
sing **chàng, chàng gē** 唱，唱歌 15
Singapore **Xīnjiāpō** 新加坡 132
singer (professional) **gēshǒu** 歌手 41
sir **xiānsheng** 先生 128
sister (elder) **jiějie** 姐姐 64
sister (younger) **mèimei** 妹妹 84
sit **zuò** 坐 159
situation **qíngkuàng** 情况 98
six **liù** 六 80
skill **gōng, jìshù** 功，技术 42, 58

sky **tiān** 天 117
sleep (v.) **shuì, shuìjiào** 睡, 睡觉 112
slender (objects) **xì** 细 127
slice (n.) **piàn** 片 94
slow **màn** 慢 83
small **xiǎo** 小 130
smile **xiào** 笑 130
snack **diǎnxīn** 点心 26
snow (n.) **xuě** 雪 135
snow (v.) **xià xuě** 下雪 135
so (pron.) **nàme, zhème, zhèyàng** 那么, 这么, 这样 87, 152, 152
so (therefore) **suǒyǐ** 所以 114
sob **kū** 哭 73
soccer **zúqiú** 足球 157
society **shèhuì** 社会 104
sock **wàzi** 袜子 120
soda (soft drink) **qìshuǐ** 汽水 96
soirée **wényi wǎnhuì** 文艺晚会 124
solve (a problem) **jiějué** 解决 64
some (pron.) **yǒude, yǒuxiē** 有的, 有些 144
sometimes **yǒushíhou** 有时候 144
son **érzi** 儿子 33
song **gē** 歌 41
soon **bùjiǔ** 不久 11
sorry **duìbùqǐ** 对不起 31
sound **shēng, shēngyīn** 声, 声音 106
sound recording **lùyīn** 录音 80
soup **tāng** 汤 115
sour **suān** 酸 113
south **nán** 南 88
south side **nánbiān** 南边 88
space **dìfāng** 地方 25
speak **shuō** 说 112
special **tèbié** 特别 116
specified **yídìng** 一定 138
speech **huà, kǒuyǔ** 话, 口语 53, 72
spend **huā** 花 52
spoken language **kǒuyǔ** 口语 72
sports **tǐyù** 体育 117
sports ground **cāochǎng, tǐyùchǎng** 操场, 体育场 13, 14
sports program **tǐyù jiémù** 体育节目 63
sports shoes **yùndòng xié** 运动鞋 131
spouse (informal) **àirén** 爱人 1
spring (season) **chūntiān** 春天 18
Spring Festival **chūnjié** 春节 18
squeeze **jǐ** 挤 58
stadium **tǐyù chǎng** 体育场 117
stamp (postal) **yóupiào** 邮票 143
stand (v.) **zhàn** 站 150
stand up **qǐlai** 起来 96
standard (n.) **shuǐpíng** 水平 106
standard of living **shēnghuó shuǐpíng** 生活水平 112
start (a journey) **chūfā** 出发 16
start (n.) **kāishǐ** 开始 69
starting from **cóng…qǐ** 从…起 19
station **zhàn** 站 150
station (bus, train) **chēzhàn** 车站 15
station master **zhànzhǎng** 站长 150
stay behind **liú** 留 80
steel **gāng** 钢 40
still (adv.) **hái, háishì** 还, 还是 48
stocking **wàzi** 袜子 120
stop (n.) **zhàn** 站 150
stop (v.) **tíng** 停 118
store (v.) **shāngdiàn** 商店 103
story (floor) **céng, lóu** 层, 楼 13, 80
story (tale) **gùshi** 故事 44
street **jiē, mǎlù** 街, 马路 63, 82
streetcar **diànchē** 电车 26
strike (v.) **dǎ** 打 20
stroll **sànbù** 散步 102
student **xuésheng** 学生 134

study (in school) **niàn** 念 90
study (n.) **yánjiū** 研究 135
study (v.) **xué, xuéxí, yánjiū** 学, 学习, 研究 134, 134, 135
study abroad **liúxué** 留学 80
stuffed dumpling **jiǎozi** 饺子 62
substance **nèiróng** 内容 89
succeed in getting **dédào** 得到 23
such as **lìrú** 例如 77
sudden **tūrán** 突然 119
suddenly **hūrán, tūrán** 忽然, 突然 52, 119
sufficient **gòu** 够 44
sugar táng 糖 116
suit (v.) **hé** 合 50
suitable **héshì** 合适 50
summer **xiàtiān** 夏天 128
(the) sun **tàiyang** 太阳 115
Sunday **Xīngqīrì, Xīngqītiān** 星期日, 星期天 133
sunshine **tàiyang** 太阳 115
supper **wǎnfàn** 晚饭 122
surely **ma** 嘛 82
surname **xìng** 姓 133
(your) surname **guìxìng** 贵姓 46
surrounding area **zhōuwéi** 周围 155
sweater (woolen) **máoyī** 毛衣 83
sweet-smelling **xiāng** 香 129
sweets **tángguǒ** 糖果 116
swim (v.) **yóuyǒng** 游泳 143

T

table **zhuōzi** 桌子 157
tablet **yàopiàn** 药片 137
Taiwan **Táiwān** 台湾 115
take **dài** 带 22
take a picture **zhàoxiàng** 照相 151
take a rest **xiūxi** 休息 133
take notice of **zhùyì** 注意 156
take off (clothes etc.) **tuō** 脱 120
take place **fāshēng** 发生 33
tale **gùshi** 故事 44
talk (v.) **huìhuà, jiǎng, tán** 会话, 讲, 谈 55, 61, 115
tall **gāo** 高 41
tangerine **júzi** 橘子 68
tap water **zìláishuǐ** 自来水 111
tape (magnetic/audio) **cídài** 磁带 19
tardy **wǎn** 晚 122
taut **jǐn** 紧 65
taxi **chūzū qìchē** 出租汽车 17
taxi stand **chūzū qìchē zhàn** 出租汽车站 150
tea **chá** 茶 13
teach **jiāo** 教 62
teacher **lǎoshī** 老师 75
teacup **chābēi** 茶杯 5
technique **jìshù** 技术 58
technology **jìshù** 技术 58
telephone (n.) **diànhuà** 电话 27
telephone (v.) **dǎdiànhuà** 打电话 27
telephone call **diànhuà** 电话 27
television **diànshì** 电视 27
television set **diànshìjī** 电视机 27
tell **gàosu** 告诉 41
tell a story **jiǎng gùshi** 讲故事 44
ten **shí** 十 107
ten cents **jiǎo** 角 62
ten thousand **wàn** 万 122
tense **jǐnzhāng** 紧张 65
terminate **jiéshù** 结束 64
test (n.) **kǎoshì** 考试 70
test (v.) **shì** 试 108
(be) tested **kǎoshì** 考试 70
text **kèwén** 课文 72
textbook **kèběn** 课本 72

than **bǐ** 比 7
thank **xièxie** 谢谢 131
that **nà** 那 87
that one **nàge** 那个 87
theatrical program **wényì jiémù** 文艺节目 63
themselves **tāmen zìjǐ** 他们自己 157
then (in that case) **nàme** 那么 87
then (next) **jiēzhe, ránhòu** 接着，然后 63, 100
there **nàlǐ** 那里 87
there is **yǒu** 有 144
therefore **suǒyǐ** 所以 114
they (female) **tāmen** 她们 115
they (male) **tāmen** 他们 114
they (non-human) **tāmen** 它们 114
thin (objects) **xì** 细 127
thing(s) **dōngxi** 东西 29
think **juéde, rènwéi, xiǎng** 觉得，认为，想 68, 101, 129
think (mistakenly) **yǐwéi** 以为 140
thinking (n.) **sīxiǎng** 思想 113
thirsty **kě, kǒu kě** 渴，口渴 71
this **zhè,** 这，这个 152
this one **zhège** 这个 152
this place **zhèlǐ** 这里 152
this year **jīnnián** 今年 65
those **nàxiē** 那些 88
though **suīrán** 虽然 113
thought **sīxiǎng** 思想 113
thousand **qiān** 千 96
three **sān** 三 102
thrilling **jīngcǎi** 精彩 66
through **jīngguò, tōngguò** 经过，通过 66, 118
throw away **diū, diūdiào** 丢，丢掉 28
Thursday **Xīngqīsì** 星期四 133
ticket **piào** 票 94
tidy up **shōushi** 收拾 109
tight **jǐn** 紧 65
time **shíjiān** 时间 107
tired **lèi** 累 76
to **gěi** 给 42
today **jīntiān** 今天 65
together **yíkuàir, yìqǐ** 一块儿，一起 139, 140
toilet **xǐshǒujiān** 洗手间 126
tomorrow **míngtiān** 明天 86
tone (of Chinese word) **shēngdiào** 声调 106
too (adj.) **yě** 也 137
too (adv.) **tài** 太 115
topple **dǎo** 倒 23
torn **pò** 破 95
(in) total **yígòng** 一共 138
totally **shífēn** 十分 107
touch (v.) **pèng** 碰 93
towards **cháo, duì, wǎng, xiàng** 朝，对，往，向 15, 31, 123, 129
town **chéng** 城 16
traffic **chē** 车 15
train (exercise) **liànxí** 练习 78
train (railway) **huǒchē** 火车 55
training (physical) **duànliàn** 锻炼 30
transform **biàn, biànhuà, gǎibiàn** 变，变化，改变 8, 8, 39
transformation **gǎibiàn** 改变 39
translate, translator **fānyì** 翻译 34
transmit **chuán** 传 17
travel **lǚxíng** 旅行 81
travel agency **lǚxíngshè** 旅行社 81
treat **duì** 对 31
tree **shù** 树 111
trolley bus **diànchē** 电车 26
troublesome **máfan** 麻烦 82
trousers **kùzi** 裤子 73
truck **kǎchē** 卡车 69
true (adj.) **duì** 对 31

Y

Z

Meaningful Character Components

Most of Chinese characters are made up of two or more component parts. "Signific graphs" (义符 **yìfú**) are components that suggest the meaning of characters. Hence, learning the meaning of these component parts will deepen your understanding of characters you know, and help you guess the meaning of unfamiliar characters. The following is a list of such meaningful character components.

冫 = freezing, ice (e.g. 冰 **bīng**, 冷 **lěng**, 寒 **hán**)

讠, 言 = word (e.g. 语 **yǔ**, 词 **cí**)

八 = dividing (e.g. 分 **fēn**, 半 **bàn**)

亻, 人 = man, person (e.g. 他 **tā**, 信 **xìn**)

刂, 刀 = knife (e.g. 利 **lì**, 剩 **shèng**)

力 = muscle, strength (e.g. 男 **nán**, 办 **bàn**)

阝 (on the left) = mound, steps (e.g. 院 **yuàn**, 附 **fù**)

阝 (on the right) = city, region (e.g. 部 **bù**, 邮 **yóu**)

氵, 水 = water (e.g. 河 **hé**, 海 **hǎi**)

忄, 心 = the heart, emotions (e.g. 情 **qíng**, 怕 **pà**)

宀 = roof, house (e.g. 家 **jiā**, 室 **shì**)

广 = roof, hut (e.g. 庭 **tíng**, 店 **diàn**)

门 = door, gate (e.g. 闻 **wén**, 间 **jiān**)

土 = earth (e.g. 场 **chǎng**, 城 **chéng**)

女 = woman (e.g. 妇 **fù**, 妈 **mā**)

饣, 食 = food (e.g. 饭 **fàn**, 饱 **bǎo**)

口 = the mouth, speech, eating (e.g. 问 **wèn**, 吃 **chī**)

囗 = boundary (e.g. 围 **wéi**, 园 **yuán**)

子, 孑 = child (e.g. 孩 **hái**, 学 **xué**)

艹 = plant, vegetation (e.g. 草 **cǎo**, 菜 **cài**)

纟 = silk, texture (e.g. 组 **zǔ**, 纸 **zhǐ**)

辶 = walking (e.g. 道 **dào**, 过 **guò**)

彳 = path, walking (e.g. 行 **xíng**, 往 **wǎng**)

巾 = cloth (e.g. 布 **bù**, 带 **dài**)

马 = horse (e.g. 骑 **qí**)

扌, 手, 攵 = the hand, action (e.g. 拿 **ná**, 擦 **cā**)

灬, 火 = fire, heat (e.g. 烧 **shāo**, 热 **rè**)

礻, 示 = spirit (e.g. 神 **shén**, 祖 **zǔ**)

户 = door, window (e.g. 房 **fáng**)

父 = father (e.g. 爸 **bà**)

日 = the sun (e.g. 晴 **qíng**, 暖 **nuǎn**)

月 = the moon (e.g. 阴 **yīn**, 明 **míng**)

月, 肉 = flesh, human organ (e.g. 脸 **liǎn**, 脚 **jiǎo**)

贝 = shell, treasure (e.g. 贵 **guì**)

止 = toe (e.g. 步 **bù**)

木 = tree, timber (e.g. 树 **shù**, 板 **bǎn**)

王, 玉 = jade (e.g. 理 **lǐ**, 球 **qiú**)

见 = seeing (e.g. 视 **shì**, 现 **xiàn**)

气 = vapor (e.g. 汽 **qì**)

车 = vehicle (e.g. 辆 **liàng**)

疒 = disease, ailment (e.g. 病 **bìng**, 疼 **téng**)

立 = standing (e.g. 站 **zhàn**, 位 **wèi**)

穴 = cave, hole (e.g. 空 **kōng**, 窗 **chuāng**)

衤, 衣 = clothing (e.g. 裤 **kù**, 袜 **wà**)

钅, 金 = metal (e.g. 银 **yín**, 钱 **qián**)

石 = stone, rock (e.g. 碗 **wǎn**, 磁 **cí**)

目 = the eye (e.g. 眼 **yǎn**, 睡 **shuì**)

田 = farm, field (e.g. 界 **jiè**, 里 **lǐ**)

禾 = seedling, crop (e.g. 种 **zhǒng**, 秋 **qiū**)

鸟 = bird (e.g. 鸡 **jī**)

米 = rice (e.g. 糖 **táng**, 精 **jīng**)

竹 = bamboo (e.g. 筷 **kuài**, 笔 **bǐ**)

舌 = the tongue (e.g. 话 **huà**, 活 **huó**)

舟 = boat (e.g. 船 **chuán**)

酉 = fermentation (e.g. 酒 **jiǔ**)

走 = walking (e.g. 起 **qǐ**)

足 = the foot (e.g. 跳 **tiào**, 踢 **tī**)

Measure Words

Measure words are a special feature of Chinese and many other Asian languages, connecting numerals to nouns. A particular measure word, or set of measure words, occurs with each noun whenever one is speaking of numbers, measures, singularity or plurality. The measure word may function like a collective noun (like a *pride* [of lions] or a *school* [of fish]), or may be related to the shape or quantity of the object.

For nouns, expressions using measure words often have the structure "number + measure word + noun," e.g.

- 两只狗 **liǎng zhī gǒu** = *two dogs*
- 一座山 **yī zuò shān** = *a mountain*

Some measure words occur with verbs, and may be related to the frequency or duration of the action. For verbs, the expression may have the structure "verb + number + measure word," e.g.

- 他说了三回了。**Tā shuōle sān huí le.** = *He's said it three times.*
- 这本书我看了两遍了。**Zhè běn shū wǒ kànle liǎng biàn le.** = *I've read this book twice.*

bǎ 把 for objects with handles

bèi 倍 fold, time

běn 本 for books or magazines

bǐ 笔 for a sum of money

biàn 遍 times, indicating the frequency of an action done in its complete duration from the beginning to the end

céng 层 story, floor

chǎng 场 for movies, sport events

cì 次 time, expressing frequency of an act

duàn 段 section of something long

dùn 顿 for meals

fēng 封 for letters

gè 个 a general measure word for nouns that do not have special measure words, or in default of any other measure word

gēn 根 for long, thin things

huí 回 number of times

jiā 家 for families or businesses

jiān 间 for rooms

jiàn 件 for things, affairs, clothes or furniture

jù 句 for sentences

kē 棵 for trees

kǒu 口 for members of a family

kuài 块 for things that can be broken into lumps or chunks; for money; *yuan*, dollar

liàng 辆 for vehicles

piān 篇 for a piece of writing

piàn 片 thin and flat piece, slice

píng 瓶 a bottle of

shǒu 首 for songs and poems

shuāng 双 a pair of (shoes, chopsticks, etc.)

tiáo 条 for things with a long, narrow shape

tóu 头 for cattle or sheep

wèi 位 a polite measure word for people

xià 下 used with certain verbs to indicate the number of times the action is done

xiē 些 some, a few, a little

zhāng 张 for paper, beds, tables, desks

zhī 只 with certain nouns denoting animals, utensils, or objects

zhī 支 with nouns denoting sticklike things

zhǒng 种 kind, sort

zuò 座 for large and solid objects, such as a large building

Useful Words

Numbers

0	零	**líng**
1	一	**yī**
2	二	**èr**
3	三	**sān**
4	四	**sì**
5	五	**wǔ**
6	六	**liù**
7	七	**qī**
8	八	**bā**
9	九	**jiǔ**
10	十	**shí**
11	十一	**shíyī**
12	十二	**shí'èr**
13	十三	**shísān**
14	十四	**shísì**
20	二十	**èrshí**
21	二十一	**èrshíyī**
22	二十二	**èrshí'èr**
23	二十三	**èrshísān**
30	三 十	**sānshí**
40	四 十	**sìshí**
50	五 十	**wǔshí**
100	一百	**yìbǎi**
200	两百	**liǎngbǎi**
300	三百	**sānbǎi**

1,000	一千	**yìqiān**
1,234	一千两百三十四 **yìqiān liángbǎi sāshísì**	
2,000	两千	**liángqiān**
3,000	三千	**sānqiān**
4,000	四千	**sìqiān**
10,000	一万	**yíwàn**
12,345	一万两千三百四十五 **yíwàn liǎngqiān sānbǎi sìshíwǔ**	
23,456	两万三千四百五十六 **liǎngwàn sānqiān sìbǎi wǔshíliù**	
100,000	十万	**shíwàn**
1 million	一百万	**yìbǎiwàn**
10 million	一千万	**yìqiānwàn**
100 million	一亿	**yíyì**
1 billion	十亿	**shíyì**
6 billion	六 十亿	**liùshíyì**

Days of the Week
Monday 星期一 **Xīngqīyī**
Tuesday 星期二 **Xīngqī'èr**
Wednesday 星期三 **Xīngqīsān**
Thursday 星期四 **Xīngqīsì**
Friday 星期五 **Xīngqīwǔ**
Saturday 星期六 **Xīngqīliù**
Sunday 星期日 **Xīngqīrì**
Sunday 星期天 **Xīngqītiān**

Months
January 一月 **Yīyuè**
February 二月 **Èryuè**
March 三月 **Sānyuè**
April 四月 **Sìyuè**
May 五月 **Wǔyuè**
June 六月 **Liùyuè**
July 七月 **Qīyuè**
August 八月 **Bāyuè**
September 九月 **Jiǔyuè**
October 十月 **Shíyuè**
November 十一月 **Shíyīyuè**
December 十二月 **Shí'èryuè**

October 24, 1942 一九四二年十月二十四日 **yījiǔsì'èr nián Shíyuè èrshísì rì**
August 2, 2006 二零零六年八月二日 **èrlínglíngliù nián Bāyuè èr rì**

Seasons
spring 春 **chūn**
summer 夏 **xià**
fall, autumn 秋 **qiū**
winter 冬 **dōng**

Time
five minutes 五分钟 **wǔfēnzhōng**
a quarter of an hour (= 15 minutes) 一刻 (钟) **yí kè (zhōng)**
half an hour 半小时 **bàn xiǎoshí**
three quarters of an hour 三刻 **sān kè**
three hours 三小时 **sān xiǎoshí**
early morning (6–9 a.m.) 早晨 / 早上 **zǎochén/zǎoshang**
morning (from 8 a.m.–noon) 上午 **shàngwǔ**
noon 中午 **zhōngwǔ**
afternoon 下午 **xiàwǔ**
evening 晚上 **wǎnshang**
at night 夜里 **yèli**
one o'clock 一点 **yīdiǎn**
two o'clock 两点 **liángdiǎn**
7:30 a.m. 早上七点半 **zǎoshang qī diǎn bàn**
10:45 a.m. 上午十点三刻 **shàngwǔ shí diǎn sān kè**
2:20 p.m. 下午两点二十分 **xiàwǔ liǎng diǎn èrshí fēn**
9:15 p.m. 晚上九点一刻 **wǎnshang jiǔ diǎn yī kè**
12:50 a.m. 十二点五十分 **yèli shí'èr diǎn wǔshí fēn**

Money

In China, the currency is called Renminbi (literally "The People's Currency"). The basic unit is the *yuan* (元 **yuán**). Each *yuan* is divided into 10 *jiao/mao* (角 / 毛 **jiǎo/máo**) or 100 *fen* (分 **fēn**)

50 cents 五毛 **wǔ máo**
$8.65 八块六毛五分 **bā kuài liù máo wǔ fēn**
$398.99 三百九十八元九角九 **sānbǎi jiǔshībā yuán jiǔ jiaǒ jiǔ**
US dollar 美元 **Měiyuán**
Japanese yen 日元 **Rìyuán**
Euro 欧元 **Ōuyuán**

Distance

meter 米 **mǐ**
meter (formal) 公尺 **gōngchǐ**
li, a Chinese unit of length, equivalent to 0.5 kilometers 里 **lǐ**
kilometer 公里 **gōnglǐ**

Weights

gram 克 **kè**
jin, unit of weight, equivalent to 0.5 kilometers 斤 **jīn**
kilogram 公斤 **gōngjīn**

Directions

east 东 **dōng**
south 南 **nán**
west 西 **xī**
north 北 **běi**
center, middle 中 **zhōng**
northeast 东北 **dōngběi**
southeast 东南 **dōngnán**
northwest 西北 **xīběi**
southwest 西南 **xī'nán**

Animals

cow, bull 牛 **niú**
water buffalo 水牛 **shuǐniú**
ox 黄牛 **huángniú**
horse 马 **mǎ**
pig 猪 **zhū**
sheep, goat 羊 **yáng**
chicken 鸡 **jī**
dog 狗 **gǒu**
cat 猫 **māo**
fish 鱼 **yú**
bird 鸟 **niǎo**

Colors

red 红 **hóng**
yellow 黄 **huáng**
blue 蓝 **lán**
white 白 **bái**
black 黑 **hēi**
green 绿 **lǜ**

Kinship Terms

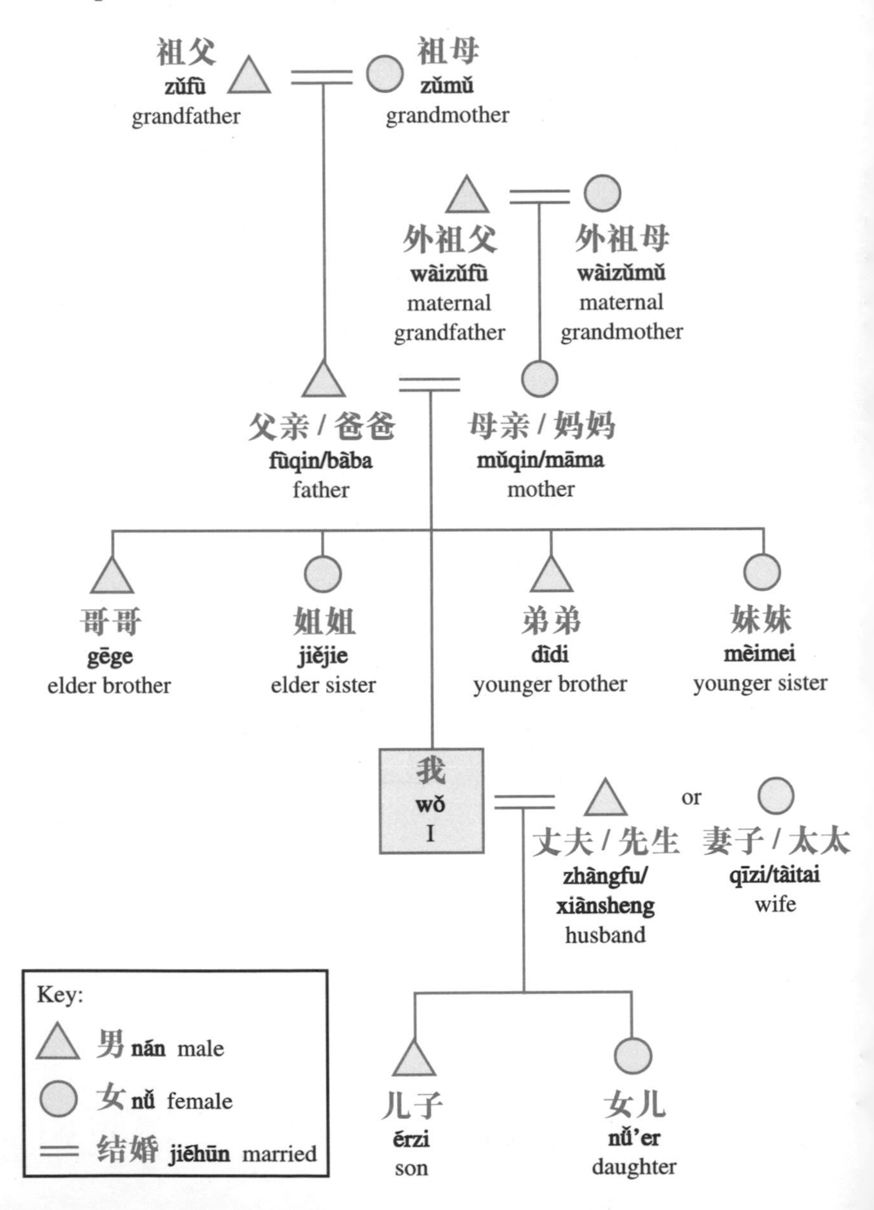